FIVE R BAD THINGS HAPPEN: HOW TO TURN TRAGEDIES INTO TRIUMPH

By Brownell Landrum

© 2006, 2016 by Brownell Landrum

Cover design by Brownell Landrum

Five Reasons Why Bad Things Happen by Brownell Landrum
Contents

Author's Note for The Revised Reasons Why:

This book is a revision to an earlier, published version of Five Reasons Why Things Happen. There are several reasons for the revision:

- First, it's been seven years since I wrote the original manuscript, and I've had quite a few life experiences since then – yes, including several "bad things" and want to share the "eureka" learnings from those with new readers. I also wanted to add new content, including a chapter on forgiveness.

- Second, I realized, in hindsight, that the first book was too big, long and cumbersome for readers to fully enjoy. After all, the Five Reasons Why are relatively simple concepts (especially if you believe in the Basic Assumptions), so I now think it's best just to focus on them instead of getting so deep into the exercises for Diagnosing and Remedying. Those exercises will be offered to readers in a separate workbook. (My agent recommended this originally – and I should've listened!)

- Third, as the song goes, "It's a new dawn, it's a new day, it's a new life" not just for me but for the world. Since I wrote the first manuscript the world has changed considerably. We went from a world mesmerized (or euthanized) by *The Secret* and "Law of Attraction" to a worldwide depression (economic and otherwise). Can the Reasons Why explain the depression? I'll leave it up to you decide. (Okay, I'll give you a bunch of hints along the way!)

- Finally, like life, writing is a journey, not a destination. Which means I keep having new insights I wanted to add! I've also read other books and discovered additional sources of information that help support the messages. Which makes this book, like life, constantly evolving. Check out the www.Reasonswhy.com website for future updates!

PREFACE: WHY LOOK FOR A REASON WHY?

A lovely, accomplished and deeply religious man and best-selling spiritual author told me he doesn't believe things happen for a reason.

I was stunned into silence.

Then I asked myself some questions:

- How can someone *not* see that things happen for a reason?
- What is required to have this belief?
- And, perhaps most importantly, does having this kind of understanding enhance someone's life?

The answers to the first two questions can come from basic laws of science, society and spiritual knowledge. First, of course, is science, which can explain the reaction to an action, whether in physics or chemistry. For example, if you heat water to 212°, it boils. Simple cause and effect. An action generates a reaction. Similarly, governmental laws are established to form a structured society, warning of a predictable response to a particular behavior. Don't run a traffic light, or you risk getting a ticket.

Universal spiritual laws of cause and effect also exist. To have faith things happen for a reason incorporates three fundamental concepts: the belief in a Higher Power, acknowledging our lives have purpose, and knowing our destiny isn't fixed, but affected by our actions (free will).

Uniting these three beliefs creates the logical conclusion of an ordered universe[1], from which flows that things happen for a reason. Said another way, our Higher Power put us on this Earth for a reason. We are not here by accident. But, because He/She gave us free will, it is up to us whether we accomplish our mission.

The next step in learning leads to question, "If things happen for a reason, what are the reasons?" The additional concepts in the chapter entitled *Basic Assumptions* establish the foundation which explains the Five Reasons Why. I'm confident that everyone who acknowledges alignment with these central principles will conclude not only that things happen for a reason, but that the Five Reasons Why offer the definitive explanation of *why*.

The answer to the third question above, "Does believing things happen for a reason make you happier? Does *not* believing make you *less* happy?" can be answered through my own experience.

My life wasn't complete, and true happiness wasn't possible, until I discovered the Five Reasons Why. When searching for an explanation of why my own personal tragedies occurred, I saw three choices, which were to (a) believe in a random universe, where there was no meaning or explanation to events; (b) fear "evil was out there" as an external, uncontrollable force; or (c) find a "higher level" explanation of why bad things happen.

The first two options were too depressing and made me feel weak and defenseless. Even in the midst of personal tragedies, I had too much faith my Higher Power not to look upward to find the answer.

My search was rewarded through a meditation that revealed the Five Reasons Why. Although they weren't entirely new concepts, the unification and completeness of the Five has

---

[1] As opposed to a random universe.

offered me a level of peace and understanding I had never known before. I feel better equipped to handle anything that happens in life.

For everyone, there are undeniable advantages in believing things happen for a reason, and even more so to be aware of what those reasons are. These benefits include added feeling of control, infinitely more optimism, advanced fulfillment, enhanced compassion, and the big kahuna: happiness.

First, let's address control.

Self-efficacy, a key component of happiness, as described by noted psychologist Albert Bandura, is our "perceived ability to manage one's personal functioning and the myriad environmental demands of the aftermath occasioned by a traumatic event."

According to Bandura, "Self-efficacy affects whether individuals think in self-enhancing or self-debilitating ways; how well they motivate themselves and persevere in the face of difficulties; the quality of their emotional life and vulnerability to stress and depression; resilience to adversity; and the choices they make at important decisional points which set life courses."

Bandura goes on to say, "the key factors of traumatic stressors include perilousness, unpredictability and uncontrollability."

The Five Reasons Why bestow self-efficacy, helping readers cope with perilousness, and explaining that everything is not only predictable but also controllable.

The skeptics out there are asking, "What if this control is an illusion?" Psychological studies have shown that optimism, even if illusory, enhances happiness, and that pessimism, even if based in reality, is a symptom of depression.[2] Interesting, right? We're happier when we feel we have some control over our circumstances. While this may not be enough to change your basic psychological makeup, hopefully it's enough to consider that skepticism won't make you happy.

---

[2] Taylor & Brown (1988), Bandura (1989).

Optimism and fulfillment are a direct result of the self-efficacy and control which comes from the Reasons Why. Fulfillment is advanced when we are living the lives we choose, rather than one forced upon us by a controlling deity or through an unpredictable random universe. Our highest, and most optimistic, destiny is the one we co-create with the Divine.

Now that we've covered control, let's look at compassion. Compassion is defined as "the humane quality of understanding the suffering of others and wanting to do something about it."[3] The Reasons Why give us the tools to "do something about it," allowing us to be more comforting and compassionate. Instead of saying "life sucks" to a friend going through difficulties, suggesting that he's at the mercy of either a random universe or a vengeful "god," the Reasons Why helps provide a framework not only for understanding but also learning and solving the problem.

Finally, the Holy Grail: happiness. When we are equipped with the awareness that things happen for a reason, and can understand and resolve (and even prevent) the Reasons Why, we are able to achieve more love, peace and joy in our life.

This, my new friends, is the *why* of the Reasons Why.

---

[3] WordNet® 2.1, © 2005 Princeton University.

INTRODUCTION

From the first moment of consciousness, human beings have asked the question "Why do Bad Things happen?" The answer that the universe is random and things "just happen" has never been satisfactory or fulfilling. And calling it the "wrath of God" has the tendency to destroy faith, not grow it.

Five Reasons Why Bad Things Happen: How to Turn Tragedies into Triumph answers that universal question, proclaiming that all Bad Things can be understood and explained by five distinct Reasons.

This book covers all kinds of problems and crises, from major catastrophes (terminal illnesses, natural disasters, being a victim of a crime) to more common troubles (having your car stolen, job loss, etc.).

I wrote this book while my life was crashing around me, forcing me to not only dig deep, but to go "higher" to gain understanding and meaning. I wrote it because I couldn't find the complete answers written anywhere (although I owe a lot of great authors and philosophers for their insight and wisdom which helped to support the messages in this book). And I wrote it so that it might help people of all faiths, backgrounds and experiences reach the deep sense of peace that can only be attained through the level of awareness and acceptance that comes from knowing the Five Reasons Why.

To get to this place of peaceful happiness requires effort from you, the reader. You'll be required to keep an open mind, be totally honest with yourself, do a lot of thinking and self-analysis and, believe it or not, have fun. But your commitment will be rewarded in ways you can't yet imagine.

Before you move forward, however, please review the Basic Assumptions and register how they mirror – or compete – with your belief system. The purpose of this book isn't to convince you of the existence of a Higher Power or life after death; it's to assure you that if these – and the other eight assumptions – are in alignment with your faith, then you now have answers to the "why" of every kind of life tragedy.

But *Five Reasons Why Bad Things Happen* doesn't end there. You're taken through the next level – diagnosing which of the Reasons Why explain your problem – and then resolving the Reasons Why to enable long-term healing.

And, finally, the part many people will want to read first: the chapter on preventing tragedies. Although this chapter is the icing on the proverbial cake, it's only a dessert that can be appreciated after the nourishing meal of the rest of the book has been consumed.

Questions that are addressed include:

- Why doesn't "The Power of Positive Thinking" always work?
- Why is prayer sometimes effective…and sometimes not?
- Why do some people have the same problems over and over again?
- Why do some people seem to lead lives of ease, while others struggle so much?
- Why does a crisis turn some people into victims and others into not only survivors but thrivers?
- What is evil?
- Do things happen for a reason? For the best?

This book makes a bold claim:

> Everything happens for one of Five Reasons.

And an even bolder claim:

> You *can* prevent Bad Things from affecting you.

Live, Learn and Love!

Introduction

CHAPTER 1: MY STORY

> Believe nothing
> just because a so-called wise person said it.
> Believe nothing
> just because a belief is generally held.
> Believe nothing
> just because it is said in ancient books.
> Believe nothing
> just because it is said to be of Divine origin.
> Believe nothing
> just because someone else believes it.
> Believe only what you yourself test and judge to be true.
> - Buddha

It shouldn't matter if I have a Ph.D. in Quantum Physics, am a Doctor in Psychology, a world-renowned philosopher or an ordained minister, for if the content of the messages in this book don't resonate with you, it won't help you, no matter who I am. It also shouldn't matter if I am a homeless transient, a spoiled socialite or an idiot savant – if you find meaning on these pages, the source is irrelevant: it's the message that counts.

But if you're curious about who I am and what compelled me to discover the reasons, here's the scoop.

WHO IS BROWNELL LANDRUM AND WHY IS SHE WRITING THIS BOOK?

I'm none of the above. I'm just a fairly average person who's had her share of doo-doo happen in her life. I guess what might make me unusual is my persistence in finding deeper meaning in life, and my willingness to open up myself – my mind and my spirit – to learning from diverse sources. I've read several hundred relevant books, articles and lectures, to help me formulate and support the information I'm providing in this book, to reinforce the Divine insight I received through my own experience.

Learning and applying the Five Reasons Why have helped me open up to a new level of understanding in my life. I frequently give thanks to the Divine for this inspiration, and for my brain and personality characteristics that have helped the Five Reasons Why be manifested in a clear and distinct way.

When I was going through my challenges, I kept asking "Why?" and nowhere could I find complete definitive answers. I read books, I listened to tapes, I researched the Internet, but couldn't' find satisfactory answers. "Bad things just happen" doesn't suffice, and that's what most of the other books say. I couldn't take that for an answer - I have a lot more faith in my Higher Power than that!

"You Create Your Own Reality" has always been too harsh an answer for me. Although many people's problems may be self-inflicted, this explanation doesn't show enough respect for the individual, and can cause great guilt if taken to heart.

So I prayed and meditated and talked with trusted, respected friends. I have a close friend to thank for engaging in repetitious, exhaustive, lengthy conversations on the subject. He proposed the possibility of one of the Reasons Why. Other friends' suggestions led to another Reason Why – but it wasn't until I started writing in my personal journal one night that the Five Reasons Why came to me clearly as a distinct, complete list.

Even though I hadn't previously seen the Five Reasons Why defined, I believe they will intuitively resonate with you. Although they're unique, in the way they collectively explain some of life's greatest miseries and mysteries, each concept, taken on its own, isn't new or earth-shattering. But I sincerely think that the concepts this book will help readers not only cope, but gain meaning and solace through life's tragedies.

YOUR STORY

What will your story be? How will you write your ending? It's up to you! Will you learn from your experience? Will you help others? Will you find happiness and bliss? Will you, perhaps, write a book of your own? Or start a cause or change your life in some other positive, profound way?

Will you turn your tragedy into a triumph?

I hope so! After all, that's the goal of this book. For you to get empowered to set your own path forward by understanding the Reason Why your tragedy happened in the first place so you can move ahead in triumph.

Will you be able to control everything that happens to you going forward? I'd like to say yes, but it's unlikely. There are numerous forces that affect everyone's life, many of which are not within your sphere of influence. (Chapter 15 has some insight here). But you can control how you handle it!

Will you actually be able to prevent future bad things from happening? Yes, and no.

There are some "bad things" that are inevitable, like death and dying. Everyone dies sometimes. That's just a fact. (After all, if they didn't, the planet would've died because it couldn't have handled the population!) But you *will* be able to look at death differently; as change, a new beginning, perhaps even as a gift, for you or the person you lost.

Will you be happy 100% of the time, every day, all day? Again, not likely. Just like we need rain for the flowers to grow, we need challenges to stretch our development muscles, to learn new lessons, to grow, change and improve.

But you should be a lot better equipped to face, feel and free the trials ahead, to get through the oppositions and pass the tests much more easily, enjoyably and meaningfully.

CHAPTER 2: COMMITMENT

The book you're looking at can take you on a unique exploration of the factors that explain the tragedies in life. I say *can*, because, in order to reach the level of understanding and peace the book promises, it will take a commitment from both of us: author and reader.

> "I know you're out there. I can feel you now.
> I know that you're afraid.
> You're afraid of change.
> I don't know the future.
> I didn't come here to tell you how this is going to end.
> I came here to tell you how it's going to begin.
> I'm going to show you a world without rules or controls, without borders or boundaries.
> A world where anything is possible.
> Where we go from there is a choice I leave to you."
> - Neo (Keanu Reeves) in *The Matrix*

Herein I'll share my commitment to you, the reader. And I'll also request your pledge on a few key topics.

THE AUTHOR'S COMMITMENT

My first pledge to you is that I've made a list of Basic Assumptions in the next chapter to help you decide if this book is for you. I don't want to waste your time if you're not aligned with these assumptions.

My second pledge is to make you think and feel – and have fun! This book has been designed to appeal to your analytical, logical Outer Self as well as your creative, fun Inner Self, or left-brain and right-brain, respectfully.

My third pledge is to provide research and quotes to support the information whenever possible. Several hundred books, articles and lectures by many of the world's greatest theologians, philosophers, psychologists, physicists and doctors contributed to this book.

My fourth pledge is that I'll provide concepts to fit with just about any religious background. Truth can be found in almost all faiths. I have no religious agenda to communicate. I do, however, provide a discussion forum on the ReasonsWhy website to answer some questions about my own particular beliefs if you're interested.

My fifth pledge is that I won't make light of what you're going through; however, I'll add just a little levity here and there.

> Nothing spoils fun like finding out it builds character.
> - Calvin & Hobbes (Bill Watterson)

My seventh and final pledge is that I won't pretend to understand the pain you're going through. As you'll see in throughout this book, there are any number of problems, tragedies and crises that categorize a "Bad Thing," each with varying degrees of challenges and pain.

Additional information is provided on the www.ReasonsWhy.com website, including:

- Online articles and activities
- The opportunity to share stories with other members
- The chance to sign up for email notices – weekly or monthly – your choice – to give tips on each RW, affirmations, quotes, new book reviews and more

© 2006, 2016 Brownell Landrum

> "I'm trying to free your mind, Neo.
> But I can only show you the door.
> You're the one that has to walk through it."
> - Morpheus (Laurence Fishburne) in *The Matrix*

YOUR COMMITMENT

> Until one is committed there is always hesitancy,
> the chance to draw back, always ineffectiveness.
> Concerning all acts of initiative and creation,
> there is one elementary truth.
> The ignorance of which kills countless ideas
> and splendid plans:
> The moment one definitely commits oneself,
> then providence moves too.
> All sorts of things occur to help
> that would never otherwise have occurred.
> A whole stream of events issues from the decision,
> raising to one's favor all manner of unforeseen
> accidents and meetings and material assistance
> which no man could have dreamed would come his way.
> Whatever you can do or dream you can, begin it.
> Boldness has genius, power and magic in it.
> - Goethe

Now your part. Here are the commitments I'd like you to make:

You need to believe in – or at least be open to – the Basic Assumptions in the next chapter.

You have to have an open mind. Some of this material may be new to you, but it will only help if your mind is open.

This is my truth. I'm convinced it is universal truth. But it's up to you to see if it is your truth. Don't just take my word for it. Experience it yourself. Read the whole book. Do the exercises in the workbook. Although you might find something you're unfamiliar with, 'try it on" to see if it fits instead of rejecting the concept because it doesn't exactly align what you've learned from another source.

If you are deeply troubled, please find professional help.

> When God grabs you by the scruff of your neck –
> you've had it. To take action, you have to know where
> you stand. You have to have a vision
> and then you have to commit to a result.
> - Archbishop Desmond Tutu, in response to the
> question, "What does it take to be a Nobel Peace Prize
> winner?"

YOUR OPPORTUNITY

Go ahead and challenge me. Make fun of me if you want. Go ahead and write me and let me know your thoughts. But before you do, please read the book with an open mind. If you make that commitment to me, I'll commit to you that I'll take your suggestions and comments the same way – with respect and honesty. (But please give me time to respond. I'm really busy!)

Keep Asking Why. Be like a toddler and always ask why, why, why. When you get an answer, keep asking why, digging deeper each time.

NOTE TO SKEPTICS, ATHEISTS, AGNOSTICS AND SCIENTISTS:

> It seems to me what is called for is an exquisite balance
> between two conflicting needs: the most skeptical
> scrutiny of all hypotheses that are served up to us and at
> the same time a great openness to new ideas. If you are
> only skeptical, then no new ideas make it through to
> you. On the other hand, if you are open to the point of
> gullibility and have not an ounce of skeptical sense in
> you, then you cannot distinguish useful ideas from the
> worthless ones.
> - Carl Sagan

On the Reasons Why website, I'll try to address the potential questions or complaints by skeptics. If, however, you're a die-hard skeptic, you probably have your own belief system – that of not believing anything – and would probably not get any value from this book. If, however, you enjoy challenging and questioning everything you read, have an open mind and are dedicated to evaluating what you learn not just based on scientific research but also on your own personal experience and empirical evidence, I encourage your questions and any challenges and ask you to email me through my website. Hopefully I can learn from your questions as I hope you've gained something by asking them.

> "Exact Science" is an oxymoron
> - Brownell

Science is never exact. It is always evolving. Every theory we accept as fact today will be challenged in the future. That's the nature of science. True scientists know this. Even Carl Sagan said, "Science, unlike many other human endeavors, reserves its highest rewards for those who disprove the contentions of the most revered leaders."

True scientists are never satisfied with the answers of yesterday. If they were, we would still think the world was flat and many other "certainties" of the past. Keep an open mind, but continue to be an explorer. Explore the theories in this book and see for yourself if they make sense and if they help make your life make sense.

> *Just because something hasn't been proven, doesn't mean it isn't true.*
> *- Brownell*

Truly, the theories in this book are actually self-fulfilling, if taken to heart. If we begin to look at our lives as being subject to the Five Reasons Why, we will create a better life for ourselves, for our families, for our communities and ultimately. for our planet.

Commitment

CHAPTER 3: THE BASIC ASSUMPTIONS

In order for this book to have meaning for you, there are nine basic assumptions that need to align with your belief system. Or you should at least have an open mind that these ways of believing might be valid.

The Basic Assumptions are:

1. There Is a Higher Power
2. God is Love/Loving
3. Our Lives Have Purpose
4. Free Will - Destiny Isn't Fixed, But Is Affected By Our Decisions and Actions
5. There is Life After Death
6. Each Human Has Three Selves or Aspects to His or Her Being
7. Survival of The Fittest
8. Evil Can Be Explained
9. Divine Guidance and Assistance is Available

BASIC ASSUMPTION #1: THERE IS A HIGHER POWER

> All matter originates and exists only by virtue of a force…We must assume behind this force the existence of a conscious and intelligent Mind. This Mind is the matrix of all matter.
> - Max Planck[4]

Whether you believe in God, Allah, Buddha, the Universe, Divine Intelligence, Love, Spirit, Cosmic Intelligence, Infinite, I Am, the Light, the Force, the Source, the Creator, Christ Consciousness or the interconnection and interaction of energy in the universe, for the Five Reasons Why to have meaning for you, it's important to have belief in a Higher Power. If you're agnostic or atheist yet still have a scientific view of the connection and effect of higher-level, creative energy, you qualify as having a belief in a (albeit somewhat different) Higher Power.

Throughout this book, you'll see references to "the Divine,[5]" as well as a Higher Power. This is to help unify the beliefs of all kinds.

> I pity the man who says there isn't a Supreme Being…Everyone who is seriously involved in the pursuit of science becomes convinced that a spirit is manifest in the laws of the Universe.
> - Albert Einstein

---

[4] Nobel Prize-winning Father of Quantum Theory.

[5] Personally, I prefer "the Divine" because to me the phrase, to me, conveys a power which is undeniably loving and compassionate.

BASIC ASSUMPTION #2: GOD IS LOVE/LOVING

No matter how you define this Higher Intelligence, as energy or as an entity, the meaning is the same: Love. God is Love. The Divine is Love. Not human, emotional love but a benevolent spiritual power that influences everything in the Universe, from atomic structure to planetary alignment. We connect with the Divine when we express and share love.

In a novel I wrote, DUET stories Volume III: *A Chorus of Voices*, the character (a guru named "Goo") offers this description of "God:"

> "Think of it like the sun. Some people are closer to the source of that love and light, and can bask in the warmth, while others are further away. Some look toward the light, while others face the opposite direction. "Now think of the sun as God or the Divine…or, let's say 'pure love." So, if God is Love, the more you love, the closer you get to God.

This might be a difficult assumption to accept, if you're going through something really tragic, because you might be inclined blame your Higher Power, either for creating the problem or for allowing it to happen. Once you understand the Five Reasons Why, you'll be able to realize the truth that your Higher Power wants the best for - and from - you. For now, you just need to want to believe that the Higher Power – the Divine – is Love.[6]

BASIC ASSUMPTION #3: OUR LIVES HAVE PURPOSE

Do you feel like your life has – or should have – a purpose or meaning? It's important that you have the desire to believe in

---

[6] Note: a discussion of the concept of God as an all-encompassing power, including love and non-loving energy can be found on the ReasonsWhy.com website. For the purpose of this book, the Divine energy we are discussing is exclusively higher, pure and loving.

some kind of Grand Plan, whether you know what it is for you or not. We are not here by accident.

> The whole history of science has been the gradual realization that events do not happen in an arbitrary manner, but that they reflect a certain underlying order, which may or may not be Divinely inspired.
> - Stephen Hawking

The Universe isn't random. Although our planet may seem random, because the events that happen don't seem to connect or make sense, that's mostly due to three factors. First, there's often a delayed reaction or result of our actions. The boomerang can take years or even lifetimes to return. Second, time is not only relative, but also influenced by our choices and awareness. Third, sudden obstacles may appear that we have to handle. These can be the result of the actions (free will) of other people, or they can be something we created.

In a children's book I wrote called, "Sometimes I Wonder," I offer the following verses:

We decide on our lessons
The paths we will take
Awards we might go for
And mistakes we might make

For life isn't easy
And not always fun
But easy is boring
Like games always won

Finding meaning and purpose can be challenging, especially during times of overwhelming stress. But, if we remember that the Divine is Love, we know the most basic explanation is that we're here to express love – to ourselves, to each other and to the planet. The way we demonstrate it, however, varies with each individual, as do the tests in our lives that can challenge and question that Divine mission.

> Love is both the question and the answer.
> From DUET stories Volume III: A Chorus of Voices by
> Brownell Landrum

In order to accept this Basic Assumption, you need to have had at least one experience in your life that provided clarity and meaning. Something happened that made you realize there is more going on than random events. Whether you experienced déjà vu, creative inspiration, telepathy, or just a strong connection with another human, you know, at least on some level, there's a higher-level force impacting your life.

> "It is an energy field created by all living things. It
> surrounds us, penetrates us,
> it binds the galaxy together."
> - Obi Wan Kenobi (Alec Guinness) explaining the Force
> to Luke Skywalker (Mark Hamill) in *Star Wars*

I distinctly remember a discussion I had with someone I knew years ago. We debated whether "things happen for a reason" or "things happen for the best." He kept arguing that things happen for the best and I took the alternate view. I won't say opposing view, because we both believed there was a reason things happen, but I wouldn't concede they're always "for the best." I had recently been through a relationship, where I had a lasting impact by being victimized, and not only was I bitter, but I could not – would not – see how it could possibly be for the best.

Depending on where you are in your process with the Bad Thing that has happened or is happening to you, you may feel the same way I did. How can what is happening to you be for the best?

> I trust that everything happens for a reason, even when
> we're not wise enough to see it.
> – Oprah Winfrey

Now that I have more perspective and have experienced several additional bad things, I can agree with the idea that things *can* happen for the best – if you understand and resolve the Reasons Why. There is the potential for a gift in every situation, no matter how horrible it may seem. What determines the success in our mission is how we use our free will.

BASIC ASSUMPTION #4: FREE WILL - DESTINY ISN'T FIXED, BUT IS AFFECTED BY OUR DECISIONS AND ACTIONS

> "Do you believe in Fate, Neo?"
> "No."
> "Why not?"
> "Because I don't like the idea that
> I'm not in control of my life."
> - Morpheus (Laurence Fishburne) and
> Neo (Keanu Reeves) in the film *The Matrix*

We have much more power and influence than we may realize. Because we are all a reflection of the Divine, we are all creators. When planning our lives with Divine Guidance, we create a kind of map that indicates significant choices and influences – potentials that can happen in our lives. Intersections and forks in the road are decisions we can make, like which job to take, where to go to school, where to live, what to major in college, whether or not to get married or have children, etc. Significant relationships will also be indicated on our self-created maps.

We have the free will to choose what course and direction to take, how fast to go down the path, whether to appreciate the scenery, focus squarely on what's up ahead or look through the rear-view mirror. The choices we make determine who we meet and where we end up.

Key lessons and individuals are probably reachable via many paths. You probably know someone who had several opportunities to connect with their mate. My friends, Lisa and Keith, are a good example. They're the same age, grew up in the same town and spent summers at neighboring beaches, but never met. They went to rival colleges and lived in the same small apartment complex, and never encountered each other. Keith and I used to go to the same park and jog and walk our dogs together, and Lisa got a dog and used to meet me at the same park, but the two of them still never connected. Then, one night she called me and told me about a guy she'd met. She revealed two or three clues and I immediately knew who she was talking about. Although the Universe (what I call Traffic Angels - see Guidance, below) had to work very hard to orchestrate the collision of events, they were clearly destined to be together.

We all have the ability to make our own decisions in life. As described above, we choose which road to take and how quickly. And we can make mistakes and have bad judgment. We can meet our soulmates[7], for example, but if we don't do our best and follow Divine Guidance, we might lose them.

> A man does not always choose
> what his guardian angel intends.
> - Thomas Aquinas

Not all roads lead to the same destination, which points to the age-old debate: is everyone always doing the best they can?

I don't believe we're all doing our best (see evil, below). We can make errors in judgment that lead us to a life of pain, evil or greed, and not reach our highest destiny. Or we can go the way of love, peace and kindness. It's up to us. This is the definition of free will.

---

[7] I believe the true definition of Soulmate is someone you have known in a previous existence that you were destined to meet. This means that we can have many soulmates in our lifetime and they can be spouses, friends, relatives or other significant relationships. You two could have met in a previous life, or on the other side, but the main component is that you were destined to meet. A Soulmate relationship may not always be a smooth and effortless connection, and often they are the relationships that offer the most challenges and opportunities to learn. I do believe, however, that our Soulmate relationships have the opportunity for the greatest amount of love, if we are willing to do the work and face the challenge.

I believe that the Divine gave us the gift of free will so we could be closer to Him/Her. If we consider the alternatives – either that everything is predetermined or that we always acted in accordance with Divine Will – what would we learn? And if we couldn't (or wouldn't) learn, how could we get closer to the ideal?

> Let men decide firmly what they won't do, and they will be free to do vigorously what they ought to do.
> - Mencius

BASIC ASSUMPTION #5: THERE IS LIFE AFTER DEATH

> Personally, I would be delighted if there were a life after death – especially if it permitted me to continue to learn about this world and others. It is really quite striking. People in different cultures, with different religious assumptions, still report remarkably similar near-death experiences about rising towards a brilliant light and having some glorious figure waiting for them. My guess is that there are just too many cases of that sort – cross-culturally homogenous – for these experiences to be just conventional descriptions or useful figures of speech.
> - Carl Sagan[8]

If our lives have reason and purpose, it follows that that our souls existed before we were born and will return to another dimensional existence after we "die."

Upwards of ninety percent of the world believes in life after death. And most, if not all, religions include some form of afterlife, the place our souls return to when they leave our earthly bodies. In fact, it's nearly impossible to have a belief in a Higher Power and not believe in some continued existence. Otherwise,

---

[8] In response to a question about Near Death Experiences and life after death.

what's the point? Even if you take the more scientific approach and think of the Divine as higher-level energy, you know from Einstein that energy continues as it evolves. I'll discuss life after death in more depth in the chapter on resolving your Reason Why, but it's important that you have some belief in (or hope for) life after death.

BASIC ASSUMPTION #6: EACH HUMAN HAS THREE SELVES OR ASPECTS TO HIS OR HER BEING

> "You are a three-fold being. You consist of body, mind and spirit. You could also call these the physical, the non-physical, and the meta-physical. This is the Holy Trinity, and it has been called by many names. Your psychiatrists have recognized this triumvirate and called it conscious, subconscious and Superconscious. Your philosophers have called it the id, the ego, and the super ego. Science calls this energy, matter and antimatter. Poets speak of mind, heart and soul."
> – "God" (Neale Donald Walsh)

Have you ever…

> …been driving and zoned out, thinking about something, and arrived at your destination without conscious effort?
> …gotten inspiration that felt outside of yourself?
> …gone to sleep with a question, and almost miraculously woken up with the answer?
> …gotten angry or upset, and you knew your reaction wasn't really rational?
> …instantly liked – or disliked – someone you've never met?
> …been searching for something, but only once you let it go and relaxed, you found it?
> …eaten something without remembering any of the bites you took?

These are all examples of the three selves, inside any of us, and how they affect our lives when we're disconnected.

Whether termed Id, Ego and Superego; Inner Self, Outer Self and Higher Self; Subconscious, Conscious and Superconscious; Basic Self, Middle Self and Higher Self; Lower Self, Mask and Higher Self; Unipili, Uhane & Aumakua; Body, Mind Spirit; Nefesh, Ruach, and Neshamah; or Father, Son and Holy Ghost, a lot of belief systems and scientific disciplines acknowledge that we're all made up of three Selves. Although the theories of Freud, Jung, Murphy, Millman, Pearsall and other experts differ somewhat on the definition of the three selves, many of the principles are the same.

- Our Inner Self or Subconscious is below the surface, usually not recognized by the conscious mind, and is the seat of our emotions. It is also the physical being and the automatic functions of our bodies. This is the "self" that reacts emotionally. It's also the self that regulates our physical bodies, and it's the part of us that unconsciously fulfills our conscious wishes, like continuing to drive to a destination without our thinking about it.

- Our Outer Self, Conscious, Middle Self, Uhane, Ego or Combined Self is the thinking, logical, conscious mind. This "self" makes decisions and is sometimes considered the parent of the Inner Self or subconscious, because it often will guide or direct the subconscious toward specific goals.

- The Higher Self, Superconscious, Superego or Spirit Self is our soul connection to the Divine, Infinite Intelligence, and Unconditional Love. This "self" is our source of inspiration. It's also the part of us that continues after we die. (See Basic Assumption #5). Napoleon Hill, in his classic book *Think and Grow Rich*, describes Higher Self guidance as Creative Imagination:

> Creative imagination: the finite mind has direct
> communication with Infinite Intelligence.
> It is the faculty through which "hunches" and
> "inspirations" are received.
> This is where all new ideas are handed over to man.
> - Napoleon Hill

Have you ever felt "in the zone" – when everything felt connected inside yourself? When you were focused on what you were doing, and you knew you were aligned physically, mentally, emotionally, and spiritually? That's how you feel when all three of your Selves are aligned toward a goal. Recognizing and understanding our three Selves is very important in understanding, resolving and preventing Bad Things. You'll get more information on the three selves and how to connect with them later in this book.

BASIC ASSUMPTION #7: SURVIVAL OF THE FITTEST

A few months ago, a friend asked, "How could people follow a leader supporting killing and violence?" My answer: "Social Darwinism."

I'm not talking about evolution here – I'm talking about the basic drive for survival on the planet. Survival of the Fittest suggests that those who are mentally, emotionally or physically stronger will survive over others. Objectively, the planet's model of Survival of the Fittest has benefits: it ensures progress and advancement.

The major problem with Survival of the Fittest is that when people are feeling vulnerable, their instinct is to find someone to subjugate (put down/overpower) to be more "fit" than another, which is known as Social Darwinism. Misaligned political leaders take advantage of this impulse by unifying the public against a common enemy, thereby instilling a sense of superiority. Certain religious figures use the same strategy: inciting a false attitude of supremacy over other groups, even going so far as to say that unless someone follows their particular faith he or she is destined for hell. Individuals follow this behavior also through condemnation, criminal acts, abusive behavior, corruption, domination and greed.

Gary Zukav, in his book, *The Seat of the Soul,* uses the term Personality to describe the Inner Self or subconscious, and Soul to describe the Higher Self. He then describes how, due to Survival of the Fittest, the Inner Self is focused on the five-sensory physical world, where "the basis of life in the physical arena is fear." Zukav said, "Fearful and violent emotions, that have come to characterize human existence, can be experienced only by the Personality (Inner Self). Only the Inner Self can feel anger, fear, hatred, vengeance, sorrow, shame, regret, indifference, frustration, cynicism and loneliness. Only the Personality (Inner Self) can judge, manipulate and exploit."

One problem with Social Darwinism is that it's in conflict with the Divine Law, "Love your neighbors as yourself." This conflict produces discrimination, intolerance and imperialism, thereby generating negative behavior and retaliatory action – making Bad Things Happen. Another problem is that by putting down our fellow citizens of Earth we're destroying our planet, thereby eventually obliterating ourselves – the ultimate final tragedy.

In addition to the three strengths mentioned above, I also suggest a fourth, and infinitely more powerful, strength that not only contributes to, but ensures survival: a strong spiritual connection. I'm calling this Spiritual Darwinism.[9]. When we're able to connect to our three Selves and with the Divine, we'll be able to eliminate the negative associations with Survival of the Fittest and find a way to prevent Bad Things from happening – to us and to our planet.

> Where love rules, there is no will to power; and where power predominates, there love is lacking.
> – Carl Jung

---

[9] More on this subject will be discussed in the chapter entitled *Spiritual Darwinism: Preventing Bad Things.*

BASIC ASSUMPTION #8: EVIL CAN BE EXPLAINED

Webster defines evil as, "morally bad or wrong; harmful injurious; unlucky, disastrous; wickedness and sin." Nowhere does Webster refer to an outside source creating the effect of evil. All the elements of the definition of the word can be – and are – created by man. All of the so-called evil in the world can be explained by both Survival of the Fittest and the Five Reasons Why.

I was talking with a close friend the other day and he said, "the evil was back" in his life. He was upset at a number of negative, Bad Things that were happening. His analogy was that we were living in dangerous woods where man-eating bears could come and attack you at any time.

My response was "Yes, there are bears in the woods, but they won't attack you unless there is a reason. There's a lot of evil out in the world, but it won't affect you unless one of the Five Reasons Why are happening in your life."

So, what is evil? Evil comes from human thought and action, whether conscious or not. Evil is separation from love, from the Divine. The *devil* is dark, destructive, low-vibrational energy, generated by collective human thoughts of anger, envy, fear and hatred, which stem from the competition generated by "survival of the fittest." When an individual has one of these thoughts himself, he separates himself from the Divine. At this point, it's up to him whether or not to join into the vicious cycle. If that individual joins the injurious energy, he will commit egregious crimes against himself, against humanity and against the planet.

> The belief in a supernatural source of evil
> is not necessary: Men alone are quite capable
> of every wickedness.
> – Joseph Conrad

However, we tend to think of evil as "out there," instead of inside us. Why is that? For two reasons. First, it feels that way. Because these feelings and actions usually come from the darker "shadow" part of our subconscious that we suppress, we're often not aware of this fear-motivated and control-dominated drive within us and our fellow man.

Second, it's a way we can take the responsibility away from ourselves and just say, "the devil made me do it." The problem with that approach is that not only is it erroneous, it disconnects us from the influence and control we have in our lives. It places the blame outside of our free will.

BASIC ASSUMPTION #9: DIVINE GUIDANCE AND ASSISTANCE IS AVAILABLE

> Ask and it shall be given you; seek and ye shall find; knock, and it shall be opened unto you.
> - Matthew (7:7)

The above statement does not mean you be able to always get what you want. But it does mean there's always help – Divine help – available. Whether you believe in Christ, Buddha, Mohammed, Allah or Energy/Science, the phrase "Seek and Ye Shall Find" applies to most belief systems. We can receive guidance if we're sincere and open in our request. Assistance is available in most situations, although not necessarily in the form we're requesting.

In addition to our own Higher or Superconscious Self, every human also has one or more angels or Spirit Guides available for support, love and direction. The responsibility of our Spirit Guides is to provide direction and guidance and love – when we ask for it. They can show us the way to achieve our earthly and Divine goals. They may not, however, intervene unless we specifically ask for their help, so we need to do this on a regular, consistent basis.

CHAPTER 4: BAD THINGS DEFINED

Bad Things are easy to recognize, but can be difficult to define clearly. Easy to recognize because, as you'll see on the list of examples later in this chapter, most people would acknowledge that each of these examples are events that qualify as tragic, or at least a significant problem.

But coming up with a universal definition of a "bad thing" can be complicated, because it depends on perspective (how you look at it), and the emotions involved. We could also look at the list and think of examples where crises like these happened to someone and either they handled it courageously, "took it in stride" or perhaps even eventually benefited from their experience.

But we certainly know a Bad Thing when we're faced with it. This is because we *feel* it. These aren't things just happening around us, they're happening *to* us, *within* us, which means they contain physical or emotional pain, or both.

HOW DO YOU DEFINE A "BAD THING?"

So, what is a "bad thing?" Is it something universally recognized or something very personal that might differ for each individual?

The Reasons Why Workbook has exercises that will take you further into this exploration, but for now just consider how you'd define a "bad thing."

Is it physical, emotional, or something else?

How do you think your definition might be different from someone else's?

Before you think that there are some things everyone would consider "bad," like cancer, for example, consider that many people who have faced cancer consider it the best thing that ever happened to them. Does that influence your view, at least a little?

WHAT "BAD THINGS" ARE WE TALKING ABOUT HERE?

This book addresses anything you would define as a "bad thing," from being cut off in traffic to a victim of a natural disaster to a terminal diagnosis. The crisis can be life changing or merely annoying. It could be something that affects every day of the rest of your life or something that hurts deeply, but is over relatively quickly. It could be an upheaval that affects every aspect of your life or an event that changes one aspect, but not others. It could be something that has yet to happen, something you're in the midst of experiencing, or something that has already happened. I'll try to address all types of traumatic events – and demonstrate that one or more of the Five Reasons Why apply, no matter what the problem is. An extensive list of the bad things this book covers is in the appendix. Some general categories include:

- Physical problems: illness, accidents, etc.
- Environmental issues and natural disasters

- Financial concerns: debt, bankruptcy, fraud, and more
- Relationship challenges
- Loss: of job, of physical or mental abilities, of home or material possessions, of relationships, of opportunities, and through death
- Emotional difficulties
- Victimization, crime, abuse, trauma and deception
- Failure of various types
- Betrayal and abuse

As you can see, the variety of bad things that can happen is unlimited. Sometimes, they can be combined. Your spouse could be unfaithful, leave you, you lose your house and your children and have serious financial difficulties and have to move in with a friend. Sometimes when it rains it pours! The purpose of the list is to show you that there are a lot of problems people face, and they can be caused by other people, acts of nature, or inflicted by ourselves.

What they all have in common, though, is the application of the Five Reasons Why. No matter what happens, the same five explanations apply.

VARIATIONS IN PERSPECTIVE

We all have different definitions of what we call "bad things." What some people consider a disaster other people call mere inconveniences. Some people sail through problems and challenges with grace and optimism, while for others, one event will evolve into more and deeper challenges.

Have you ever seen people in the same situation react differently? Take the same problem: a job layoff. Several people in a company I worked for were involved in a downsizing at the same time, but their response varied widely. Craig was running around scared and nervous, applying for every job he heard about, fearful he wouldn't find work and desperate to find anything, even though he had several months of severance pay.

Andrew was taking it in stride, grateful for the month or two of severance to help him find work that he would find meaningful and rewarding. Larry's confidence was destroyed and he was immobilized with depression. Shelley had been anticipating the layoff and was excited about the opportunity to pursue her own entrepreneurial venture. And Mary was glad for the time off and didn't plan to start looking for another job until she had taken a vacation and "chilled out."

How do you feel about teenagers with a broken heart? Do you brush it off as "puppy love," or do you recognize the feelings can be as deep and profound as a divorce? The truth is, the feelings can be as powerful at any age. The difference may be the elements of the person's life that can be affected. Did the breakup affect the person's identity and self-image? Did it have an effect on their friends and social system? How about a financial impact? Did it necessitate a move? Change long term plans? The answers depend on the situation and the people and feelings involved. In actuality, the teenager's grief may be stronger than the adult's. The elements of the events are important in determining the effect of the crisis.

CHARACTERISTICS OF CRISES

Now that we've discussed the elements, let's look at a list of the potential characteristics of various crises. These characteristics can apply to just about any traumatic event.

Change in Future Direction

When something major happens, it usually means that something we had planned for is now either interrupted or ended entirely. When someone loses a child, for example, he comes to a painful realization he they won't have the opportunity to witness her graduation, marriage and possibly grandchildren. When we lose a job, we have to acknowledge that the pension we had planned won't happen.

In Maxwell Maltz's classic book, *Psycho-Cybernetics*, he says our brains are like a heat-seeking missile in quest of a target. When something occurs to eliminate the possibility of what we had earlier set as a goal, we become confused and frustrated. That is, until we adjust.

Sometimes pessimism makes us think our previous goals are now "impossible," when they may just be delayed or changed. As you'll learn in the fifth Reason Why, it may even be better than planned in many cases. Inability to have children may result in a more rewarding future by adopting. Losing a job may lead to a successful entrepreneurial adventure. In the meantime, however, our original plans are interrupted.

Change in Day-to-Day Activity

Most major events have two phases. The first phase is when our lives are turned upside down with a flurry of activity. We need to focus on the problem at hand, which means that we abandon other important things in our lives: family, friends, work, and engaging in pleasurable activities. Usually, we're too busy to even think about what we're missing, but occasionally it sets in and we get lonely, resentful or reminiscent of "the good old days."

In the second phase, a whole different set of emotions and situations occur when the major elements of the crisis have subsided. We have more time on our hands, and we also have to address the people and responsibilities we had put off.

In my hospice work, I've learned that one of the most challenging aspects families face is the sometimes dramatic change in their day-to-day schedules. While caring for a person who is seriously ill (or in trouble), family members' schedules are completely shifted toward taking care of the other person. The family might feel resentment and loss for the activities they were no longer able to experience. When the patient has passed on (or the trouble is over), the daily plans become wide open, sometimes causing loneliness and pain.

My sister was exceptionally attached to her 17-year-old dog. Being single and childless, this companion meant the world to her. Every day she spent most of her time with her beloved animal, knowing that she needed her extra care and that their time together was probably limited. When her pet died, I was not only very worried about her grief, but also concerned about the emptiness of her day-to-day life, so I "loaned" her my dog to take care of for a few weeks. It proved to be a significant contribution to her life. She could dote on my pet, filling up her schedule, but since she already knew him and was aware that he wasn't in her long-term future, she wouldn't have the problems often associated with getting another pet too soon, and she could return him to me when she was better able to cope.

Reduction/Elimination of Pleasurable Activities

When we're faced with upsetting incidents we're often forced to cut back on enjoyable activities - or potentially give them up. People entrenched in the aftermath of a natural disaster, for example, would often do anything for a hot bath. When we suffer a financial setback we feel deprived when we can't go out to dinner or buy something we want. When someone close to us dies, we often feel guilty when we do things fun or pleasurable, thinking that somehow it "isn't fair to their memory."

Change in Relationships

Relationships can change dramatically during a crisis. I've noticed when times were bad for me, I've lost a lot of friends. At first, it was very upsetting, and it caused me to challenge my faith, not only in the people I called friends, but also in my ability to choose the people to whom I would become close.

Because of my work with hospice patients, I know that the first few weeks following a death, the survivors will often be besieged with flowers, food and notes of sympathy. But after this initial period, they're often, in contrast, left very alone and sometimes forgotten.

When a close friend went through two major painful events at the same time, (the death of her mother and a divorce), she became aware of the changing nature of relationships during a crisis. Some people, she found, were right there at the beginning of the crisis, doing whatever they could do. She was grateful, but then she also saw that some weren't in for the long haul.

When we lose a job, we often lose the relationships that go along with it. When we go through a divorce, friends and family often "take sides." Relationships change even more dramatically when we have direct responsibility for causing our own crisis.

Separation from Others

Not only are we less able to see our friends and lose contact with other people, but we also can feel a sense of separation, of being different from them. We might fear we're being judged or condemned, so we avoid them. Of course, if we're incarcerated or in the hospital, then we have a literal physical separation from others.

Challenge of Faith or Trust

Our faith is challenged when we don't understand the Reasons Why the event occurred. We won't understand why our Higher Power could "let this happen," which makes us question His/Her power and concern.

And a crisis can also make us question and doubt the motives of other people, sometimes even making us distrust everyone.

One of the primary goals of this book is to provide understanding in this area and re-instill faith, in the Divine and in others.

Repeat Patterns and Downward Spiraling

> If you are caught in a situation of emotional turmoil, or if your ego has taken over, or if you find that something you are trying to accomplish is more difficult than it should be, that too many obstacles have come across your path, stop and ask yourself why.
> Your spirit knows, your intuition knows,
> but you have to be awake enough, and have enough self-awareness, to hear the message.
> - Carmen Harra

Sometimes the same, or a similar, problem can show up again and again. This can be a sign of a pattern repeating itself. For example, some people get one illness after another. Others may keep losing the same kinds of jobs.

Downward Spiraling is when one tragic event evolves into more and more problems. Someone can be a victim of crime and then become so upset or paranoid, he loses his job. Then he may experience the resulting financial problems and losses, which can put a strain on his relationships. What's the trigger that starts the spiral? By becoming aware of the Five Reasons Why, you'll be able to stop your patterns from repeating and spiraling downward.

EMOTIONS AND FEARS

Emotions

In addition to the emotional pain you identified at the beginning of this chapter, other feelings may be involved in your crisis. These emotions may be manifested in one of four ways:

- Toward us
- By ourselves (in general or toward ourselves)
- By us toward others
- Around us

Fear

Because fear is so significant throughout a crisis, it needs to have special attention. Fear is usually present in situations of disaster, no matter what the time perspective (if the crisis has already occurred, is in process, or still to come), although it's most pronounced when we're still facing problems ahead of us. Most (if not all) types of fear can be summarized by the following list.

Kinds of Fear:

- Fear of death
- Fear of God

- Fear of lack of love
- Fear of not being good enough
- Fear of loss
  - of love
  - of money/property
  - of mental abilities
- Fear of being trapped
- Fear of the unknown
- Fear of the future
- Fear of pain and/or ill health
- Fear of betrayal/misplaced trust
- Fear of evil

In the next chapter you'll be asked to look at your own crises and identify the elements involved, as well as to achieve clarity on how each of these characteristics relate to you.

Bad Things Defined

CHAPTER 5: UNDERSTANDING YOUR CRISIS

Before we begin looking at the Five Reasons Why, it's important to get a clear understanding of the crisis you're going through, including your role in the event, what is causing the problem, the time and the areas of life that are affected.

EVENTS AND POTENTIAL ELEMENTS

There are several elements that define tragic events, including:

- The *Role* of the individual and how he/she is involved
- The Cause of the event
- The Time Perspective – whether the event has happened in the past, is happening now or is expected to happen in the future, and
- The *Areas of Life* that are affected.

Role

To whom is the event happening? It's important to recognize whether the event is happening to you directly, or to someone close to you. If it's happening directly to you – you're the one with the health crisis, the job loss, or the broken heart – your experience will be very different than if you're indirectly involved. You may feel guilt or a degree of responsibility for how your calamity is affecting those close to you. *You* may know that you can handle the financial impact of a job loss, but you may be having profound feelings of the sacrifices your family will have to endure, for example.

If the disaster isn't yours specifically, it can still affect you deeply. For example, if your parent is diagnosed with a terminal illness, you may need to take on more responsibilities or you may not be able to receive comfort for your own challenges and distress. Your colleague may lose his or her job and not only will you miss their companionship and contribution, but your own workload will increase.

Or, perhaps the challenge may not be yours directly or indirectly, but you still feel profoundly affected by the stories of the anguish other people are going through, which makes it affect you personally. Millions of people mourned the death of Princess Diana, but to many the grief was personal: it brought up memories of their own divorce, or eating problem, or perhaps thinking of the children's loss of their beloved mother.

To understand your crisis, you'll also want to see if an event that has happened to someone else has caused a fear in yourself. If a hurricane can hit New Orleans, what natural disaster could affect your home? If your sister could get cervical cancer, could you? If terrorists could attack New York, what is the possibility they could attack your home town? Fear, as I'll discuss in the chapter on Subconscious Sabotage, has a powerful effect on our lives and we need to identify the source.

Cause

Identifying the cause of the event is a valuable way to get more understanding, and the more you're able to take some level of responsibility, the greater your potential for healing and learning. As you'll learn later in this book, the cause for a tragedy may or may not be one of the Reasons Why the event occurred. In the chapter on Karma I'll talk about causes and effects that affect individuals. In the chapter on Subconscious

Sabotage, I'll discuss how our thoughts – conscious and unconscious – create reality.

In their book *Predictable Surprises*, Max H. Bazerman and Michael D. Watkins define large-scale events (using examples including Enron and the 9/11 attacks) that are both predictable and preventable, yet which come as surprises, either because leaders refuse to see the evidence and ignore the warnings or they "don't think it can happen." Their book is a caution to business and political leaders to look for potential threats, respond in a timely manner and learn from mistakes.

Similarly, individual trials and tribulations should be analyzed as to whether they could've been predictable or preventable. Some things, of course, can't be prevented. Every one of us will die, but we can have some control over how we die. We will all experience the loss of a loved one, but we can be better prepared to cope. Other tragic events may be prevented completely, like many illnesses, relationship problems, business and financial failures and even accidents and being a victim of a crime. The chapter on Spiritual Darwinism includes tools for preventing these future adversities and will show how you can avoid being personally disturbed by large group events like attacks, and natural disasters.

> It's time to change the mind-set
> that natural disasters are inevitable.
> - Gordon McBean

Analyzing the cause of a situation helps us become more aware of our responsibility, which then can empower us to resolve the Bad Things that happen.

Time Perspective

Getting the proper perspective on the timing of the Bad Thing happening can help you deal with it more precisely and effectively.

> We have nothing to fear but fear itself.
> - Franklin Delano Roosevelt

Worry and Fear are focusing on dealings that have yet to take place. When I was in my darkest times, it was mostly due to worry or dread. I was unsure whether I could cope with horrors I saw coming on the horizon. I found out, however, that worrying about an event is always worse than it happening. For example, when I realized that selling everything I owned could be a freeing experience, it changed my perspective and made me realize the truth of President Roosevelt's statement above.

The following quote is from A Very Special Epilogue I wrote to DUET stories Volume III: *A Chorus of Voices*. Writing the following statement was a very powerful experience for me, because I finally "got it." I hope you do, too!

> Fear doesn't come from lack of love; it comes from lack of trust. The solution is to trust yourself, to trust each other and to trust your connection with the Source of all Love and Light. To trust God.
> from A Very Special Epilogue to DUET stories Volume III: A Chorus of Voices by Brownell Landrum

Guilt and resentment are emotions created by things that have already happened. Guilt and remorse can keep us trapped in the past and paralyze us from moving forward, either because we don't feel worthy or because we're afraid we'll make the same mistake again. Resentment is also an emotion caused by living in the past, but instead of regretting something we did in the past, we're angry with someone else for what she did to us.

Subconscious Sabotage, one of the Five Reasons Why, demonstrates the power of the emotions of worry, fear, guilt and resentment and how they can actually bring about the things you fear the most.

Both fear and guilt can be helpful emotions, however. Just as fear can be a healthy way to tell us what to avoid in the future, guilt or remorse is an opportunity to learn from our mistakes. Resentment gives us the opportunity to experience one of the most positive, loving and healing emotions we can feel: forgiveness.

Therefore, knowing the time perspective helps us know how to deal with the problem.

Areas of Life Affected and Degree

What areas of your life have been or are being affected the most by the crisis? Sometimes an event that affects one area of our lives can expand to affecting other areas of our lives. I've noticed in my own life, years ago, that I've lost people I considered friends when times got tough for me. Perhaps they did not know what to say. Or maybe they didn't want to catch the problems I had, as though failure or loss was some kind of virus. A friend of mine realized there were a number of people who were there for her when her mother died, but for only a short period of time, then they were gone.

By looking at the areas of your life (Relationships, Financial, Home, Job/Career, Future Direction, Self-image, and Physical) and examining the degree in which each are affected by what you're going through, you'll have the tools to cope with the experience.

Length of Impact

As with time perspective, how we look at the length of an event provides us with more realization. Chronic illnesses can cause a lifetime of pain. The death of someone close to you can be a long time unfolding or a quick, horrifying shock, but we can pass through the stages of mourning and, although forever changed, are able to move on with our lives. Parents with an abducted child may find at some point they need closure, even if the news is bad.

Just as we can be living in the past with carried-over fear, we can be dragging out a crisis beyond its actual life span. Some crises are unremitting and affect us significantly every day of our lives. But most aren't; they just seem that way. For example, we can be mourning the loss of a relationship for an overwhelmingly long period of time, and blaming the past instead of putting the past where it belongs and dealing with today's feelings today.

Recommendation #1 for Understanding and Resolving Your Bad Things:

Either get the Reasons Why Workbook or start a journal on your own. You've probably read this a dozen times and may have one started or still have one going. Journaling is especially important in times of crisis. In his book *Stumbling on Happiness*, author Daniel Gilbert conveys that "simply writing about a trauma – such as the death of a loved one or a physical assault – can lead to surprising improvements in both subjective well-being and physical health. What's more, the people who experience the greatest benefit from these writing exercises are those whose writing contains an explanation of the trauma."

Your Reasons Why Workbook or Journal will have a distinct purpose: to recognize, process and get to the bottom of the bad things in your life, to help you identify and appreciate the gifts, lessons and rewards in your life.

HOW IT FEELS

It doesn't matter what you're going through, relative to anyone else's problems. Any pain you're feeling is real to you – and understandable. You may have experienced feelings of despair; without hope. You might have felt like you were trapped in a pitch dark room, with no windows or doors open and nowhere to turn. You might have felt abandoned by someone close to you – or by The Divine. You might be exhausted with defeat and fear the feelings will never end.

There's a great book, called *Lost Between Lives* by Daniel Holden that I recommend. For me, his words felt very real, as if he understood what I was going through. It isn't a book of platitudes or feel-good affirmations. It's a book that allows you to realize you're not alone, that someone knows how you feel.

Although I'm convinced the Five Reasons Why can explain your trauma and help you cope with the problems you're facing, I never want to diminish the power of your anguish. It's very real and very palpable and can be extremely life-shattering.

Harold Percival, in his book, *Thinking & Destiny*[10], said the following:

> "If (you do) not run away from the indistinct apprehension of some disaster or from the fear of some definite calamity, (you have) an opportunity to change the desire that helped to conceive or entertain the thought that has to be balanced. All (you) need or can do, is to feel that it wants to do right and is willing to do or to suffer whatever is necessary to that end."

What he's saying here is that we need to feel the feelings. We need to be willing to feel the suffering. He goes on to say:

> "When (you get yourself) into that feeling, (you have) strength; strength comes. If (you hold) that feeling of strength (you) will be able to go through any disaster."

We should not ignore our feelings and we definitely should not medicate ourselves to cover them up. We need to experience them deeply, bringing them to the surface to be processed. When we have the courage to face our feelings of misery, loss and hopelessness, we'll find the strength to get through them. If we don't face our emotions, they'll continue to fester and swell below the surface, creating longer-lasting and more profound pain. Clinical research proved this to be true: "Suppression of emotional thoughts, particularly those thoughts that arouse negative emotions" increases "susceptibility to illness" via a weakened immune system (lower T-cell count).[11]

---

[10] I recommend this book if you have a voracious appetite for complex and detailed explanations for the ways of the world. It nearly 1000 almost overwhelmingly deep pages. Alternatively, you could read Richard Matheson's book called *The Path; A New Look at Reality*, which is based on Percival's book, is 144 pages and easier to read.

[11] Pennebaker, Petrie and Booth, "Immunological Effects of Thought Suppression"

Feel the Feelings

In the chapter on Subconscious Sabotage, you'll learn how to connect with your Subconscious or Inner Self. In the meantime, make sure you allow yourself to consciously feel the feelings you're going through. Don't mask them or cover them up with drugs. Don't distract yourself with work or other interferences, only to find you can't sleep or the feelings come out in the most inopportune moment.

In an episode of one of my favorite TV shows, Lost, the main character, a surgeon, said he had a situation when operating on a patient when he felt immense fear. He allowed himself five seconds to "let it in," to let the fear take over him. Then he was able to concentrate.

So throw a temper tantrum. Get on the bed on your back and kick and scream and cry. You can yell at someone you trust or just at air molecules. Just let your frustrations out.

The Reasons Why Workbook has a number of exercises to help you "face it, feel it, free it."

WHAT DO *YOU* THINK?

Why do you think it happened to you?

I was talking with Melissa, a lifelong friend of mine who had a serious problem with her brain – an inoperable abscess had appeared suddenly and she was having major problems with the antibiotics, the only known treatment. I asked her why she thought she had gotten the ailment.

First she described how she had been suddenly paralyzed and rushed to the hospital, and the whole course of diagnosis and treatment she endured. Then I asked her again, "Why do you think it happened to you?" She gave a very different answer. She said that by facing death, she no longer feared it and, although she's prepared for it, she's not ready. She also said she had put huge effort into her job that, in the end, wasn't meaningful for her. She was grateful for the understanding and support of her previous employer and the long-term disability made available.

She realized she was given an opportunity to find work that would allow her to have a more balanced and rewarding life. She praised her husband for his unwavering love and support. And she recognized the opportunity to explore her spiritual faith and get closer to the Divine.

Wow! I thought. I was so impressed and proud of her strength and insight. You'll see, when you explore the Five Reasons Why, what else she's learning from her experience.

Ask Friends and Family

Ask your friends and family, people you trust to be honest and who have your best interest at heart, what they think.

Most people (except perhaps our parents) are hesitant to be direct with us. They may not want to sound critical or unloving, or are afraid they won't seem compassionate. But often they know and can see what's going on with us more than we can.

The best way to get advice from your friends and family is to make it easy and comfortable for them to help you. Using the questions below, discuss your crisis with them.

Ask them to be as specific as they can. Why do they think you got cancer? Why do they think your spouse cheated on you? And so on.

- Why do you think it (the bad thing) happened to me?
- Have I ever done anything like this to anyone else?
- Do you think I caused this event in any way, either consciously or subconsciously? If so, how?
- How do you feel about what is happening (or has happened) to me?
- Do you think this could've been prevented? If so, how?
- Do you see any Lessons that I could be learning?
- Do you see any Tests that could be involved in what I'm going through?
- Do you see any possibility for a Reward or Blessing in Disguise? If so, what do you think that could be?

CHARACTERISTICS OF CRISES

Crises, even those vastly different from each other, often have some of the same characteristics. Looking at your event, which of the following has happened to you, and to what degree?

Change in Future Direction

- What plans that you had previously made for the future are now changed?

Change in Day-to-Day Activity

- How has your daily life changed?
- What are you doing now that you didn't do before?
- What are you not doing?

Reduction/Elimination of Pleasurable Activities

- What enjoyable activities are you now doing less of?
- Are any pleasures you previously enjoyed now not possible? Is this a short-term or a long term problem?

Separation from Others

- Do you feel separated from other people for some reason? Why?

Challenge of Faith or Trust

- Has your faith or trust in the Divine or your Higher Power been challenged? If so, in what ways?
- Has your confidence or reliance in others been compromised? Who, and how?

Harmful Habits

- Do you have any addictions or harmful habits? They could include anything done to an unbalanced level, including drinking alcohol, smoking, sleeping, eating, and even watching television or exercising. Describe.
- Have any of these habits increased – or decreased – since your crisis began?

Responsibility and Burden

- Do you feel like you're burdened with overwhelming responsibility – either more than you can handle, or more than you think you should have to deal with? If so, describe, and be specific.

Repeat Patterns and Downward Spiraling

- Have you experienced the same problem repeatedly? Are you always losing the same kinds of jobs, for example? Are you always in the same kinds of relationships? Are you constantly getting one illness after another? Explore and study any repeating patterns in your own life.

- Could you be in a Downward Spiral? Has one tragic event evolved into additional problems? Get clarity on the initial event – what started it all? How did one event roll into the other events? Was the trigger event the worst of it all, or were the subsequent events worse?

EMOTIONS AND FEARS

As you'll learn in the chapter on Subconscious Sabotage, emotions and fears are very influential in our lives, and if they aren't a source of unhappiness, they can be at least major contributors.

Emotions

Emotions can be on the surface, readily acknowledged and expressed, or they can be hidden and/or suppressed. They can be a result of what is happening now in our lives or be a residual effect of something from our past. And they can be something that "attaches" to us from others, almost like a virus that enters our system. Because of the impact of emotions, both ours and those of people around us, we need to dig deep to unearth the deepest, and darkest ones in order to heal.

Emotional Responses

The following is a list of emotions. Have you experienced any of these emotions, feelings or actions – toward you, by you toward yourself (or in general), by you toward others, around you?

Aggression, agony, anger, anguish, annoyance, arrogance, bitterness, cowardice, cruelty, deceit, denial, depression, despair, despondency, discrimination, distrust, envy, exhaustion, fear, frustration, gloom, gluttony, greed, grief, guilt, harassment, hatred, hypocrisy, ingratitude, irresponsibility, jealousy, judgment, malice, meanness, menace, pain, pessimism, prejudice, rage, rancor, remorse, resentment, revenge, seething, selfishness, self-loathing, sloth, sorrow, torment, torture, vindictiveness, violence, worry.

> The first step toward change is awareness. The second step is acceptance. The third step is action.
> - Nathaniel Branden

Fears

Do you have any of the following fears? In the form below, indicate the degree of fear you have in each area. And, while answering think of the *why* behind your answers. For example, if you fear God, why? If you fear loss, what are you afraid of losing? If you're afraid of the future, what are you worried about happening?

Types of Fear

- Fear of death
- Fear of God
- Fear of lack of love
- Fear of not being good enough
- Fear of rejection
- Fear of loss
- Fear of loss of money/property
- Fear of loss of mental or physical abilities
- Fear of being trapped
- Fear of the unknown
- Fear of the future

- Fear of pain and/or ill health
- Fear of betrayal/ misplaced trust
- Fear of evil

LOOKING FORWARD

How Do You Think You Will Feel About Your Experiences in the Future? How do you think you'll feel two weeks from now? Six weeks from now? Six months from now? A year from now? Two years from now? Ten years from now?

Sometimes we can't see through the darkness. Just like on rainy days we can't imagine the sun ever shining again. But guess what? The sun will, as the song goes, come out tomorrow. It always has!

Understanding Your Crisis

CHAPTER 6: THE FIVE REASONS WHY

There are Five Reasons Why Bad Things happen:

1. Karma
2. Subconscious Sabotage
3. Lessons
4. Tests
5. Reward

Each of the Five Reasons Why are described in depth in their own individual chapter. But what do they have in common and how do they interact?

WHAT THE FIVE REASONS HAVE IN COMMON

- The Reasons Why are straightforward and relatable
- All crises are explainable by the Reasons Why.
- All of the Reasons Why are driven by a higher purpose.
- It is necessary to understand the Reasons Why to achieve long-term healing.

- The power to heal is within each of us.
- The Reasons Why can all be diagnosed and resolved.
- The Reasons Why may be used to help us learn how to prevent future bad things from happening.

The Reasons Why Are Straightforward and Relatable

Although you may learn some new explanations and techniques, the Reasons Why are straightforward so that everyone can relate to them. No matter what your crisis is, and regardless of your spiritual beliefs, anyone can recognize and appreciate the messages herein.

All Crises Are Explainable by the Reasons Why

As established in the Basic Assumptions, our lives have a purpose and things happen for a reason. Although Bad Things can seem to be random "attacks," you'll see how they can explain every kind of event, from seemingly "evil" acts, like terrorist attacks and rape, to personal illness to natural disasters.

All of the Reasons Why Are Driven By A Higher Purpose

The Divine is loving, generous and compassionate. He (or She) wants only the best for us. He/She isn't angry, vengeful or full of wrath – these are purely human emotions. In fact, He/She gave us free will, so we could have the freedom to choose whether to be like the Divine – caring and kindhearted – or away from Him.

The underlying purpose for each of the Reasons Why is to help learn to be more loving toward ourselves, each other and the planet.

It is Necessary to Understand the Reasons Why to Achieve Long-Term Healing

The best doctors in the world can provide medications or surgery to treat an illness, but unless the Reason Why the disease came about is healed, their efforts are temporary, or another, similar problem will likely develop.

The Power to Heal is Within Each of Us

Because the power to heal is within each of us, to be healed of your Reasons Why you won't need to follow a new guru or see a new doctor or change your belief system. This doesn't mean you should abandon whatever method of physical, psychological or spiritual healing you're pursuing; it just means that the true cure comes from within.

They All Can Be Diagnosed and Resolved

Through the use of this book, everyone who reads and follows closely can have their Reasons Why diagnosed and resolved, which is where real healing begins.

> Generally, a difficult situation gives us an opportunity to see where we are stuck or fearful so we can take appropriate new steps. It could be an opportunity to heal an old wound, to discover an unconscious behavior pattern, to stand up for ourselves, to accomplish a dream, or to learn a crucial piece of information that we need for our evolving journey. Once our learning is accomplished, life makes sure we move along.
> - James Redfield and Carol Adrienne

The Reasons Why Can Be Used to Help Us Learn How to Prevent Future Bad Things from Happening

Because the Reasons Why explain any crisis, they can also be used to help you prevent Bad Things from affecting you. The chapter on Spiritual Darwinism will demonstrate this rather ambitious claim. However, it won't do any good to move straight to that chapter, because the pre-requisite is reading the earlier chapters.

How They Interact

At least one of the Five Reasons Why can explain what happens to you – but not necessarily all 5. You could have one, two, three, four or all 5 of the Reasons Why in your situation, and they can also be combined in one several ways.

Important Things to Remember about the Reasons Why

Two important things to keep in mind about the Reasons Why. First, there is always a Reasons Why. Second, no one should judge anyone else's Reasons Why.

There is Always a Reason Why

> If everything continued "happily ever after" we would remain in an undisturbed and permanently dulled state. Nothing of interest would happen, no development would be possible...
> – Edward Whitmont

The mystery of our misfortunes will be revealed. Like the beams of light flowing through the clouds after a storm, you will be enlightened with understanding how problems can be explained. This is the gift I received through my ordeal, which I'm sharing with you.

This might be difficult for you to adopt initially. Therefore, a leap of faith is required at this stage. But this book will clearly explain that everything that happens to us is a result of one or more of the Five Reasons Why.

No One Can or Should Attempt to Determine or Judge Anyone Else's Reasons Why

"Judge not yet ye be judged." (Matthew 7:1) Although this book will suggest some *possible* explanations of the Reasons Why certain problems manifest, only you can determine the explanation for yourself. By reading this book, you'll have the tools to uncover your own Reasons Why.

If you're faced with comforting someone else while he's going through turmoil, make sure you don't pass judgment on why you think he's experiencing their crisis. The last chapter will provide suggestions for helping others through their misfortunes and setbacks.

The Five Reasons Why

CHAPTER 7: THE FIRST REASON WHY: KARMA

The first of the Five Reasons Why is Karma. Karma is perhaps the most obvious Reason Why. Although it doesn't apply in all situations, it's a commonly recognized form of cosmic justice. But what is Karma?

KARMA QUIZ

Let's start out by seeing how much you know about Karma.

1. True or False?
   a. You have to believe in reincarnation to accept the principles of Karma.
   b. Karma = Punishment
   c. You pay for your Karma in the next lifetime.
   d. Karma is a form of Cosmic Justice – to make people pay for their sins.
   e. You cannot be Christian and believe in Karma.
   f. Karma is predictable but not preventable.
   g. We sometimes choose Karma to teach us and help us evolve.
   h. Karma always includes Lessons, but Lessons don't always involve Karma.

  i. You can't prevent group Karma.

  j. We should always try to help other people resolve or remove their Karma.

2. Where does the word Karma come from?
  a. A song in the 80's by Culture Club
  b. Sanskrit: meaning "to do" or *deed*
  c. Pali: meaning *action, effect, destiny*

3. Who or What administers Karma?
  a. An all-powerful God
  b. A Jury or Tribunal "up there'
  c. Our Spirit Guides or Guardian Angels
  d. It is all Energy – Like Attracting Like, the interaction and reaction of forces, the balancing of power.

4. Which of the following statements does *not* describe Karma?
  a. You Reap What You Sow
  b. Do Unto Others As You Would Have Them Do Unto You
  c. To Everything There is a Season
  d. For Every Action There is a Reaction
  e. What Comes Around Goes Around
  f. Cause and Effect
  g. An Eye For An Eye

5. Can you believe in the concept of Karma and not believe in reincarnation?
  a. No, they go hand in hand. You have to believe in one to believe in the other.
  b. Yes.
  c. I don't know.

6. How does Karma relate to punishment?
  a. They are the same thing.

   b. They can be the same thing, but Karma can be positive, too.
   c. Karma is never negative or punishment, it's only positive or good.

7. You decide to steal someone's idea at work. Which of the following examples describes Karma that could result?
   a. The idea turns out to be a bad one and your company loses millions and you lose your job
   b. The person you stole the idea from bad-mouths you to everyone else in the company.
   c. Years later, you leave the company and apply to a new company, and then find out that the hiring manager is the person you stole the idea from.
   d. Someone steals your idea.

8. What is Instant Karma?
   a. A song by John Lennon
   b. When you miss the next shot in racquetball after lying about he serve being "out."
   c. When the effect immediately follows the cause.

9. What do you do when you get emails that say "if you don't forward this email something bad will happen?"
   a. I always send them on – I don't want any bad luck coming my way!
   b. I get angry with the person who sent them.
   c. I ignore them. If you don't believe in that stuff it won't affect you.
   d. Sometimes I don't send them and then something bad will happen to me, like smashing my finger in the computer when I shut it down.

10. What religion or belief system has a version of Karma?

     a. Hindu
     b. Christian
     c. Buddhism
     d. New Age

11. What is a way to clear up negative Karma?
     a. Apologize to the people you've harmed and try to make it up to them.
     b. Take your punishment and get it over with.
     c. Avoid the person you harmed.

12. What is the best way to create more positive Karma?
     a. Give money to charity anonymously.
     b. Do a favor for someone.
     c. Eat your vegetables.
     d. Pray for the health and well-being of others, including strangers.
     e. Forgive people who have harmed you.

WHAT DO YOU KNOW ABOUT KARMA?

What are your feelings about the following phrases?

- Cause and Effect
- You Reap What You Sow.[12]
- Do Unto Others As You Would Have Them Do Unto You (or If You Do Unto Others They Will React by Doing Unto You.)
- Punishment or Reward for Past Deeds
- For Every Action There is a Reaction.[13]

---

[12] "A man reaps what he sows. The one who sows to please his sinful nature, from that nature will reap destruction; the one who sows to please the Spirit, from the Spirit will reap eternal life. Let us not become weary in doing good, for at the proper time we will reap a harvest if we do not give up." – Galatians 6:7-9

[13] "To every action there is always opposed an equal reaction" from Sir Isaac Newton's Laws of Motion III.

- You Will Be Punished for Your Sins
- What Goes Around Comes Around
- He Who Lives By The Sword Dies By The Sword.[14]
- He got what's coming to him
- An Eye for an Eye.[15]

Most people, most cultures believe in some form of Karma. And most Bad Things can be explained by Karma.

The concept of Karma is reaching the mainstream. The best example of this is the television show, *My Name is Earl*, on NBC. The premise of the show is that the main character, Earl, learns the meaning of karma – that, basically, bad luck follows bad deeds and good luck follows good deeds. Earl has a list of all the bad things he has done in his life. Each episode shows not only he tries to set his Karma right, but also how he knows that any questionable act he could do from now forward would create more negative Karma.

The creators, producers, writers and actors on this show should be applauded for bringing consciousness of conscience to the public. And what Earl demonstrates is that Karma isn't necessarily instant – it can have its effects many years in the future.

It's also interesting how the show doesn't address particular spiritual beliefs. Karma seems to have its own energy and driving purpose.

An Eye for An Eye – A Tragic Misinterpretation

It's this author's assertion that this phrase from Exodus has been depressingly misinterpreted, leading to additional harmful

---

[14] "He that leadeth into captivity shall go into captivity; he that killeth with the sword must be killed with the sword." - Bhagavad Gita (Song Celestial: 4)
[15] "And if any mischief follow, then thou shalt give life for life, Eye for eye, tooth for tooth, hand for hand, foot for foot. Burning for burning, wound for wound, stripe for stripe." -- Exodus 21: 23-25

Karma being generated in the world. Too often, people use this Old Testament quote to justify human revenge (otherwise known as evil), instead of its actual intent of communicating the effects of Karma: if you take an eye, be prepared to lose an eye.

WHAT IS KARMA?

> I believe that we are solely responsible for our choices,
> and we have to accept the consequences of every deed,
> word, and thought throughout our lifetime.
> - Elisabeth Kubler-Ross

Karma is derived from Sanskrit, meaning "to do" or *deed,* and from Pali: meaning *action, effect, or destiny.* The general concept of Karma is common in most of the mainstream religions, including but not limited to, Hindu, Buddhism, Christianity, Judaism, Muslim, and more. Many people think of Karma as justice or punishment for our sins, handed out by a threatening all-powerful God who should be feared. Or, perhaps, that all our transgressions are evaluated and dispensed by an otherworldly jury.

But if we stay with our Basic Assumptions that the Higher Power or the Divine is Love/Loving and there is a purpose for our lives, the more logical and loving explanation of Karma is to teach, to make us better people and make the world a better place. If there were no repercussions to our actions, what kind of world would we create?

Until all humans become fully enlightened beings and can recognize the inner, personal hurt that comes from harming others – and, conversely, the positive, beautiful, feeling that comes from acting in a generous, loving way, we need to know that our actions have consequences.

> How would you live your life differently, if you
> instantly felt the harm you inflicted on another?
> - Brownell

Dannion Brinkley said in his autobiography about his near death experience, *Saved by the Light,* that when we die, we experience a Life Review where we not only we re-live all the experiences of our lives, but we also re-live them *from the other person's point of view.* Anyone we were ever mean or cruel to, we experience how they felt. Anyone we were ever angry with, we feel how our anger affected the other person. If we lied, we learn how it felt to be lied to. If we physically harmed someone, we feel the pain ourselves. If we judged someone, we feel the judgment ourselves. Every unkind thought and all wounding actions are relived from the other person's point of view.

Conversely, anyone we were ever generous with, or loving or thoughtful to, we get to feel how they felt. We experience every kind touch, every considerate gesture, and every good or loving thought we have ever demonstrated to others.

> Karma is harsh in its fairness. It is so fair that all appeals to chance, accident, or luck are ruled out. It means that it is hopeless to drift through life waiting for the breaks to come our way. We are the breaks.
> – Larry Dossey, M.D.

The following quote from Richard Matheson's book, *What Dreams May Come,* is a nice illustration of karma and the life review: "Not only did I rediscover every sense experience of my life, I had to live each unfulfilled desire as well – as though they'd been fulfilled. I see that what transpires in the mind is just as real as any flesh and blood occurrence. What had only been imagination in life now became tangible, each fantasy a full reality. Still, always the balance. The scales of justice: darkness paralleled by light, cruelty by compassion, lust by love. And always, unremittingly, that inmost summons: *What have you done with your life?"*

KARMIC TIMING

Karma isn't just in a Life Review; it occurs throughout life. And, although it can be instant, it usually isn't, and can take years or even lifetimes. This means that we never know when our

Karma can cycle back to us. Harold Percival, in his book, *Thinking & Destiny,* uses the term *exteriorization of thought* as a description of Karma: "This is the law: Every thing existing on the physical plane is an exteriorization of a thought, which must be balanced through the one who issued the thought, and in accordance with that one's responsibility, at the conjunction of time, condition, and place."

Instant Karma

Instant Karma, in addition to being a song by John Lennon, is the most obvious demonstration of the cause-and-effect relationship. We have all experienced it. One of my favorite examples is when I play racquetball. Inevitably, when either my opponent or I make a bad call, we miss the next shot. For example, he might say that my serve was "out," but without conviction, and I know he's wrong. So we play the point again and I win the point. Instant Karma happens so much in our games together that we automatically, and jokingly, accept the outcome of the successive point is karmic retribution.

Can you think of times when you've experienced Instant Karma? Have you ever had something happen to you immediately following something you've done? Most of us know how it feels to receive instant repercussion from a behavior or action – if we smile at someone, they usually smile back, and if we're rude or inconsiderate (or even mean), we'll feel their response right away.

Present Life Karma

Most Karma happens later in our lives, waiting for the best opportunity or circumstance. Here's an example of an experience I had with Karma: One day I told Karen[16], a good friend whom I had worked with previously, about a job opportunity I was pursuing through a recruiter. Immediately after we hung up, she contacted the recruiter and told her that she (Karen) was more qualified for the job than I was. Karen tried to get the recruiter to cancel my interview and send her instead. Instead, the recruiter

---

[16] The name has been changed.

called me immediately and told me what Karen had done, not believing the underhanded nerve that Karen showed.

Fast forward two years. I was working for a competitor in the same kind of prestigious job we had both wanted, and I got a call from the Human Resources department. He asked if I knew someone with Karen's name, noticing that we'd worked together years previously. I told him what she'd done and he promptly discarded her resume. Then, a month or two later, I was traveling for business and ran into Karen at the airport. She asked who I worked for and I told her. She was in visible shock.

Did Karen get her Karma? I don't know – it's her Karma, not mine. And I don't know if she learned a Lesson or not. But I learned a Lesson. I didn't have to do anything for Karen to get her Karma. I never had to get angry with her. I wasn't malicious about her, bad-mouthing her to others. I just told the truth to HR. And let Karma do the rest.

An alternative experience was when I was working in a job that I absolutely hated. My boss was a nightmare, making life hell for all his subordinates. I had moved halfway across the country for the job and felt lost and desperate for a way out. One of my peers (Trey) was excited about a job he for which he had an interview and I was jealous. I wanted the job! I talked with the Trey. I asked him to keep me apprised of his interviews and status. I also asked if he'd let me know if it didn't look like he'd get the job and if he'd be upset if I pursued it, should that happen. When he knew he wasn't being considered, I got an interview. Neither of us was hired, which turned out to be a blessing in disguise, when the man with whom we'd both interviewed was arrested for embezzling.

Karma? I don't know, but I do feel like I passed the Test, and it was a blessing that I didn't get the job.

Past Life Karma and Reincarnation

Reincarnation is a basic premise behind many religions' views of Karma and is a powerful explanation of Bad Things that happen to someone at birth.

A lot of excellent books have been written about Reincarnation and how past lives affect subsequent ones, including those by Brian L Weiss, Richard Sutphen, James Van Praagh, Helen Wambach and several more. If you're interested in this topic and want to learn more about how present-day problems may be explained by a past life, I recommend you explore books by these authors.

If you don't believe in Reincarnation, you can still believe in Karma. While it is true that you would be precluded from using Karma as an explanation for some Bad Things, one or more of the other Reasons Why would still apply.

FAMILY KARMA AND GROUP KARMA

Karma doesn't just affect individuals – it can be a factor in group and family events as well. Examples of Family Karma would be if your home was the only one in the neighborhood destroyed by a tornado, or if all members of a family had a genetic disorder.[17] If every member of a family is responsible for a harmful behavior or action, all will probably be concerned with repercussive Karma.

Family Karma can extend generations. Some of your experiences may be traced back to those of your grandparents. For example, if you're a descendant of the Mayflower, you may have a naturally strong survival instinct. If your grandmother was sexually abused, it could explain your mother's distrust of men. A grandfather's involvement with illegal alcohol trade in the time of Prohibition could translate into alcoholism in the family.

Several years ago, I met a woman whose family was always sick with different ailments. When one member would get ill, another would get something more serious. This could be family Karma. Or it could be Subconscious Sabotage or even a Lesson or a Test – or a combination!

---

[17] Please note, however, this doesn't mean that Karma necessarily caused these events – these are just possible examples.

Group Karma

Group Karma could refer to a group of any size: a small gathering of two or three friends, a team of twenty or more, a city, or even a nation. When one nation attacks another country, it disturbs the Karma of everyone in the assaulting nation, whether they supported the war or not. If a group of two or three people get together to gossip or put down someone else, all members of the group are subject to karmic repercussions.

Group Karma could explain all kinds of events, from terrorist attacks to airplane crashes to natural disasters. The decisions and actions of the leader of a nation or a company have an effect on the entire group under their influence. In this way, the expression "one bad apple spoils the whole bunch" can apply. Karmic events can happen, even when we aren't personally involved, but "allow" things to happen.

Conversely, the actions of a few people within a group or territory can positively involve the larger group. For example, studies have proven what is called the "1% Solution." When 1% of a population of a town meditates regularly, crime drops significantly. This fact is expanded into a theory that if 1% of the people of the Earth were to meditate regularly we would have world peace. Group thought with intention is powerful!

What If Everybody Did?

When I was a child, one of my favorite books was a book called *What if Everybody Did?*[18] The message of the book was to look at your actions and ask yourself what would happen if everyone took the same action. They used the examples of picking a flower and then showed a garden with no flowers, only stems. And I think they used the example of throwing a piece of trash, on the highway and then how the street would be overwhelmed with pieces of trash if everyone did the same thing.

We may feel like our actions are not so significant (and thereby at any risk of generating negative Karma for us), when

---

[18] I don't remember the author, and haven't been able to locate the book – it may no longer be in print…

done in isolation, but we need to consider, "What if everybody did it?"

The "Why" of Karma and How Karma Explains Bad Things

So why does Karma exist? Why would a loving Higher Power create a world with Karma? Could Karma actually be a loving concept?

From the higher perspective, Karma is a concept of love. Have you ever realized that you learned more from touching the hot stove than from having someone tell you that it was hot and not to touch it?

Have you ever had a teacher who challenged you – who was fair, but wouldn't accept cookie-cutter answers or lazy reports – and knew their motive was for you to learn? It worked, didn't it? You put in extra effort and received the Reward of additional knowledge. The Divine works that way. Maybe you haven't always realized that Bad Things are ways for us to learn, that a higher purpose was involved. But now you do. Karma gives us a chance to balance our past transgressions and learn how to stop the cycle.

> Karma encourages soul and planetary progress.
> - Brownell

Karma and Predictable Events

In the earlier chapter on the Five Reasons Why you learned about Predictable Surprises. How do they relate to Karma? Simply, Karma can be a way of predicting an event that will happen to us. We may not be able to determine the time, place and condition of the repercussion of our actions, but the law of Karma predicts that we'll "reap what we sow."

REVENGE, RESENTMENT AND CYCLICAL KARMA

How people treat you is their karma;

> how you react is yours.
> - Wayne Dyer

Karma isn't revenge, and should *never* be used as a justification for revenge. As discussed earlier, the biblical phrase "an eye for an eye" has been misinterpreted. It does not mean that revenge is justified. It means that if you take an eye, an eye will be taken from you – which is Karma.

When someone engages in revenge, it escalates the karmic cycle into horrifying consequences for all involved.

There's a memorable scene in the movie *The Interpreter*[19], where Nicole Kidman's character, Silvia Broome, describes the way the people in a fictional African country called Matobo deal with grief and revenge. They use a powerful ritual that offers victims' families a way to relive their grief, by ending the karmic cycle.

> "Everyone who loses somebody wants revenge on someone - on God if they can't find anyone else. But in Africa, in Matobo, the Ku believe the only way to end grief is to save a life. If someone is murdered, a year of mourning ends with a ritual that we call the Drowning Man Trial. There's an all-night party beside a river. At dawn, the killer is put in a boat, he's taken out on the water and he's dropped. He's bound, so that he can't swim. The family of the dead then has to make a choice. They can let him drown or they can swim out and save him. The Ku believe that if the family lets the killer drown, they'll have justice, but spend the rest of their lives in mourning. But if they save him -

---

[19] *Written by* Charles Randolf, Scott Frank and Steven Zaillian and directed by Sydney Pollack.

if they admit that life isn't always just - that very act can take away their sorrow."

The beauty of this story is how it gives us a different perspective on grief and vengeance. We may have tried to justify our actions as "human nature" when we want to blame someone for the Bad Things that happen to us, but this story is more than a screenplay. It makes us realize that, not only is vengeance a lazy form of grief, but it can cause a lifetime of pain. Karma tells us this anguish is a *result* of the revenge we hold in our hearts.

However, if we learn the Lesson and accept the Reasons Why tragedies occur, we can recognize the opportunities provided to us to truly heal – and end - the cycle created by Karma.

Justice, Jail and Legal Resolution

We all need to avoid being part of someone else's Karma. As soon as we get involved in another person's Karma, we become subject to that Karma ourselves. But what should we do when someone attacks us? What should we do when someone steals from us? Should we take her to court? Or let it go? Should we fight or walk away?

It's a personal choice but, to avoid negative Karma, we need to be mindful of our motivation. If you're angry or want revenge, you'll be lowering yourself to the perpetrator's level and continue the karmic cycle, while destroying yourself physically and mentally in the process.

Conversely, if you're able to release any resentment and forgive, yet still understand that you need to play out your role and help protect society by factually and unemotionally explaining the course of events, you're less likely to create negative Karma and you may even be creating positive Karma, instead. In addition, you need to be open to whatever apologies, amends or compensation the perpetrator can provide.

I'll give you an example. The other day, someone illegally cut me off in traffic. I clearly had the right of way, but she recklessly disregarded my rights or my feelings in the matter. So I showed my annoyance. I didn't have any anger or thoughts of revenge, however. I just wanted to make it clear they did something wrong. The next person, however, might not be so nice. They might have even enacted revenge – either with vengeful thoughts or actions to make her "pay" for her disregard. For me, however, I didn't hold any anger or resentment toward her, I just let it go. In the past, I might have let the experience ruin my day, which would have done more harm to me than it would have done to the guilty party.

In the next chapter, I discuss the ways our thoughts can create the events that happen to us.

INDIRECT KARMA

Often what happens to us is the result of someone else's Karma, but it still can affect us. For example, if your brother's car is stolen, it may affect your outlook on life, (you may be angry, etc.) and you may have to become his chauffeur. The World Trade Center attacks on 9/11 directly harmed less than 4000 people, but thousands, perhaps millions, more have been impacted by the tragedy.

KARMA AND INTENTION, THOUGHTS AND FEELINGS

It's pretty clear that Karma is a result of our actions, but can our thoughts and/or feelings also create Karma? How about the role of intention? Does it make a difference if we intend to hurt someone or if, on the other hand, we harm them through reckless disregard or even by accident? How important are our feelings and thoughts?

Questions To Ponder: What Is The Role Of Intent In Karma?

In your journal, answer the following questions:

- If you do something with a positive intention, yet others consider your actions harmful, are you creating negative Karma?
- What if others are actually harmed?

- If you do something and upset or hurt someone without realizing it, do you create negative Karma?
- Would it make a difference if they were hurt physically, emotionally, or both?
- If you do something that hurts others, but it's for their benefit, are you creating negative Karma?
- Someone does something to you and you react by doing the same thing back to him. Are you ending the Karmic cycle, or are you creating more negative Karma?
- Suppose you're warned that someone is planning to harm or attack you, so you go after them first. Is this creating negative Karma? Or is it preventing it?
- Someone is attacking your family and you pull out a gun and kill her. Are you immune from negative Karma or will you have to pay? What if the harm is more mental or emotional than physical? Does that make a difference?
- You steal something from someone who has more than enough – food, for example. Does this act create negative Karma?
- If you do something that might be considered a sin, but have reason or justification for your actions, is it still a sin?
- If you do something destructive to someone, either with ill intent or with reckless disregard for their well-being, but instead of being hurt, he either doesn't care or finds Reward in the outcome, are you still creating bad Karma?

The following quote from Gary Zukav summarizes the role of thoughts, feelings and intent in Karma: "Every action, thought, and feeling is motivated by an intention, and that intention is a cause that exists as one with an effect. In this profound way, we are held responsible for our every action, thought, and feeling, which is to say, for our every intention."

A friend of mine was driving down the highway in the right lane and cut off the person trying to merge in the lane. I called his attention to what he did, and he said that since he didn't mean to do it, he shouldn't feel guilty and wouldn't have any Karmic repercussions. Do you agree? I didn't. Whether he intended to hurt the other person or not, they were probably upset. He could have even caused an accident. Ignorance of the law of Karma is no excuse. He and I've talked about this a few times since, and my friend has come to realize that his actions had repercussions, and he has become more aware ever since.

Just a couple of weeks ago, another event happened that clarified the situation. A friend's niece was in a serious accident, in nearly the same location, because someone cut her off in traffic. Whether that person intended to hurt her or not, his carelessness and inconsideration caused her car to flip, trapping her upside down and crushing her hand, resulting in a partial amputation.

Even if we may not see the result of our actions, the lessons of Karma will probably come back around to teach.

The Law of Karma holds that two factors are involved: intent and effect of your actions.

Intent is an indication of your emotional state, at the time of the event. Deliberately hurting someone else is, of course, the most severe kind of a negative Karmic act, but even if you are indifferent to the feelings of others, you'll also have a karmic consequence. In all cases, if the other person is harmed by your actions, you'll most likely experience a Karmic aftermath.

Effect is the result of how someone felt because of what you did. Although we cannot always be responsible for how others feel, Karma can swoop in and give us the Lesson: How would you feel, if it was done to you?

We need to be very careful, when we rationalize or try to justify our actions. I remember clearly a discussion with a woman I used to work with about the war in Iraq. She considered herself a devout God-fearing Christian, but some of her views on revenge and pre-emptive action didn't match those of Christ's teachings. Instead of following the commandment, "Thou Shalt Not Kill" she admitted that she would, without remorse, quickly end the life of someone who was trying to harm someone in her family. Instead of the 'turn the other cheek" approach, she felt "we should get them before they attack us." She felt fully justified in her position, even though her proposed actions were in complete conflict with her religious doctrine.

Let's suppose, for a minute, her approach is defensible. What kind of a world would that create? I explained to her the pre-emptive attitude of "get them before they get us" creates a very slippery slope. How do you know they will "get' us? How can you be absolutely certain? Even if you're sure, doesn't that make you as "bad" as they are? Wouldn't the result be a paranoid world where everyone is constantly fearful of anyone "different" than they are? And since every human being is, in essence, individual and unique, then potentially everyone "out there" would be someone to fear – or attack.

Karma in Your Own Yard

Let's look at a simpler, less controversial example. Let's suppose you woke up and found that your neighbor had driven a deep rut in your yard the night before. How would you react? Would you confront him? If so, would you react in rage, or would you calmly ask him what had happened? Or would you hire an attorney to take action? Or, instead of confronting him, would you do the same, to "show" him? Or perhaps, in your rage, would you do something even worse?

If your answer was to react in anger or even rage, how loving do you think that response is? How effective? Suppose you went over to him and got furious, how do you think he would respond? How do you think he'd react if you did something similar back to him (the old interpretation of "an eye for an eye")?

I'm confident you recognize the harmful effect of responding in anger – it creates more anger – in you and the other person. And reacting in revenge creates an escalating cycle.

Now let's look at another way to respond to the situation. Yes, you're angry. You have the right to feel violated. As you'll learn in the next chapter, it's not healthy or advisable to hold in your negative emotions. Face the anger inside of yourself. Feel it. Get the emotion to the surface and even find a safe way to express it. Hitting a pillow is a good way. Physical exercise also works very well. Expressing your emotions allow you to be free and free them.

Following this release, you're able to get grounded and ask for Divine Guidance. You can go next door and talk rationally to your neighbor. You can show him what he's done and ask him, calmly yet confidently, to make it up to you – perhaps to not only fix the lawn but offer another gesture to demonstrate their appreciation for your understanding. You may find out he was really embarrassed and afraid to talk with you – and that he's grateful for a chance to make it up to you.

Okay, you may be asking, "But what if the neighbor hates you?" What if you're sure she did it to "get you?" If this is the case, then you should do whatever you can to find out why. Was she angry for something you had done to her? Is it possible she's angry, for something you might not be aware, but she never confronted you, she just held in the feelings?

"No," you may be saying to yourself. He's just acting irrationally. He's jealous or resent you for something you possess. Then remember Basic Assumption #7: Survival of the Fittest. Humans react very predictably when they're challenged. They'll try to "survive" by demonstrating an advantage of superior strength, often by putting someone else down in order to survive. Understanding the motivations and reactions in human beings can help you know how to resolve conflict with them. Your neighbor may be going through some very difficult times and their rutting your yard was a way to act out their emotions. She may need your pity and understanding not your anger.

As previously discussed, when each of us departs this world, we face a review of our lifetime, including not just everything we experienced from our own point of view, but also from the perspective of everyone we interacted with in our lifetimes. Not only that, but we're also confronted with others who were impacted by what we did *in*directly. For example, the person who cut off my friend's niece (in the previous example) will not only have to meet her and feel how she felt, but also experience the emotions and torment felt by her family and close friends.

OTHER PEOPLE'S KARMA

Just as we should avoid being a part of another person's Karma, we should also never place judgment on whether someone else deserves, or is receiving, Karma. Every time we judge others, we create negative Karma for ourselves.

Before becoming too involved with helping someone else, especially when choosing a side in a dispute, we need to carefully watch our motivations and judgment. When we get involved with another person's Karma, we're often guilty of judging what they're going through. Most so-called handicapped people would prefer to be treated like everyone else, not to be pitied or "cured" in any way. And their situation has its own Reason Why.

If a child dies early in its life, we do not know what agreement was made between that child's soul and the soul of its parents, or what healing was served by that experience. Although we are sympathetic to the anguish of the parents, we cannot judge this event.

> If we, or the parents of this child, do not understand the impersonal nature of the dynamic that is in motion, we may react with anger towards the Universe, or towards each other or with guilt if we feel that our actions were inadequate. All these reactions create Karma,
> and more lessons for the soul to learn –
> more karmic debts for the soul to pay – appear.
> - Gary Zukav

A woman might choose, for example, to experience life in a wheelchair in order to learn compassion. Or, perhaps, she had a subconscious desire to have someone take care of her. In this case, removing their handicap would remove her opportunity to learn.

We should especially be careful when choosing sides in other people's disputes, either on an individual basis or on a global basis. History is ripe with examples of international disagreements where military assistance is provided to a so-called ally who ended up turning on the nation who provided the help.

There are always two sides in an argument, and there's almost always some level of "fault" on both sides. Each role could've been performed differently, because there was one or more critical decisions made on each side.

What if someone asks us for help? In the last chapter I'll discuss ways to help others through their crisis.

Evil Explained by Karma

If we recognize evil to be described and identified in our Basic Assumptions as being generated by human thought and action, then the law of Karma suggests that acts against us we would call "evil" are likely to be the result of what we have done to others.

KARMA AND THE ROLE OF THE DIVINE

> The Wrath of God is an Oxymoron.
> - Brownell

"The Wrath of God" is a contradiction in terms. Wrath is defined as "intense anger, rage or fury."[20] The Divine does not exert any kind of wrath or punishment. How can He/She? As established in the Basic Assumptions, The Divine is Love. Love is the opposite of anger, rage and fury.

> Love is patient, love is kind. It does not envy, it does not boast, it is not proud. It is not rude, it is not self-seeking. It is not easily angered, it keeps no record of wrongs. Love does not delight in evil, but rejoices with the truth. It always protects, always trusts, always hopes, always perseveres. Love never fails.
> - I Corinthians 13:4-8

Neither is our Higher Power totally indifferent to the calamities that befall us. But He/She won't interfere with our

---

[20] Webster's Dictionary

free will, won't intervene in a dispute. He/She created a beautiful, peaceful planet, with everything we need to survive and thrive.

The Divine – and our Spirit Guides – will provide Lessons to help us learn. They're more like loving parents, who will sometimes let a child make his or her own mistake when they won't listen or make beneficial choices.

"Go ahead and eat all your Halloween candy, but don't come crying to me when you feel sick," is an analogous example. Or, "I told you you'd be too tired to go to the amusement park if you stayed up all night." In similar ways, the Divine has shown us the best ways to take care of ourselves and our planet, but so often we won't listen. Karma is the universal law of balance – and the Divine purpose is to help us learn and keep learning.

The planet, however, does have the potential to dole out retribution to any creature (including humans) who mistreats it. Mother Earth or Gaia has an arsenal of tactics to react to human mistreatment: hurricanes, floods, fires, viruses, harmful insects, tsunamis, tornadoes, mudslides and more. In some ways, we could use the analogy of fleas on a dog. At first, the dog may be an annoyed and just scratch here and there, but eventually it will jump in the water to get the fleas off its back. The more we annoy the planet with pollution, overcrowding and destruction, the more potential for substantial reaction from the planet.

> Whether it is to be Utopia or Oblivion will be a touch-and-go relay race right up to the final moment…Humanity is in 'final exam' as to whether or not it qualifies for continuance in Universe.
> – Buckminster Fuller

In the chapter on Spiritual Darwinism, you'll be given the tools to be able to take better care of the planet and prevent even large scale group events.

NEGATIVE KARMA AND HELL

An episode of the TV Show, *Lost,* described an interesting story of Karma and Hell. We hear of a story of a young boy who strikes a dog viciously with a shovel, killing the animal because the dog had attacked and bitten his little sister in the face. When the boy is asked by a priest if he's wondering if he would go to hell for killing the dog. "No," the boy replies. "I was wondering if the dog will be in hell when I get there."

Just as evil is created by human thought and action, hell can be another word for Karma. How we handle it, however, can depend on whether we can get out of "hell" and instead move toward a life of love, peace and ease.

HOW KARMA COULD EXPLAIN VARIOUS EXAMPLES OF BAD THINGS

Theoretically, most (if not all) of the categories Bad Things identified in the chapter on Bad Things Defined (and in the complete list in the appendix) have the potential to be explained by Karma, but Karma doesn't necessarily apply to every situation, and may or may not apply to yours. But let's look at how Karma *could* possibly explain a few following situations.

You're diagnosed with a chronic, painful illness
- In this. or in a previous life, you had someone close to you with a painful illness and you showed no compassion.
- In this. or a previous life, you caused harm to someone that caused her physical (or emotional) pain.

Your business fails and you lose everything
- You were ruthless/ unethical in your business deals.
- You sabotaged someone else's business.
- Your business was harmful to others.

Your home or property is destroyed
- You destroyed something that belonged to someone else.

Someone close to you is diagnosed with a terminal disease
- It could be *their* Karma.
- You didn't take care of someone who needed you before, and now you have another opportunity.

Your spouse leaves you for someone else

- You didn't treat him/her very well.
- You were unfaithful and abandoned a previous relationship and/or You had either a physical or emotional affair.
- You didn't believe in/support him/her.

Could Karma be involved in your crisis?

Questions to ask yourself:

- Have I ever done anything just like this to someone else?
- Have I ever done anything similar to this?
- Have I ever thought of or considered doing anything like this to anyone?
- Have I ever wished this on someone?
- Is it possible I could've done something like this and not remember?
- Is it possible I could've done something like this in a previous lifetime?
- Have I ever enabled someone to do something like this to someone else?
- Have I ever wanted harm to come to someone?
- Have I ever shown disrespect, judgment or contempt toward someone who had a similar condition/problem?
- Have I fully appreciated and taken care of what I have in my life?

KARMA QUIZ - ANSWERS

Now – go back to the Karma Quiz. Can you answer the questions now?

1. True or False
   a. False. Although reincarnation does explain some kinds of Karma, it doesn't explain all. The principles of Karma are found in many faiths and religions that don't necessarily believe in reincarnation.
   b. Not really. First of all, some Karma is positive or good. Also, the purpose of Karma is not to punish – it is to teach.
   c. Not necessarily. There's also Instant Karma that happens immediately.
   d. Again, not really. Karma isn't punishment; it's a way to learn. The question is, does paying for your sins help you learn?
   e. False. Much of the foundation of Christianity includes Karmic principles.
   f. True and false. Karma is predictable but it can also be preventable if we stop the karmic cycle and learn the required Lesson. But since Karma can be negative or positive, we wouldn't want to avoid positive Karma, would we?
   g. True! We are often, if not always involved on some level of our own Karmic learning.
   h. True. The purpose of Karma is to teach a Lesson, but, as you'll learn in the chapter on Lessons, Lessons are not always a result of Karma.
   i. Trick question. You, individually, may have minimal ability to change group Karma. But you can make a huge difference by getting a group together to use your collective energy to transform others.

    j. False, sort of. There are some things we can do for others to help them with their karmic lessons, but we need to be careful. We can always pray for Divine Guidance or send love to someone. But before becoming too involved with helping someone else or especially when choosing a side in a dispute, we need to carefully watch our motivations and judgment.

2. b and c

3. Trick question! It could be any or all of the above.

4. Answer: c - This phrase from Ecclesiastes is probably not intended to explain Karma, although it does help give some explanation to how things in life may be balanced.

5. Answer: b – although anytime you answer "I don't know" and want to learn more is a good thing – bonus point!

6. Answer: None of the above. As discussed above, Karma can be positive or negative, but it isn't intended to be punishment, it's intended to be a tool for learning.

7. Answer: Any of the above could be Karmic retribution and a way to help you learn.

8. Answer: All of the above.

9. Answer: Another trick question – but an opportunity to demonstrate how Karma and Subconscious Sabotage may interact.

10. All of the above

11. a; "b" could also be accepted if learning was involved.

12. Answer: All of the above, although "c" is a different form of Karma – the things we can do for ourselves to create positive things.

CHAPTER 8: THE SECOND REASON WHY: SUBCONSCIOUS SABOTAGE

> All that we are is the result of what we have thought.
> The mind is everything. What we think, we become.
> - Maharishi Mahesh Yogi

Subconscious Sabotage is, in essence, the way we can sabotage ourselves without knowing it and cause Bad Things to happen in our lives. Of course, the challenge here is the subconscious or "without knowing it" part. How can we diagnose and fix – not to mention prevent – the problems we don't know we're causing? This chapter will explain the most complicated of the Five Reasons Why – Subconscious Sabotage.

First, let's look at some relevant definitions of the word Sabotage:
- Treacherous action to defeat or hinder a cause or an endeavor; deliberate subversion
- A deliberate act of destruction or disruption

Subconscious Sabotage could explain:
- Why we eat things that are bad for us
- Why we get illnesses
- Why our resolutions often fail

- Hurricanes, earthquakes and other natural disasters
- Why we spend more than we make and get ourselves in debt (or are one step away from it)
- Why our favorite team loses a playoff game
- Why we don't get the promotion we want (and deserve)
- Why someone is wrongly accused of a crime
- Accidents
- Emotional outbursts, including child abuse

In truth, Subconscious Sabotage could possibly explain just about any kind of unfortunate event.

TYPES OF SABOTAGE

To understand sabotage, we need to look at it from the following perspectives:

- *Conscious* Sabotage, by You Toward Yourself
- *Conscious* Sabotage Between Individuals
- *Conscious* Group Sabotage
- *Subconscious* Sabotage, by You Toward Yourself
- *Subconscious* Sabotage Between Individuals
- Group *Subconscious* Sabotage or Collective Unconscious Sabotage

CONSCIOUS SABOTAGE

Conscious Sabotage is self-explanatory. It occurs when someone is aware of their actions and is deliberately interfering with the activities or goodwill of another.

Conscious Sabotage by You, Toward Yourself

This is when you're completely aware of how you're sabotaging yourself. Many times we know what we're doing to ourselves, but we keep on doing it. However, even though we have awareness of the problem, the underlying reason we don't change our behavior is usually lodged in our subconscious.

Conscious Sabotage Between
Individuals

This kind of sabotage is also done consciously, but is between individuals. It's usually done to prevent the other person from accomplishing something, or to make something happen to them. A person may spread stories about someone he doesn't like, or complain about a competitor at work, for example.

Larry Dossey, M.D discusses this kind of sabotage in his remarkable book, *Be Careful What You Pray For...You Just Might Get It*[21]. Dossey said that a Gallup poll in 1994 found that 5 percent of Americans have prayed for harm to come to others. One in twenty - and that's just the people who admit it, and define their conscious intentions as prayers.

> "Anyone who is intolerant and narrow can be a source of harm to others. This does not mean such people are consciously praying for the harm of another. It's more likely, rather, that the negative thoughts originate in the unconscious mind and that the individuals are totally unaware they're harboring harmful attitudes about another."[22]

Thoughts are prayers, too. Every thought we have, both conscious and unconscious, is form of prayer, and can be loving and helpful or negative and harmful. And, as this chapter demonstrates, there's enormous power in thought and prayer.

> If the gods listened to the prayers of men, all humankind
> would quickly perish since they constantly
> pray for many evils to befall one another"
> - Epicurus

I used to work for a company where this kind of behavior was frightfully common, especially by a particular individual. He would routinely go to someone in senior management and blame

---

[21] A fascinating, well-researched book!

[22] Quote from Larry Dossey's book, *Prayer is Good Medicine*.

someone else for a mistake he made. His strategy was to be the first one to explain the situation, forcing the other (innocent) person to defend herself against something she didn't do! I don't know if it has caught up with him – yet – but I do know he was fully aware of what he was doing. (And he will probably get his Karma someday, without my having to worry about it or want it or to be involved with it.)

Conscious sabotage can occur with thoughts and feelings, as well as actions, as long as you're aware of them. Your thoughts can have an unknown effect on someone else. I used to know someone who told me she sent nasty thoughts to an inconsiderate and threatening motorcycle driver and almost immediately afterward he crashed his bike. Coincidence? Maybe. But there *is* power in thought.

Most of us are guilty of this more often than we think. Just recently I was talking with a friend about a particular movie star, who we felt had treated others badly, and I surprised myself when we admitted we were happy that his recent film wasn't doing well. We didn't consciously go out to sabotage his box office, by protesting or telling people we know not to see the movie, but just by adding our thoughts to the collective unconscious (see below), we were consciously involved in wanting to "teach him a lesson."

In another story of malicious manipulation, a friend of mine was horribly frightened by an internet group sending emails to her, warning that unless she subscribed to their service for "protection and advice," all kinds of terrifying things would happen to her. They used just enough information they had on her to make her believe that they had psychic abilities.

I get disgusted and upset at these kinds of "curse" tactics, including the chain emails that start with an uplifting message, but warn of something bad happening if you don't send it on. The truth is, any time you send an email out to someone that warns of bad luck if the recipient doesn't forward the email – even if the rest of the email has an upbeat message – you're guilty of perpetuating conscious sabotage.[23] Not only is it not a nice thing to do to your friends, it can also create negative Karma for the sender.

It's a natural – although nasty - response of Survival of the Fittest to seek this kind of competitive advantage. Dossey quotes writer George Williams when describing the motivation between both conscious and unconscious sabotage: "'Natural selection…can honestly be described as a process for maximizing short-sighted selfishness. I would concede that moral indifference might aptly characterize the physical Universe. But for the biological world, a stronger term is needed.' The only one that will do, it seems, is evil."

Conscious Group Sabotage

Conscious Group Sabotage happens when a number of people collectively try to influence either an individual or another group. The group could be trying to negatively influence someone (or some group) from succeeding. An example of this is when half a sporting arena is sending thoughts that a player for the opposing team would miss a shot/pass/goal, etc.

A group could be trying to communicate their advantages over a competitor or opponent by emphasizing the other's weaknesses. Competitive marketing strategies are an example in the workplace, where a company will have a campaign designed to "smear' another company's reputation.

Conscious Group Sabotage can occur when an organization tries to use a form of conscious sabotage to influence another group, warning of serious consequences if the second group doesn't comply. This can be seen in some forms of government propaganda when political leaders generate communications that are intended to influence – and often inflame – their constituents, in order to garner support for a particular strategy, law or shift in governmental authority or actions.

---

[23] If you are superstitious and are concerned that if you don't send the message on, something bad will happen to you, send it on – but please DELETE THE HARMFUL WARNING beforehand.

Some religious groups consciously try to influence other groups' behaviors using destructive or harmful methods. I recently learned of an example of this that really floored me. I had heard of particular religions, and even denominations within a religion, professing to be the "only way" to God or heaven, but apparently there are actually specific churches that declare that unless an individual is a member of that exact church they're destined for hell! So, what they're saying, is that 99.99999% of the population is destined to be eternally damned. This is an outrageous, yet horrifyingly true example of elitist Social Darwinism.

> Collective fear stimulates herd instinct,
> and tends to produce ferocity toward those
> who are not regarded as members of the herd.
> – Bertrand Russell

Similarly, I received a flyer on my car a few months ago, which warned of all kinds of natural and man-made disasters, generating all kinds of fear in the reader. But wait! If you join their church, you will be saved.

All of the above are examples of groups consciously trying to manipulate and sabotage (put down) others.

SUBCONSCIOUS SABOTAGE QUESTIONS

- Have you ever said, "I just *knew* that would happen!"? Or, "I was afraid that would happen?"
- Have you ever eaten something and finished before you realized you had even eaten it?
- Do you ever think about someone and then he or she calls?
- Do you ever just "know" something is going to happen before it does?
- Have you ever experienced déjà vu?
- Has something ever happened to you that you know was something someone secretly wished for (or on) you?

- Have you ever said about someone "he's not acting like himself?"
- Have you ever secretly wanted harm to come to someone?
- Is there any reason someone could hate you and want harm to come to you?

Each of us has a personality below the surface. Freud called it the id. Jung called it the Unconscious or Subconscious. Gary Zukav calls it the Personality. Other names for this part of us can be Inner Self, Basic Self, Inner Child.[24], Unipili, Lower Self. You could even use the terms Physical Self, Body, or even "Son.[25]"

Extensive scientific research exists about the power of the Subconscious mind, which I'll discuss throughout this chapter.

Like Conscious Sabotage, Subconscious Sabotage can take place with thoughts and feelings as well as actions, but in this case you aren't sentient of what you're doing. Because Subconscious Sabotage exists when the interfering, destructive performance is happening below the surface, outside of the awareness of the conscious mind.

> When an inner situation is not made conscious,
> it appears outside as fate.
> – Carl Jung

Subconscious Sabotage by You, Toward Yourself

Believe it or not, you can sabotage yourself without knowing it. Specific emotions and thought patterns can create events in our lives, both positive and negative. In fact, this is the most

---

[24] The Inner Child and the Subconscious or Inner Self have many similarities in that they all reside below our conscious thoughts and are defined by our emotions. However, much of the work on the Inner Child is based on healing wounds from childhood – which is a very powerful and important tool with which to process these traumas if it applies to you. But, the Inner Self is a part of every human being, no matter their life history.

[25] As in Father, Son, Holy Spirit. To some people, this interpretation of this Biblical phrase is inappropriate or inaccurate. No problem! If this is how you feel, ignore it!

common way we sabotage ourselves – or, I should say this is the way the subconscious part of ourselves sabotages our whole being. Examples include all the things that negative thoughts and feelings produce, including procrastination, self-criticism, rationalization, addiction, distrust and many more.

Subconscious Sabotage Between Individuals

This kind of sabotage ensues when someone is sending out subtle negative messages or doing destructive things to someone else without consciously knowing it. An overprotective mother may be subconsciously raising a timid child, for example. Or a jealous spouse may be driving their mate to cheat without knowing it.

Here are some phrases that illustrate Subconscious Sabotage between individuals:

- You can't do that.
- If you do/eat/try that, _____ will happen.
- Rich people are greedy.
- You'll never amount to anything.
- You'll fail.
- You haven't got a chance.
- You are always wrong.
- Things are getting worse.
- He'll never make it.
- I hope someone teaches him a lesson.

We can unconsciously sabotage others – and they us – when we pray for something at the expense of someone else. For example, when we pray for our sports team to win, we're also praying for the other team to lose. When we pray to get a specific job, we are, consciously or not, praying that someone else doesn't get the job. As Larry Dossey said, "Like most types of negative prayer, this is usually done casually, without considering the potential harm it may cause." But it *does* come with a price. As discussed in the chapter on Karma, not only do our actions create negative Karma, but our thoughts, and especially our prayers do, too.

Subconscious Sabotage toward others can happen between family members, friends or colleagues, and it can also be anonymous. If you've cut someone off in traffic, for example, he might've "cursed" you in his anger. This can have an effect on you and could even create Bad Things.

Subconscious Sabotage between two people can be described as sabotage between the two Subconscious Inner Selves of the individuals involved. This can happen in a number of ways: through our actions, emotions, dreams, gestures and energy. We can even affect the energy of a room just by walking in it. Have you ever noticed how a nasty-tempered person can change everyone's moods when they join a group? Subconscious Sabotage between individuals is very powerful and can have an influence on a wide span of people.

> Because of our inherent suggestibility,
> we can easily reinforce the unconscious parts of each
> other, as if we are mutually hypnotizing each other
> in a self-perpetuating feedback loop.
> - Paul Levy

We can generate Subconscious Sabotage from others by the way we behave. For example, a friend of mine purchased an extremely large, attention-getting vehicle. His intent was to have a car that would impress; however, his decision could backfire on him. Yes, some people could be awed, but others could be jealous. And yet others could resent him and even "curse" him for taking up space, consuming more gasoline, and contributing more destruction of the environment.

> What happens when you set yourself out to impress
> others? You might trigger off envy.
> It makes you feel strong and powerful
> at the expense of another person's smallness.
> - Pathwork Lecture #56

Group Subconscious Sabotage and Collective Unconscious Sabotage

Every day, we hear dozens of news stories that generate feelings of fear, anxiety, futility, hatred, anger, disgust, failure and imminent tragedy. "If it bleeds, it leads" is the motto of the news business because they know fully well that the more emotional reaction they can generate, the more likely we'll become glued to the set/paper/radio.

- The _____ (media/government/expert) is predicting _____ (war, failure, economic decline, weather problems, etc.).
- This _____ is expected to be worse than last year.
- "Amber alert"
- _____is warning not to _____.

> Where are we going and why are we in this handbasket?
> - Unknown

Dr. Joseph Murphy describes the influence of these kind of negative suggestions in his landmark book, *The Power of Your Subconscious Mind*, "In all ages and in every part of the world, the power of suggestion has played a dominant part in the life and thought of humankind. Political creed, religious beliefs, and cultural customs all flourish and perpetuate themselves through the power of heterosuggestion[26]...If you accept them and take them in, these thoughts of fear can cause you to lose the will for life."

The Collective Unconscious

Jung coined the term Collective Unconscious to describe the "collective psychology" of a group. Jung defines the Collective Unconscious as the "sum total of all the concepts, the hopes and wishes and desires (for good or ill) which Man as a whole has ever had." An individual's subconscious mind connects to a

---

[26] Suggestions from person to person.

combined group mind, which is common to all human beings The Collective Unconscious arises in each individual from shared emotions, common experiences and united culture.

The collective, unconscious thoughts and actions of large groups have an influence on a lot of the things that happen. Any time there's a groundswell of emotion – hatred, fear, anger, jealousy, ingratitude, greed, judgment, frustration, etc. – there's a risk of something harmful – and even horrifying – happening as a result of the energy from the collective unconscious. Independent terrorists and suicide bombers may not have been on a specific, directed mission, but may have been acting on the collective emotions of the people around him. If enough people hate another person or group, there will be a reaction. If enough people send out thoughts of envy or fear, there will be a reaction. And, thankfully, if enough people convey thoughts of love, peace or hope, there will be a reaction.

An example of the unknown influence of the collective unconscious is the 100 Monkey Effect, which explains a story that began in 1952 on the island of Koshima. Scientists provided the native monkeys with sweet potatoes dropped in the sand. An 18-month old female monkey tried washing her sweet potato in the stream and decided that it tasted better. Gradually, other monkeys on the island joined in and started washing their sweet potatoes as well. The fascinating thing is, when the one hundredth monkey on the island began washing its sweet potatoes, colonies of monkeys on other isolated islands began washing their sweet potatoes.

Whether the story is a theory or actual fact isn't important: the effect is common and established throughout history. How else can we explain the nearly simultaneous adoption of various cultural phenomena, from the controlling of fire to the development of a written language, when the cultures had no contact with each other?

The Collective Unconscious is very powerful. In addition to generating progress, "it" can produce great tragedy, because of the combined power of the evil, destructive, vindictive, mean and vicious thoughts of humans in their fight for supremacy in order to survive.

The Energy of Planet Earth

Many cultures believe that the Earth itself has an energy or consciousness. Mother Nature, Gaia, or Mother Earth are terms often used for this energy. The following quote.[27] is a quite beautiful way to look at our planet:

> "Earth has a soul. She wants to be the nurturer of all those who live on her, whom she loves so dearly. She is quite dismayed at the amount of disrespect and destruction that's being done in the name of progress. The Earth initially was created with a highly spiritually evolved soul and was very pleased to be given the opportunity to be created to house the new beings that came to live upon it, whether they be humanoid or animal or vegetable. As man continued to evolve and destroy much of earth, it has brought a great sadness to earth, and as Earth sees less natural things happening to her, to weathers and climates, to the reproduction of living creatures, Earth feels that it's not understanding its role any more in giving and providing the substance for all to be living upon as people continue to destroy that. So Earth looks with great dismay upon the events that are happening."

This energy can explain natural disasters. The more we, as humans, disrespect and disregard our planet, the more likely the planet will fight back, with hurricanes, floods and other environmental calamities, plus physical problems like viruses, pollution, global warming and more. It is an established fact that human disrespect has already created much of this destruction. If

---

[27] From the website: www.afterlife101.com

we continue our damaging and disrespectful behavior, the planet will respond forcefully.

Just like relationships between people, there needs to be love, appreciation and respect between us and the planet, otherwise the relationship is in jeopardy. I'm not offering this as a threat intended to generate fear, but as a suggestion to consider: how are we handling our part of the relationship between humans and our planet? There are so many more of us now – over six billion people – that we're looking for some other planet to house us. But how does that make us different from the "aliens" in the movie *Independence Day*?

HOW SUBCONSCIOUS SABOTAGE WORKS

So, we can sabotage others – but we can also sabotage ourselves, whether consciously or unconsciously/subconsciously. Conscious self-sabotage is easier to identify when we consciously know we are sabotaging our success at work, for example, or if we are habitually late or are rude to our boss. These are conscious choices. Or are they? Do we *intend* to be late, or does time get away from us? Do we make a decision to be rude to our boss, or does it just seem to happen?

Let's look at another example. Let's say we want a leaner, healthier body but, for some reason, we eat something indulgent, like a donut. Why did we eat the donut? Maybe it was so we could make our inner selves feel more appreciated – we *deserve* that donut. Or we may eat a donut without remembering the experience. It's almost like we zoned out while eating the donut. Why does that happen? Subconscious Sabotage explains this phenomena, which can be better analyzed when we look at the three Selves.

THE THREE SELVES

As established in the Basic Assumptions, each human being has three selves to our being:

- The Conscious, Ego or Outer Self
- The Superconscious, Superego or Higher Self
- The Subconscious, Id or Inner Self.[28]

One way to look at the three selves is to consider that each of us has an everlasting soul, the one that exists before we are born and continues after our death. To experience life on earth, the soul chooses a body. The soul is our Superconscious, or Higher Self. The body is our Subconscious or Inner Self. And the merging of the two "beings" is the Conscious, or Outer Self.

Another parallel is to look at the terms Father, Mother and Child, with Father describing the Higher Power or Higher Self, Mother as Earth or the physical/Subconscious, and Child as the Outer Self or Conscious, combined being created by the merging of the two energies.

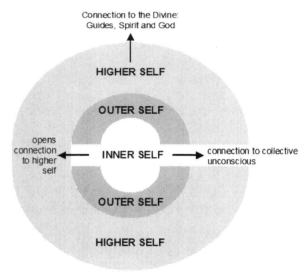

---

[28] I do not use the term "Lower" self for several reasons. First, it is not a complimentary term, and since we need to make friends with this part of ourselves, it is not a good way to start if we designate that part of ourselves as "lower." Second, we should love all parts of ourselves, including and even especially our Inner Self or Subconscious Self. Third, this part of our selves is not inferior at all. In many ways it has superior information and talents that we can each benefit from!

The above diagram shows the relationship between the Three Selves.

The Outer Self or Conscious Mind

The Conscious or Outer Self is a pretty obvious concept for us to grasp: "it" is the part of ourselves that's the thinking, logical, conscious mind. This "self" makes decisions and is sometimes considered the "parent" of the Inner Self or subconscious, because it often will guide or direct the subconscious toward specific objectives.

The Conscious or Outer Self is the part of us we know and recognize all the time. It's the thinking part, the part that's awake and pays attention and makes conscious decisions. Your Outer Self is the logical part of you.

If our Outer (Conscious) Self was always in control, we would always make decisions based on research and reason. We would have no intuition or higher consciousness, but only logic.

The Higher Self or Superconscious Mind

Many people believe that a pure scientific mind is one of pure Conscious Self – with no inspiration or innovation. However, Albert Einstein, arguably one of the best scientific minds of all time, made the following quotes:

- "The gift of fantasy has meant more to me than my talent or absorbing positive knowledge."
- "Imagination is more important than knowledge."
- "I am enough of an artist to draw freely upon my imagination. Knowledge is limited, whereas imagination embraces the entire world, stimulating progress, giving birth to evolution."

Where does this fantasy, inspiration and imagination come from? Not from the rational, conscious mind. It comes from communicating with your Higher Self and Infinite Intelligence (the Divine).

Napoleon Hill discusses inspiration in his classic book, *Think and Grow Rich*. He suggests that ideas or "hunches" come from one of four sources: (1) Infinite Intelligence; (2) our Subconscious Mind or Inner Self; (3) from the mind of someone else's conscious thought or (4) from the mind of the other person's subconscious.

The Superconscious, Superego or Higher Self is our connection to the Divine, Spirit, Infinite Intelligence, and Unconditional Love. This "self" is our source of inspiration, love, and universal peace. This is our true soul, which existed before our birth, and will continue on after our physical bodies die. The following excerpt from the afterlife101 website describes the Higher Self.

> "The higher self is your spirit that continues to live through all three-dimensional lifetimes and is always there... by that we mean the unconditional love, the unconditional forgiveness, acceptance, knowing that you are perfect in all ways."

Wow! Incredible stuff! But of course, this isn't the part of us that sabotages, so I'll wait until we get to later chapters to discuss connecting with your higher, Divine self.

The Inner Self or Subconscious Mind

The Subconscious or Inner Self is the part of us that underlies Subconscious Sabotage. It's below the surface, usually not recognized by the conscious mind and is the seat of our emotions, habits and automatic reactions.

Dan Millman, in his book, *No Ordinary Moments – A Peaceful Warrior's Guide to Daily Life,* describes the relationship between the Basic (Inner) Self and the Conscious Self: "When working in harmony, our Conscious Self guides, educates and reassures our Inner Self, as a parent would a child, helping it to understand life, while allowing the Inner Self to express its own unique capacities."

The Inner Self is sometimes assumed to be our Inner Child because it functions in a childlike way, due to its emotional response. But it's much more than our childhood memories. It's also our connection to the Earth and survival, and is the part of us that runs our autonomic body systems (breathing, digesting, etc.) Our Inner Self also unconsciously fulfills our conscious wishes, like continuing to drive to a destination without our thinking about it.

This is the "self" that reacts emotionally. Joseph Murphy describes the Subconscious/Subjective mind, "Your subjective (subconscious) mind perceives by intuition. It's the seat of emotions and the storehouse of memory. Your subconscious mind performs its highest functions when your objective senses are not functioning. Your subconscious mind sees without the use of the natural organs of vision. It has the capacity of clairvoyance and clairaudience; it can see and hear events that are taking place elsewhere. Through your subjective mind, you can read the thoughts of others, read the contents of sealed envelopes, or intuit the information on a computer disk without using the hard drive."

Science tells us our conscious minds can process about 2000 bits of information per second, but our subconscious processes about 4 billion per second! Said another way, scientific and medical research has shown that up to 95% of our thoughts, emotions and learning occur in our subconscious mind. That means we're not consciously aware of 95% of our decisions and actions!

In the bestseller *Blink*, author Malcolm Gladwell discusses what he calls the adaptive subconscious:

> "The mind operates most efficiently by relegating a good deal of high-level, sophisticated thinking to the unconscious...Whenever we meet someone for the first time, whenever we interview someone for a job, whenever we react to a new idea, whenever we're faced with making a decision quickly under stress, we use that part of our brain."

Some of the "Rules" that Govern the Inner Self

The Inner Self:

- Fulfills every command (as directed by the Outer Self) at face value. This is why affirmations and visualization can be effective.

- Is our emotional self.

- Is our physical being: breathing, cell regeneration, eyes blinking, hunger, thirst, etc.

- Is our physical and emotional "Survival of the Fittest" instinct. This is how "fight or flight" comes out when we are threatened.

- Stays "awake" at all times. This is why we'll wake up when alerted, and why we can ask him or her to wake us up at a specific time.

- Will "take over" when our Outer Self "lets" them, usually when a strong emotion is present, especially fear and guilt. This is why we often don't remember eating something we shouldn't, and other addictive behavior.

- Has no concept of the passage of time. Have you ever noticed when you sleep you can't tell how long it has been?

- Is controlled by programming and past conditioning. This is where habits come from: i.e. waking up every morning at the same time.

- Takes everything *literally*. If we say to ourselves, "I'll stay up all night to finish that project" but decide instead to go to bed, we might find ourselves awake all night anyway.

- Can relate to the Inner Self of others, no matter where they are. Have you ever been thinking about someone and he calls? This communication happens because of our Inner Self connections.

- Blocks – or opens – our connection to our Higher Self, depending on whether he/she is happy.

> The subconscious is the intermediary, which translates one's prayers into terms which Infinite Intelligence can recognize, presents the message, and brings back the answer in the form of a definite plan or idea for procuring the object of the prayer.
> - Napoleon Hill

The first time I realized the power of my own Subconscious Sabotage was about fifteen years ago, when I was involved in a legal dispute. It had only been eight months since the legal papers were filed, but I was getting antsy to move on, to have the matter resolved. However, as any attorney can tell you, these kinds of disputes can take years to get to court; my wanting it over so soon was naïve and wishful thinking. Nevertheless, I decide to see a therapist trained in Kinesiology[29] that a friend of mine recommended. Her specialty was to use kinesiology (muscle testing) to access the subconscious. After one or two sessions with her, she found the source and cleared the blocks I had hidden inside, and the defendant settled the lawsuit within a week. A week! Amazing. I didn't care how it worked; I was just thrilled that it *worked*!

THE IMPORTANCE OF KNOWING AND CONNECTING WITH THE THREE SELVES

You've probably known about the three selves for years, whether you've studied basic psychology in school, read authors like Napoleon Hill, Joseph Murphy and Maxwell Maltz, or identified the spiritual part of you. Or, perhaps, instinctively, you know about these aspects of yourself. Maybe you always wondered if you have multiple personalities! It's difficult to

---

[29] Kinesiology is a form of diagnosis in holistic health care based on the theory that the body's subconscious knows what is "good" and "bad" or "right" or "wrong" for the body. Various forms of muscle testing determine the best form of therapy for patients, whether diagnosing emotional, chemical or structural sources for a patient's issue or concern.

deny these descriptive aspects of ourselves, and it isn't much of a stretch to make distinctions between the characteristics, to be able to separate them into the three groupings discussed.

> Who looks outside, dreams; who looks inside, awakes.
> - Carl G. Jung

What you may not have done before, however, is to take this a step further and pull apart these three personalities into three distinct "beings" or people. I had read all these books over the years, and had even had the above described experience with the power of connecting with my Inner Self, but the real breakthrough came from a friend of mine, who follows a Polynesian faith called Huna. In that belief system, they say that we should actually assign a different name to each of our Selves.

Naming Your Selves

Remember, in chapter on Commitment, I said you would be strongly encouraged to follow a few exercises? The following is very important. You should be prepared at this point to come up with a name for each of your three selves. When I get to the chapter on Diagnosing you'll at least have to have determined the name for your Inner Self.

The name for your Outer Self is easy. It's your given name in this lifetime. Mine is Brownell.

Next, you need a name for your Inner Self. All you have to do is ask your Inner Self to tell you what his or her name is.

A name may not "pop up" immediately, although it could. I've met some people who know theirs instantly. For me, it took a day or two and "came to me" when I was distracted from conscious thought and my physical body was content. This is usually when he/she is most likely to communicate to you. Try asking right before you go to bed to wake up with "his" or "her" name.

The name for your Higher Self may take longer to come to you. Often, it opens up after you've connected with your basic self.

Note to skeptics: You'll have to trust me on how important this step is. You can call this hokey or stupid, but please oblige this request.

What separating and naming does is give us clarity on the force behind our emotions, thoughts and actions. When I first named my Inner Self, I felt a kind of freedom and understanding I had never felt before. Now, crazy as it may seem, I talk with "her" all the time. I ask "her" what she wants to do, eat, etc.

Just as you have to recognize a problem, before you can fix it, you have to separate your three selves, before you can become a fully integrated being. Naming your Inner Self is a critical step in understanding this crucial part of yourself.

HOW SUBCONSCIOUS SABOTAGE IS RESPONSIBLE FOR BAD THINGS

> "We have met the enemy and he is us."
> - Pogo (Walt Kelly)

Okay, so we have all kinds of thoughts and actions swirling all over the place – from us and to us consciously, from us and to us subconsciously, and then from groups to groups and groups to individuals. It's a bombardment of energy all over the place!

Napoleon Hill's *Think & Grow Rich* lists thirty-one causes of failure, including everything from dishonesty to lack of ambition, procrastination, an uncontrolled desire for "something for nothing" and many more. More than twenty of these thirty-one causes of failure can be attributed to Subconscious Sabotage and the Inner Self.

Subconscious Sabotage can create the following kinds of "Bad Things:"
- Repeatedly losing your job
- One-hit wonders in the music business
- Disease and illness
- Marriage problems and divorce

111

- Business failure
- Loss of friendships
- Criminal activity – as a victim or a perpetrator
- Being falsely accused of a crime
- Abuse
- Financial failure
- Depression or other emotional problems
- Eating the wrong thing
- Not paying attention and allowing accidents to happen
- Not allowing intuition, inspiration or Divine Guidance to come through
- Reacting emotionally
- Unhealthy emotional responses, resulting in relationship problems
- Interfering with what your conscious mind wants to do, like forgetting your keys, turning off alarms, leaving your door unlocked, etc.
- Memory blocks
- Repercussions from bad judgment, i.e. criminal activity, drinking and driving, and much more

Group or Collective Unconscious Sabotage can underlie the following:
- Natural Disasters
- Punishment for famous people – i.e. criminal sentences, career failure, etc.
- War
- Pollution
- Violence

How can Subconscious Sabotage create these events? Because *thought has enormous power*.

All strife, such as war, poverty, quarrels,

> difficulties of all sorts, sickness and dying
> are the expression of humanity's expression of
> humanity's confusions, its state of consciousness
> which clings to destructive emotions.
> - Pathwork[30] Lecture #130

HOW THOUGHT CREATES

The power of conscious thought has been established in physics, particularly quantum physics/quantum mechanics, as well as medical science.

Here's an oversimplification of the basic principles in quantum mechanics. We all learned about protons, neutrons and electrons in school – the building blocks for all matter. Most physicists now believe these "blocks" are actually not physical particles, but waves of energy. This means nothing in our "physical" world is physical at all – it's all energy.[31] The pages you're reading are nothing but energy. The same with your body. The same with the planet and everything in it and on it.

When you realize everything is basically energy, vibrating at different speeds in different combinations, you have to acknowledge that thought itself is energy. In fact, not only is thought energy, but it's very powerful and influential energy. Some physicists say "consciousness collapses the wave function" thereby creating reality itself. Another way to say this is that science has proven that the expectations (thoughts) of the experimenters have an influence on the outcome of an event. Mind over matter has new meaning, because there's very little difference between "mind" and "matter," when everything is energy. Thought is energy. Energy creates. Thought creates.

Okay, not so simple. Sorry. But interesting, huh?

The movie and book, *What the Bleep Do We Know?*, by William Arntz, Betsy Chasse and Mark Vicente (which I highly recommend!), includes insights on quantum physics from various

---

[30] International Pathwork Foundation: www.pathwork.org.
[31] This is called the wave vs. particle theory in physics. Please forgive me for my simplistic explanation.

physicians, meta-physicians, scientists, philosophers and spiritual teachers, with the overarching theme of how our thoughts create our reality. The scientists explore the subject of quantum physics, including citing the experiments by Dr. Masaru Emoto (and written about in his book, *The Hidden Messages in Water.*) If "seeing is believing," Dr. Emoto's work demonstrates, through photography, how water reacts to human consciousness. Photographs show how water molecules with positive messages form beautiful crystals, while those with negative messages are ugly and malformed.

Dr. Emoto took water from a single source, put the water in separate bottles with various words on the bottles, and photographed the water crystals. The effect was, in a word, awesome. The water crystals with positive, loving words were beautiful, and the water crystals with harmful and negative words were deformed and ugly. Dr. Emoto went on to repeat the study numerous times with water from sources all over the world: the effects of words – of thoughts – were the same.[32]

What the Bleep Do We Know? takes Dr. Emoto's research a bit further, to suggest that if our bodies are 90% water, and if thoughts have such an effect on water, then our negative thoughts of ourselves have the potential to be powerfully destructive.

The Power of Prayer

In Larry Dossey's book, *Prayer is Good Medicine*, he discusses the power of prayer and its relationship to what are called "N*onlocal events*" in quantum physics: "Nonlocal events have three common characteristics. They are said to be unmediated (the distant changes don't depend on the transmission of energy or on any sort of energetic signal); they are unmitigated (the strength of the change does not become weaker with increasing distance); and they are immediate (the distant changes take place simultaneously)."

What he's saying is that the power of prayer (thought) isn't restricted by distance or time. It's also not restricted by

---

[32] For further information, refer to Dr. Emoto's book or website: www.masaru-emoto.net.

conscious awareness. Physicist John Eccles' theory said, "our minds exist outside the material world and interacts with our brains at the quantum level." In other words, our Superconscious "minds" can affect our physical (subconscious) brains.

I myself have witnessed the positive effect of prayer from a distance, where someone projected healing messages to a friend over 300 miles away, without her knowledge - and she was completely cured of an incurable, chronic disease within a week! The downside of this kind of power is, if negative or uncontrolled, it can also sabotage and produce all kinds of calamities.

The Mind-Body Connection

We all know that stress causes all kinds of diseases and accidents to occur. Some physicians even believe that just about everything that happens to us is a result of stress, including cancer, heart disease, headaches, indigestion and even accidents of every kind.

> I admit thoughts influence the body.
> – Albert Einstein

The medical community is fully aware of the placebo effect, which describes treatments that have no specific therapeutic value but which nevertheless help make many people better. But there is also its reverse: the nocebo effect. Dr. Larry Dossey[33] explains, "The nocebo and placebo are opposites. The latter refers to the positive physical effects that occur as a result of belief, expectation, and suggestion. In contrast, nocebo effects are the negative results of negative beliefs, feelings and emotions. Nocebo effects are essentially self-curses." Robert A. Hahn, an epidemiologist at the Centers for Disease Control and Prevention in Atlanta, has said that "nocebo effects are a matter of life or death." Dossey then follows up with examples of how the belief in impending disease actually causes or worsens the disease.

---

[33] Reference: *Be Careful What You Pray For...You Just Might Get It* by Larry Dossey, M.D.

The scientific evidence for the mind's influence on the body comes from three converging areas of research:

- Physiological research, which investigates the biological and biochemical connections between the brain and the body's systems.

- Epidemiological research, which shows correlations between certain psychological factors and certain illnesses in the population at large.

- Clinical research, which tests the effectiveness of mind/body approaches in preventing, alleviating, or treating diseases.

> "What is real? How do you define real? If you're talking about what you can feel, what you can smell, what you can taste and see, then real is simply electrical signals interpreted by your brain."
> - Morpheus (Laurence Fishburne) in the film The Matrix

Biochemical Brain Function

Neuroscientist Dr. Candace Pert, an established expert on biochemical brain function, describes her research: "Your subconscious mind is really your body. Peptides are the biochemical correlate of emotion. Emotional memory is stored throughout the body. Emotions, ranging from anger to fear, sadness, joy, contentment, courage, pleasure, pain, awe, and bliss, engender a constellation of bodily changes, of which facial expressions are simply the most obvious.".[34]

"And," concludes Pert, "you can access emotional memory anywhere in the network." How else, she speculates, could therapies based on massage, therapeutic touch and chiropractic trigger profound transformations? "Repressed emotions and memories might actually be stored in receptors throughout the body." In fact, said Pert, body and brain are not separate. "We are one bodymind."

---

[34] Excerpt from Psychology Today article entitled *Impertinent Ideas*" by Jill Neimark.

You Can Heal Your Life

In her revolutionary, bestselling books, *You Can Heal Your Life* and *Heal Your Body,* Louise Hay breaks new ground in the identification of emotional causes for physical disease. "I believe we create every so-called illness in our body. The body, like everything else in life, is a mirror of our inner thoughts and beliefs. The body is always talking to us, if we'll only take the time to listen. Every cell within your body responds to every single thought you think and every word you speak. Continuous modes of thinking and speaking produce body behaviors and postures and "eases" or dis-eases.[35]"

Hay includes a list of illnesses matched to what she calls "Probable Mental Patterns." For example, she said, "Cancer is a dis-ease caused by deep resentment held for a long time until it literally eats away at the body."

Louise Hay suggests that resentment, envy, jealousy and hatred are a contributing factor to the following diseases: abscess, bad breath, bleeding, boils, burns, bursitis, carpal-tunnel syndrome, cellulite, conjunctivitis, dementia, dysentery, fever, gout, infection, injuries, laryngitis, mononucleosis, periodontitis, rabies, sores, sprains, thrush, urinary infections, vaginitis, warts, wounds and more. Hay said that the following four emotions "cause more problems than anything else:" Resentment, Criticism, Guilt, and Fear.

Subconscious = Inner Self = Body = Emotions

In the chapter *Understanding Your Crisis* we identified a vast number of emotions you may be experiencing. Now you know they're being expressed by _____. (the name for your Inner Self).[36] Now let's review some basic negative emotions, attitudes and behaviors and how they may create destructive events.

---

[35] Excerpt from *You Can Heal Your Life.*
[36] Do you have a name yet?

EMOTIONS AND YOUR INNER SELF

Your subconscious is the source of your emotions. We don't consciously wake up in the morning and tell ourselves, "I'm going to be angry today," or "Let's see, what should I be afraid of?" We just *feel* them. Whatever you focus on, you draw to yourself. If you focus on the things you're afraid of, you'll manifest them in your life. If you focus on hatred, you will draw hatred; if you focus on anger, you'll perpetuate anger. If you're guilty of judgments against others or yourself, you'll continue to spiral in a world of prejudice and discrimination.

> "Emotion is the power which attracts. That which you fear strongly, you will experience.
> Emotion is energy in motion.
> When you move energy, you create effect.
> If you move enough energy, you create matter.
> Thought is pure energy."
> - "God" (Neale Donald Walsh)

When we ignore, deny or try to cover up our emotions, we're neglecting our Inner Self. I don't agree with the theories that all we have to do is think positive and instantly we'll be happy. No, our Inner Self is much too sophisticated for that. Suppressed or repressed emotions are still there, below the surface. Jung called this part of our psyche "the shadow." In William A. Miller's book, *Make Friends with Your Shadow – How to Accept and Use Positively the Negative Side of Your Personality*, he said, "The shadow is like a foreign personality – a primitive, instinctive, animalistic kind of being. It's the collection of uncivilized desires and feelings. The shadow is everything we don't want to be...everything we don't want others to know about us. It's everything we don't even want to know about ourselves and have thus conveniently 'forgotten' through denial and repression."

> The fearful and violent emotions that have come to characterize human existence can be experienced only by the Personality (Inner Self). Only the (Inner Self)

> can feel anger, fear, hatred, vengeance, sorry, shame,
> regret, indifference, frustration, cynicism and loneliness.
> Only the (Inner Self) can judge, manipulate and exploit.
> – Gary Zukav

How Inner Self Shadow Emotions Produce Subconscious Sabotage

The emotions listed in the chapter on Understanding Your Crisis all produce some form of Subconscious Sabotage – by you toward yourself or between individuals:

Anger, Rage, Malice, Seething	Produces	Damage to your body, and sends negative, sabotaging emotions to others
Attachment to the Outcome	Produces	Inability to receive the things you want and prevents the Divine from bringing what is best for you
Cowardice	Produces	Failure to take action that will release you from your problems and create a better future
Cruelty	Produces	Negative energy sent to others, and causes you to receive their anger in return – which is how negative karma is created!
Deceit, Hypocrisy and Distrust	Produces	Distrust from you and toward you; prevents you from connecting with others; puts up an impenetrable shield
Denial	Produces	The inability to heal and move on
Frustration and Annoyance	Produces	Repeated patterns of behavior
Gloom, Despair, Pessimism, Exhaustion, Despondency and Depression	Produces	Inaction and festering

Grief	Produces	Inability to look forward to the future
Ingratitude	Produces	Inability to appreciate the things you have, which prevents good from flowing into your life
Irresponsibility, Gluttony and Sloth	Produces	Self-destructive behavior and addictions
Judgment of Self	Produces	Damages to our Inner Self and prevents us from achieving our higher Divine Purpose.
Judgment of Others	Produces	A destructive message to them and then returns to us in the form of their judgment of us – producing a never-ending karmic cycle
Pain	Produces	Physical pain produces emotional pain; emotional pain produces physical pain – both prevent healing
Resentment, Envy, Jealousy, Rancor, Hatred, Meanness and Bitterness	Produces	Failure - Keeps us from doing our best and learning to love ourselves
Revenge, Vindictiveness and Harassment	Produces	Reciprocal behavior (Karma)
Selfishness, Arrogance and Greed	Produces	Separation from others and from the Divine
Self-Loathing	Produces	Physically and emotionally destructive behavior, and prevents us from receiving Divine Assistance.
Sorrow, Anguish and Agony	Produces	Inability to see the gifts in our lives; keeps us tethered to the past
Violence Torment, Menace and Torture	Produces	Reciprocal behavior (Karma)
Worry and Fear	Produces	Inaction; reduces faith, and brings toward us that which we fear.

The following true story.[37] demonstrates how a negative emotion – distrust in others – creates Subconscious Sabotage:

Larry was really struggling in his career. For some reason he couldn't understand, he had bad luck holding onto a job. It seemed like every time he thought he had a good job the company would go through a downsizing and he would lose his job. He blamed it on unfortunate timing, the economy, corporate volatility and, if he took any responsibility for his plight at all it was that he made poor choices of companies and/or bosses.

I told him it looked like a clear case of Subconscious Sabotage. Larry was keeping a secret: he's gay. I explained that the problem wasn't in his sexual orientation, but in Larry's secrecy and shame. He was so afraid his co-workers would find out and judge him, he walked around in fear. And when you're afraid of something and keeping it inside of you, other people will know you're hiding something and not trust you. So, who will be on the chopping block at every management meeting determining who stays and who goes? Larry. Every time.

I suggested that Larry look for a company – and boss - more open minded and accepting, so that he could be honest and really be himself. He would be able to make friends easier and hold onto jobs longer. He would likely become more trusted (as well as trusting others more).

When we don't trust others, we exhibit a "vibe" or energy that separates us from others – a very sabotaging approach to life, because distrust harbors more distrust, leading potentially to paranoia.

Whichever emotion is present, it's a sign that our Inner Self is crying out for attention – and an opportunity for healing.

> "Fear is the path to the Dark Side. Fear leads to anger,
> Anger leads to hate; Hate leads to suffering."
> - Yoda (Frank Oz) in Star Wars Episode I:
> The Phantom Menace

---

[37] Names have been changed.

NEGLECTING THE NEEDS OF YOUR INNER SELF

Subconscious Sabotage occurs when we neglect the needs of our Inner Self. As discussed above, your Inner Self *is* your body. Just as with our emotions, when we neglect the physical aspects of our Inner Self, we're sabotaging ourselves.

Ways to neglect our Inner Self:

- Not enough rest / Too much stress
- Not having enough fun
- Eating the wrong foods
- Not exercising
- Not enjoying nature/the sun
- Not listening to physical problems
- Covering problems with drugs, alcohol and other addictions

What can happen when we disregard our Subconscious Self:

- We get depressed and discouraged
- We try and try, but can't get ahead
- We're in debt
- We have weight struggles
- We procrastinate, or we don't complete tasks
- We're angry, fearful, frustrated, anxious, and experience a whole array of negative emotions
- We can't sleep – or sleep too much
- We have digestive problems (indigestion, constipation, diarrhea, etc.)
- We have relationship problems.
- We over-indulge in food, drink, drugs, shopping, or other excessive behavior
- We never learn how to appreciate life.
- We becoming workaholics.
- We isolate ourselves socially, afraid to get involved with other people, for fear we'll be found out to be inadequate, not normal, or a misfit.

ADDICTIONS AND THE INNER SELF

Addictions are embedded in our Inner Self, whether as a result of a physiological disorder or because we're not in touch with the needs and desires of our subconscious selves and 'they" are crying out for us to notice them. In many ways, just as a child wants to repeat an activity over and over again, our Inner Selves will repeat the same pursuit. They may be responding to a deeply embedded command from the will of the Outer Self "I am an addict." "I *need* the drink/ drug/food/activity." "I can't stop." "I deserve the _____." These are all commands our conscious minds imprint on the subconscious.

Addictions may also be created by an Inner Self who isn't getting enough attention. This is why many of our addictive behaviors happen when we "zone out" – our conscious minds have left our bodies. We'll engage in the activity without receiving any of the pleasure – or guilt – associated with it. For example, we may eat a whole package of snacks and not remember eating them. Or we could watch hours of mindless television, in order to avoid doing a project. Of course, the Inner Self will often leave the repercussions to the Outer Self, forcing the conscious self to deal with the hangovers and posting bail.

The movie *Fight Club* illustrates the ways the character's Outer Self detaches and allows his Inner Self take over, performing all kinds of self-destructive (and externally devastating) behavior.

> The images of the unconscious place a great
> responsibility upon a man. Failure to understand them,
> or a shirking of ethical responsibility,
> deprives him of his wholeness and
> imposes a painful fragmentariness on his life.
> – Carl Jung

WHY THE SUBCONSCIOUS SABOTAGES

The Subconscious sabotages for the following reasons:

- To get our attention
- When we're upset and don't want to cope
- When we feel threatened
- When we don't feel loved
- To replay the programming and patterns that have been set by us, by individuals we encounter and established by our leaders and the media
- When looking for the "easy way out"
- To "follow the pack" – to "jump off the cliff because everyone else does" (as a rationalization for not listening and taking personal responsibility)
- To justify doing what we want to do (and not doing what we don't want to do)
- To "win" the battle for Survival of the Fittest

> Always remember – always remember – that any destiny arranged for man is not arranged for him by some arbitrary, extraneous power but is offered to him, made easy or forced on him, by his own past thoughts.
> – Richard Matheson

SUBCONSCIOUS SABOTAGE AND THE ROLE OF THE DIVINE

What is the role of the Divine in Subconscious Sabotage? First of all, It/He/She won't interfere with our free will (Basic Assumption #4). Without free will, how are we ever going to learn? "Love and fear are feelings which open one or limit one to their spiritual evolution. The Divine gives free will in how one lives their life. God the highest power won't intercept an individual's free will no matter what direction it is taking."[38]

---

[38] www.Afterlife101.com

In the movie, "Oh God!" George Burns, starring as the Almighty, sends the message that God exists, that He cares, and that people can change the world for the better, but it's up to them to do so because they have *free will*.

> Love cannot exist
> where there is not the freedom to choose.
> - Unknown

As discussed earlier in this chapter, we have three selves, including a Higher Self or Superconscious, which is our connection to the Divine. But our subconscious or Inner Self can block us from our spiritual connection. Unless we can connect and "make friends" with this shadow self, we have difficulty connecting with the Divine.

Subconscious Sabotage and Predictable Events

We can predict future events caused by Subconscious Sabotage, when we realize that we bring to us what we think and feel. In this way, we "create our own reality." Feelings can be the most powerful creative energy, and the most potent feeling of all is fear, because it directly manifests that which we fear.

Evil Explained by Subconscious Sabotage

Evil comes from human thought and action, whether conscious or not. Evil is separation from love, from God. The devil isn't an external being whom we can blame for our woes. No. "It" is dark, destructive low-vibrational energy generated by collective human thoughts of anger, envy, fear and hatred which usually stems from the competition generated by "survival of the fittest." When an individual has one of these thoughts himself, he separates himself from God. At this point, it's up to him whether or not to join into the vicious energy cycle. If he joins the injurious energy, he will commit egregious crimes against himself, against humanity and against the planet.

125

How Subconscious Sabotage Could Explain Various Examples of Bad Things

Each of the dozens of Bad Things identified have the potential to be explained by Subconscious Sabotage. This doesn't mean that these explanations apply every time. Remember, no one can judge anyone else's Reasons Why. But let's look at how Subconscious Sabotage *could* possibly explain a few situations:

You're diagnosed with a chronic, painful illness
- You've been worried your whole life about getting sick
- You haven't been taking care of yourself
- You want someone to take care of you

Your business fails and you lose everything
- Your competition or enemies wanted to see you fail
- You didn't feel you deserved success
- You wanted to "destroy" the competition
- You didn't enjoy the business and it showed through your Inner Self
- Someone said, 'You'll never amount to much"

Your home is destroyed by fire/flood/ hurricane/tornado
- You didn't really like your home, neighborhood or lifestyle.
- Your Subconscious/Inner Self was ready for a change
- A group of people resented your neighborhood
- You wanted a change
- There was angst (or other negative energy) in the neighborhood
- You didn't appreciate what you had

Someone close to you is in an accident or diagnosed with a serious illness

- You wanted to feel needed/to have someone to take care of
- You felt guilty for not being a better son/daughter/mother/father/sibling
- You were afraid he would injure himself or get sick
- She was reckless and/or didn't take care of herself
- Subconsciously he craved a rest from a stressful life
- She wanted someone to take care of her
- You/they were paranoid that something would happen

Your spouse leaves you for someone else
- You were afraid he/she would leave you and were very jealous and/or controlling
- You fantasized about other partners (or cheated yourself)
- You wanted a break

These are just a few examples. Can you see a pattern? Some explanations are from self-sabotage, some are from others and some are from groups or the collective unconscious. More examples can be found on the reasonswhy.com website.

COULD SUBCONSCIOUS SABOTAGE BE INVOLVED IN YOUR CRISIS?

- Have I ever worried that this would happen?
- Have I ever thought of or considered doing anything like this to anyone?
- Have I ever wished this on someone?
- Have I ever put down someone else (or a group of people)?
- In the past, how have I judged people who this kind of thing has happened to?
- Is it possible that someone could've wished this on me? If it was a group/mass event, is there any reason someone could've wished this on a group you're associated with?
- Is there any reason someone could be jealous of me?

- Could someone have negatively judged me/us?
- Is there anyone who benefited by this happening to me? Is it possible that they could've wanted the benefit to happen (whether they realized or not that it could've resulted in what happened to me?)
- Are there any (however subtle) benefits in my crisis that I might've somehow wanted?
- Have I been taking good care of myself?
- Am I aware of the "shadow" side of myself – my negative, non-loving or destructive emotions and thoughts?
- Is there anything or anyone I'm too attached to?
- Am I addicted to or obsessed with anyone or anything?
- Are my prayers or desires too limiting?
- Have I ever prayed for – or wanted - something for myself that was ultimately to the detriment of someone else? (In other words, have I ever inadvertently created a negative prayer for someone when I prayed for something for myself?)
- Have I ever said, "I just *knew* that would happen!"? Or, "I was afraid this would happen."?
- Have you ever secretly wanted harm to come to someone?

CHAPTER 9: THE THIRD REASON WHY: LESSONS

> After close to forty years of maintaining an ongoing relationship with the souls in the hereafter, I have come to understand this one statement to be true above all: We are, each of us, born into our exact situation in life in order to fulfill our spiritual journey on the earth.
> It makes no difference who you are or what you will be
> – if you are here, lessons will be learned.
> – George Anderson

We embark on our experiences on this planet in order to learn and contribute. Lessons are an important part of life; from the first moment we're born. We immediately need to learn how to communicate our basic needs for food, love and comfort – and to get the attention of others who can help us. Scientists tell us that, in the first few years of life, we're constantly learning, expanding our brain synapses exponentially. However, after the age of five or six, these synapses not only stop growing, but actually start dying off, indicating that even at that early age we have a propensity to select the things we want to focus on and develop and learn.

As we get older, we become more and more selective about the things we want to learn, often rejecting opportunities for

Lessons. But our brains, our bodies, our *souls* still have a driving need for activity, for development, for progress.

Some of us embrace learning and growth, trying new things, taking risks, enrolling in courses, reading books, seeking out professional guidance, exploring, discovering, searching, investigating, opening up and challenging ourselves.

I'll often tell friends, with a gleam in my eye, that my mantra is "I want to learn through Joy." Not a bad goal, right? The problem is, most of us need a little nudging – some more than others – to branch out, to expand, to change, to grow, to learn.

This means we often need problems in order to motivate us to change. The more we're stuck in our ways, the more steadfast we are in maintaining our way of life, the bigger the problems can be. As you saw in the chapter on Bad Things Defined (and in the Appendix), there are a lot of very, very Bad Things that can happen!

As discussed in the chapter on Karma, all Karma includes Lessons. And in the chapter on Subconscious Sabotage, you found out how the energy of thought (your own and others') can create tragic events – an important Lesson!

Sometimes, however, neither Karma nor Subconscious Sabotage can explain a crisis. Sometimes the main Reason Why the crisis occurred is to teach a Lesson to be learned.

You wouldn't be reading this far into this book if you hadn't already been open to, and probably accepted, the idea that things happen for a reason and that reason is always to learn, to change. Within virtually every single "bad thing" that happens is a plethora of all kinds of lessons. In fact, talk with just about anyone who's been through a calamitous experience of any kind and I'm confident they can tell you something they learned through the process. Hopefully, the Lesson "stuck," so they won't have to repeat the learning – and hopefully it will have "stuck" for you, too!

> Those who cannot remember the past
> are condemned to repeat it.
> - George Santayana

EARTH SCHOOL

> The school of hard knocks is an accelerated curriculum.
> - Menander of Athens

Each of us has enrolled in Earth School. The campus is beautiful (except where we have destroyed it). There is a lot to learn here, and the experience is rewarding, stimulating and exciting. But the classes can be very challenging and the teachers (each other) are often demanding. The grading system is unique in that we all evaluate our own progress and there's no "bell curve." Everyone has the potential to graduate with honors.

Earth School has a wide and varied curriculum. Many of the classes we signed up for in advance, but we forget our major and class load, once we were here. The reason we have this amnesia is so that we can be born anew, with pure innocence. For most of us, our lapsed memories are a gift; we may not have had the courage to take some of our most rewarding classes if we had known how much work it would require.

But then, it would have been nice to know what to expect – and that's the purpose of this chapter: to discuss the kinds of Earth School Lessons involved in tragic events.

As you'll see, Lessons can take many forms. We can learn through joyful things like appreciation, acceptance and peace, or we can learn through distressing experiences like loss, pain, despair and deception. You can probably already identify several things you've learned through your challenging experience. The following provides a brief description (organized alphabetically) of nearly 100 of the potential "classes" you may be taking.

◆ Acceptance, Awareness and Denial ◆

> Acceptance of what has happened is the first step to
> overcoming the consequences of any misfortune.
> - William James

The Serenity Prayer, a hallmark of most 12-step programs, is a perfect model for acceptance, and has helped countless people going through a personal crisis of one kind or another: "God grant me the Serenity to accept the things I cannot change, the Courage to change the things I can, and the Wisdom to know the difference."

Often we're faced with a crisis because we've been denying our problems for too long. Everyone has heard of stories of people with large tumors (sometimes weighing several pounds!), or people who have stayed in abusive relationships (or jobs) for years – out of denial.

Acceptance is the opposite of denial, but before we can accept someone (including our self) or something, we need to have awareness and clarity of our problems, their causes and the Reasons Why.

◆ Accepting Others– Even Accepting That Some People Are Not Fully Evolved ◆

> When people whose spiritual development is on
> different levels are involved with one another,
> it is always the more highly evolved
> who is responsible for the relationship.
> - Pathwork[39] Lecture #180

One opportunity for learning, inherent in many traumatic events, is an opportunity to accept others for who and what they

---

[39] International Pathwork Foundation: www.pathwork.org.

are. As previously established, judging others is a way to create harmful events through Karma, Subconscious Sabotage, or both, and either of these is an opportunity to learn acceptance of others.

Anne Frank, in the quote below, exemplifies acceptance of others, even those committing egregious acts:

> In spite of everything I still believe that people are really good at heart. I simply can't build up my hopes on a foundation consisting of confusion, misery and death.
> - Anne Frank

Why would the Divine want us to learn this Lesson? Because we cannot love God unless we have the ability to find something loving in all of His/Her creatures, including those that might be defined as wayward or even evil. And if we cannot love God, we're ultimately unable to love others – or our Selves.

I like to use the analogy of keys on a piano. Some are higher and some are lower, some in a major key and some minor, but all are needed to make music.

> Truly loving another means letting go of all expectations. It means full acceptance, even celebration of another's personhood.
> - Unknown

♦ ACCOUNTABILITY AND RESPONSIBILITY ♦

Accountability is keeping commitments. Honoring your word. Taking responsibility for your actions. Owning up. Taking your lumps. Confessing and accepting the consequences. Recognizing the role you played in whatever happened to you. A crucial lesson! Perhaps the most important one of all! (Good thing it comes up early in the alphabet!)

The challenge with accountability is that often we're not "conscious" of our actions! We have that pesky subconscious/Inner Self that does things without our being aware of them! Which makes it easier for us to say, "I didn't mean to," or "I had no idea!" But, as you know, not only is this no excuse for our behavior, it's also destined to...you guessed it...keep producing more bad things, both for ourselves as well as to other people!

In addition to being the author of this book, I'm also the author/creator of a program called DrawSuccess. (www.DrawSuccess.com) It's an interactive, engaging program used to help people to "draw out" solutions to work better together by understanding their strengths and differences. One of the most powerful programs offered through DrawSuccess is one on Contribution & Accountability, which includes activities designed to build awareness about the importance of accountability within organizational teams and workgroups. One of those exercises is a quick, fun and *very* powerful way to ensure accountability among team members. The keys with that activity, and with any function of accountability, are two things: consciousness and consequence. To make you aware of what you do, and have ways to recognize the possible negative effects (to us and others) produced by our actions.

The gift in learning the Five Reasons Why is to be able to understand the need to take responsibility for our actions, whether the explanation for our crisis is Karma, Subconscious Sabotage, a Lesson, Test or Reward. Responsibility provides us with the gift of knowing what we can control – ourselves, our thoughts and our actions.

Dr. David R. Hawkins, in his book, *Power vs. Force*, explains the impact of having accountability for not only your actions but your perceptions: "By taking responsibility for the consequences of his own perceptions, the observer can transcend the role of victim to an understanding that 'nothing out there has power over you.' It isn't life's events, but how one reacts to them and the attitude that one has about them, that determines whether such events have a positive or negative effect on one's life, whether they're experienced as opportunity or as stress."

Accountability also means we cannot deny our role in the conditions of Earth, including pollution, global warming, natural disasters and other global conditions. Leading scientists have established the direct link between three things: the way we treat the Earth, how it causes planetary changes, and how the climate crisis is not only threatening our future, but is, indeed, causing many of our recent environmental tragedies, including hurricanes, drought, flooding and many diseases and viruses.

> The world is a dangerous place to live, not because of the people who are evil, but because of the people who don't do anything about it.
> – Albert Einstein

◆ ACTION ◆

> I believe life is constantly testing us for our level of commitment, and life's greatest rewards are reserved for those who demonstrate a never-ending commitment to act until they achieve. This level of resolve can move mountains, but it must be constant and consistent.
> As simplistic as this may sound, it is still the common denominator separating those who live their dreams from those who live in regret.
> - Anthony Robbins

Crisis gets us moving and forces us to take immediate action: something many of us need to learn. Whether the action is to express love or to just take step after step, it's important to "keep focusing forward with energy."

All too often, we wait until the last minute of someone's life – or our own - to express our love and appreciation. This is one of my big soap box pitches, and something I sincerely hope you learn, because there are serious repercussions when we delay. What happens is that we often feel so guilty, we try to put off the inevitable – death – by prolonging life through extreme, and even undignified ways. We put loved ones in hospitals and plug them into machines to assuage our guilt. The problem with this is that we don't allow them to die with dignity or with peace.[40], which isn't fair to them.

Another problem with this is that we're needlessly wasting precious medical resources, because of the guilt of our inaction. It has been estimated that as much as seventy-five percent of the medical expenses in this country are spent extending terminal patients lives an additional fourteen days. Seventy-five percent to extend the lives by two weeks of people who are already going to die! Just think of how useful that money could be in disease prevention or offering health care to people who cannot afford it...All because we lived in denial and failed to take action – to tell them we loved them – when we had the chance.

In his book, *Stumbling on Happiness*, author Daniel Gilbert said that "in the long run, people of every age and in every walk of life seem to regret *not* having done things much more than they regret the things they did..."

But you, the reader, are learning the Lesson of action because just by reading this book you're saying to your Higher Self, "I'm ready to learn – and to focus forward with energy to improve my life and the lives of others." Now, the next step is to keep learning and demonstrate that you're ready for magnificent transformation – for yourself and the planet!

> Action is just focusing forward with energy.
> - Brownell

◆ ADAPTABILITY VS. STAGNATION ◆

> One should act in consonance with the way of heaven and earth, which is enduring and eternal. The superior man perseveres long in his course, adapts to the times, but remains firm in his direction and correct in his goals.
> - I Ching

---

[40] The alternative is to choose hospice care, where patients are cared for with respect and comfort through their final days.,

When we fear the future, the loss of security or of change, we're exhibiting our unwillingness to adapt, to transform. We hold onto the past, even if painful, because we are unwilling to prepare for the future.

However, because of the disturbances we experience in a crisis, we're forced to adapt, to transform ourselves. Learning to change and evolve gives us incredible strength to be able to handle whatever life throws at us.

> It's easier to put on slippers
> than to carpet the whole world.
> - Stuart Smalley (Al Franken)

◆ ADVENTURE ◆

> The opposite of Insecurity isn't Security.
> It's a Sense of Adventure.
> - Brownell

One thing we learn very quickly, when faced with a crisis, is the elusiveness of security and stability. In tragic situations, our lives are turned upside down.

One aspect of this Lesson is that we find we often hold onto situations, places and relationships because of a false sense of security or a fear of the unknown. Sometimes we need a Divine nudge, to find our true and highest destiny. Attachment and fear of losing something – especially security – will often come to us as a Lesson to learn to look at our lives with a sense of adventure.

> Security is mostly a superstition.
> It does not exist in nature,
> nor do the children of men as a whole experience it.
> Avoiding danger is no safer in the long run than outright
> exposure. Life is either a daring adventure or nothing.
> –Helen Keller

The above quote by Helen Keller instills a sense of adventure. Her own life could've been one of crisis and self-denial, but instead she broke through her physical limitations of sight, hearing and verbalization and experienced a life of amazing accomplishments. Seems pretty clear she not only learned a powerful Lesson, but is also an inspiration for the rest of us to learn.

◆ AMBITION AND DRIVE ◆

The interesting thing about ambition is that it's often used to rationalize people's behavior. When I was looking to find a quote, I realized that there are two divisive philosophies regarding ambition. For the people who have it, they want to know that others endorse their behavior. But this comes with a price, because those with too much ambition often ignore other, often more important things in life.

But then there are those who are living a life of complacency and lack ambition completely who could use a little motivation.

What's the key? Knowing that what you strive for is something that will create Functional (or internal) Happiness, not Circumstantial (external) Happiness (see category later in this chapter).

◆ ANGER: HARMFUL AND USEFUL ◆

> It is a waste of time to be angry about my disability.
> One has to get on with life and I haven't done badly.
> People won't have time for you
> if you are always angry or complaining.
> – Stephen Hawking

As discussed in Subconscious Sabotage, anger can be extremely destructive and can perpetuate harmful Karma. Understanding the devastating nature of anger is a powerful Lesson.

Anger results from one of two things. Either it is a result of frustration because we feel we aren't being heard, or because we feel powerless and trapped. Realizing this can help us not only understand the reason behind the anger, it can help us know how to resolve it. What are the most effective ways to get someone to listen? What is the best way to react when we feel trapped?

> Healthy anger will never weaken you,
> it will give you strength and freedom.
> - Pathwork lecture #102

Anger can be useful if it is a motivator for change. For instance, injustice stimulates people to work for justice. War can encourage people to rally for peace. Outrage at global warming can increase awareness and communication. Irritation with unreasonable health care practices incites people to protest traditional medicine. If no one had transformed their anger into action, we would still be facing the tyranny, social injustice, and human rights violations that plagued the past.

> Nobody got anywhere in the world
> by simply being content
> - Louis L'Amour

♦ APPRECIATION AND GRATITUDE ♦

> Count your blessings. Once you realize how valuable
> you are and how much you have going for you, the
> smiles will return, the sun will break out,
> the music will play, and you will finally be able
> to move forward the life that God intended for you
> with grace, strength, courage, and confidence.
> - Og Mandino

It may seem like there's a fine line between attachment and appreciation. But in fact there is a big difference. With attachment, there's fear involved, while appreciation is purely for enjoyment and comes from love, not fear.

Appreciation is a way of expressing our love of God. Appreciation is the pure and true way to change your life through positive thinking, because it's a life approach that allows you to acknowledge the gifts in your life. And it grows with awareness and practice, because the more you appreciate your blessings, the more prominently they show up.

Not only do other humans increase their generosity to those who are grateful, but the Divine works in the same manner. When we give thanks, our Spirit Guides not only rejoice, but it also opens them up to help us more.

> Now is no time to think of what you do not have. Think of what you can do with what there is.
> - Ernest Hemingway

♦ ASKING FOR GUIDANCE/TO SEE THE SIGNS ♦

> The most wonderful aspect of the universal scheme of things is the action of free beings under divine guidance.
> - Joseph Marie de Maistre

Happy, spiritually connected people are able to unite with the Divine on a smooth and frequent basis. All they have to do is settle their minds and ask for guidance.

Conversely, unhappy or externally-focused people are either too busy or too troubled to make the connection. This could be the single reason crises happen – to remind us to look inward and upward for love and guidance.

♦ ASKING FOR – AND RECEIVING - HELP AND LOVE♦

> Refusing to ask for help when you need it is refusing someone the chance to be helpful.
> - Ric Ocasek

For some of us, asking for help can be the most difficult Lesson of all to learn. Often we don't ask at all, and try to get through things on our own, which makes the process of healing more difficult and takes longer. Sometimes this turns us into a martyr (one who chooses to suffer).

Or, we have an unexpressed hidden expectation that someone should "know" what we need and miraculously provide it, and when they don't, we get hurt or angry.

Either way, learning how to ask for help graciously is especially important as we face a crisis. There's much to gain by asking others to help us. We enrich relationships; improve our chances of success, and speed up our progress. Just as importantly, we give others the opportunity to feel the marvelous, life-enriching elation that comes from helping us.

Just about anything you're going through has happened to someone else who can help you. You just have to find and reach out to them. There are a number of resources to meet people who can help you, including therapists, healers, books, websites, organizations, self-help groups, and many others.

We need to allow people to love us in their way – not ours. When we don't feel loved, we need to check our emotions, check our facts, and check our fears.

Some of us need to learn to receive help – we're used to being the helpers. But that can actually be selfish because, to be truly loving, we need to allow others to love us also. Be gracious and appreciative of others' help and love. It's a precious gift!

♦ ATTACHMENT/DETACHMENT/ SURRENDER ♦

> "Attachment leads to jealousy.
> The shadow of greed that is."
> Yoda (Frank Oz) in Star Wars Episode III—Revenge of the Sith

When we say "I can't live without" something, we're taught a valuable Lesson: that we're wrong. We *can* live without something. Attachment is a fear of loss – and by now you know what happens when we fear something – we actually push it away from us!

I had a breakthrough moment, when facing the worst of my business/financial problems, when I entered what I called "the happy land of apathy." It wasn't what most people would traditionally call apathy – that I didn't care about anything or anyone – but it was a moment of releasing my worries. Que Sera Sera – "what will be will be" – is a good motto at times of great stress and tragedy, because when we "let it be" and relinquish control in an uncontrollable situation, a certain level of peace can enter us and "there will be an answer.".

> And the reason it was life changing for me is because in that moment of surrender, I realized that when you've done everything that you can do, when you've given it the best that you know how, you surrender it to that which is greater than yourself. You survive everything. And when you make peace with that, that is when you open up the space for what is to come to you, to come. And that lesson has changed me forever.
> - Oprah Winfrey

◆ AUTHENTICITY ◆

> An authentic life is the most personal form of worship.
> Everyday life has become my prayer.
> - Sarah Ban Breathnach

When we're deceitful or false, life has a way of knocking us off our blocks to teach us the importance of authenticity. Authentic people are genuine, reliable and credible they are not only true to others but true to themselves.

◆ AWARENESS ◆

> Let us not look back in anger or forward in fear,
> but around in awareness.
> - James Thurber

Have you ever tried to get someone's attention, to notice something? First, you call to him, then you start to yell. Eventually, you physically try to move him to look in your direction.

The Universe does this, too. It gently nudges, then it gets a little more obvious, until often the only way it can get us to look is to throw us into a crisis.

Awareness, however is simple: pay attention! James Redfield's wildly popular book, *The Celestine Prophecy*, stresses the importance of looking for signs. Written as an adventure novel, the messages are commanding: coincidences are everywhere and happening all the time – we just need to become aware of them!

◆ BALANCE ◆

> Even a happy life cannot be without a measure of
> darkness, and the word happy would lose its meaning if
> it were not balanced by sadness. It is far better to take
> things as they come along with patience and equanimity.
> - Carl Jung

Tragedies often happen when our lives are out of balance, when we're too focused on one area of our life and missing the other, and often more important, things.

Balance is an important Lesson, because we need to recognize that, even though we may not consciously want Bad Things to happen, our lives would be pretty boring if we always got everything we wanted all the time and nothing exciting ever happens. The above quote by Carl Jung exemplifies this sentiment.

143

♦ BEING A SUPPORT TO OTHERS ♦

> I've learned that people will forget what you said,
> people will forget what you did, but people
> will never forget how you made them feel.
> - Maya Angelou

Sometimes it takes a disaster to bring out the best in us, to be able to recognize and demonstrate how we can be a powerful support to others.

♦ BLAME ♦

> When you blame others,
> you give up your power to change.
> - Dr. Robert Anthony

Bestselling author Dr. Wayne Dyer said the following about blame, "All blame is a waste of time. No matter how much fault you find with another, and regardless of how much you blame him, it won't change you. The only thing blame does is to keep the focus off you when you're looking for external reasons to explain your unhappiness or frustration. You may succeed in making another feel guilty about something by blaming him, but you won't succeed in changing whatever it is about you that is making you unhappy."

There is a big difference between identifying the cause of a problem and placing blame. The difference is energy and responsibility. Because blame is a negative feeling, energy is usually mixed with anger, directed out towards someone or something else. Blame takes the responsibility away from us and places it in someone else's hands. Identifying a cause allows us to assess our responsibility for what has happened. When we put blame outside ourselves and fail to take responsibility, to see the Reasons Why the event occurred, we lose our ability to take control of the situation and make necessary changes.

Or, as comedian Al Franken's alter ego Stuart Smalley said, "when you point one finger at someone else, three fingers are pointing back at you."

♦ BOREDOM ♦

> Once thought I had mono for an entire year.
> It turned out I was just really bored.
> - Wayne Campbell (Mike Myers) in the movie *Wayne's World*

The above quote, while amusing, is often sadly true. People are likely to experience one of two outcomes when they're bored. They may become lazy and lethargic and apathetic - the kind of apathy when they truly don't care about anything or anyone. In his book, *Power vs. Force,* David R. Hawkins, M.D. Ph.D. suggests this form of apathy is one of the lowest levels of human consciousness, "Apathy is a state of helplessness; its victims...lack the energy to avail themselves of what may be available." This kind of boredom can produce depression, listlessness and illness.

Alternatively, boredom can also create "drama addicts," people who look for – and even create – dramatic events, in order to keep some excitement in their lives. These people thrive on the news, staying glued to the latest crisis, worrying about everything from terrorist attacks to the latest flu epidemic to being struck by lightning.

Drama addicts seem to get energy by telling everyone else about all the problems of the world that they should be worried about, because it helps feed their fears. An extreme example is the perpetuation of all the urban myths circulating through the internet, which, until they're disproved, can radically change people's behavior – all created by fear and generated by boredom.

The truth about either reaction to boredom is that we can learn that we have a choice in how we respond. We just have to recognize it.

◆ CHOICE ◆

> Our lives are a sum total of the choices we have made.
> - Wayne Dyer

One of the fears identified in the chapter on Understanding Your Crisis was the Fear of Being Trapped. Often, the Lesson within this fear is to recognize we all have many choices and options in any situation. We may *think* we can't quit the job or live without something or someone, but when we are able to open our eyes and see a variety of alternatives, we find we hold the power to select our own future.

It may not feel like we had a choice in what has happened to us. On a conscious level, that may be true. But on some level we have chosen to learn the Lessons we're being faced with. It's up to us whether we learn the Lessons and pass the Tests so we can move forward.

◆ COMPASSION ◆

> From wisdom, understanding.
> From understanding, compassion.
> From compassion, love.
> - Richard Wagner

A tragedy can instantly transform a shallow, inconsiderate person into one with compassion. Sometimes it happens as an innate response. The public reaction to Princess Diana's death, the victims of terrorist attacks, and sufferers from natural disasters are all examples of where compassionate people rallied to help others.

But often we only learn compassion by direct experience. When we have experienced a crisis, it provides us with more compassion when someone experiences a similar crisis. For example, once I had felt the darkest of despair myself, I became able to relate to others in despair, because I truly know *what it feels like*.

Compassion should not be judgment or pity however; instead demonstrate understanding and a willingness to help.

◆ CONNECTEDNESS ◆

> A human being is a part of a whole, called by us 'universe', a part limited in time and space. He experiences himself, his thoughts and feelings as something separated from the rest...a kind of optical delusion of his consciousness. This delusion is a kind of prison for us, restricting us to our personal desires and to affection for a few persons nearest to us. Our task must be to free ourselves from this prison by widening our circle of compassion to embrace all living creatures and the whole of nature in its beauty.
> - Albert Einstein

In Marcus Buckingham and Donald O. Clifton's book, *Now, Discover Your Strengths*, the authors identify Connectedness as one of the thirty-four strengths one can possess, "...In your soul you know that we are all connected.... You gain confidence from knowing that we are not isolated from one another or from the Earth and the life on it. The feeling of Connectedness implies certain responsibilities. If we are all part of a larger picture, then we must not harm others because we will be harming ourselves. We must not exploit because we will be exploiting ourselves."

When we live in relative isolation, "in our own world," we may think we don't need anyone else. Tragic events often teach us otherwise – we all have responsibility to each other and to the planet, because we're all connected.

◆ CONNECTING WITH INNER SELF ◆

> When there is no enemy within,
> the enemies outside cannot hurt you.
> - African Proverb

The chapter on Subconscious Sabotage demonstrated how important it is to go inward and connect with your subconscious or Inner Self. This is an important Lesson for this book – and for your life. I'll give you the tools to accomplish in subsequent chapters.

◆ CONNECTION WITH YOUR HIGHER SELF AND YOUR HIGHER POWER ◆

> If only God would give me some clear sign! Like making a large deposit in my name in a Swiss bank.
> – Woody Allen

Tragedy has a way of making us look outward and upward, as well as inward. If we choose to connect with the Divine, we're guaranteed to feel loved and loving. We just have to ask!

◆ CONSCIOUSNESS ◆

> Each Personality contributes, in its own special way, with its own special aptitudes and Lessons to learn, consciously or unconsciously, to the evolution of its soul.
> – Gary Zukav

Consciousness is conscious thought and conscious action – being aware of our feelings and how we act – what we're doing every moment. Pain can teach us to be acutely aware of everything we do. But we don't need anguish, all we have to do is wake up!

◆ COURAGE ◆

> It takes great courage and personal strength to hold on to our center during times of great hurt.
> – Marianne Williamson

Facing and getting through calamities takes enormous courage. It often forces us to go out on a limb and take the road less traveled.

Have you ever been skiing, looking down at the hill below and wondering how you'll ever make it down without recreating the famous "agony of defeat" scene from sporting programs? But when you do make it, have you ever looked back up at that enormous hill with amazement at your accomplishment? That's the glory of the Lesson of courage!

> Being deeply loved by someone gives you strength
> while loving someone deeply gives you courage.
> - Lao Tzu

♦ DESIRE ♦

Desire is defined by Webster's as "to long for, to crave, to ask for." Desire can be both healthy and unhealthy. It depends on the reason for the desire (is it in the best interest of all concerned?) and the degree of attachment or detachment to the outcome.

> It is a miserable state of mind to have few things to
> desire, and many things to fear.
> - Francis Bacon

Often a Lesson that comes with unhealthy desire is to "be careful what you ask for." When we're too specific, too attached to a particular longing we may indeed get what we desire and either not be satisfied or, perhaps, be devastated by the result.

An example of this is what's called "affluenza," which describes problems that arise when people achieve sudden wealth. There may be a false sense of entitlement, loss of future motivation, low self-esteem, loss of self-confidence, low self-worth and/or preoccupation with externals.

Desire is healthy when the goal is enlightenment, love, joy, peace or bliss. In this kind of desire, we're pursuing an internal state of mind that's an expression of love, instead of an external "thing." In essence, our desire is for functional happiness, versus circumstantial happiness, and the effect is not only longer lasting, it's infinitely more fulfilling.

◆ DESPAIR AND HOPE ◆

> There is no despair so absolute as that which comes with the first moments of our first great sorrow, when we have not yet known what it is to have suffered and be healed, to have despaired and have recovered hope.
> - George Eliot

Despair is one of the most overwhelming emotions there is, because it is the immobilizing loss of hope. Whenever you find yourself feeling a sense of despair, it usually means you have an interruption in your plans for the future and either don't know where to turn or are afraid you can't get through what's ahead of you. If you don't know where to turn or what to do, ask for help. Believe it or not, there can be two benefits of despair. First, it helps us seek and find help. Second, it makes us look for and discover hope. Hope is the antidote to despair.

> When the human is exhausted by grief or remorse, covered with shame and abandoned by the world, hope glimmers and brightens into a ray of light. The human, in his darkest hours, looks for hope. While he looks for hope he cannot fail altogether. Hope shows the way by which one can save himself and earn his conscious immortality.
> – Harold Percival

Like Divine love, hope is avaliable to all of us, all the time. All we have to do is close our eyes and ask, and open our eyes and remember.

> Despair is a cruel companion. It robs you of everything; especially the choices that still lie within your control.
> Goo the Guru in DUET stories Volume III: A Chorus of Voices by Brownell Landrum

◆ ENTHUSIASM ◆

> Success is the ability to go from one failure to another
> with no loss of enthusiasm.
> - Winston Churchill

Enthusiasm is an evocative word. It comes from the Greek worth entheos, which means inspiration, to be filled with God, or in the presence of the Divine. It's a near cousin in meaning and impact to Appreciation, because both words evoke assistance from our Higher Power.

In times of tragedy, we sometimes lose our enthusiasm and zest for life. But, like love, it's available to us all the time; we just have to look within and ask for it.

ETHICAL BEHAVIOR

> A man's ethical behavior should be based effectually on
> sympathy, education, and social ties;
> no religious basis is necessary. Man would indeed be in
> a poor way if he had to be restrained by fear of
> punishment and hope of reward after death.
> - Albert Einstein

When people are unethical or demonstrate immoral or inconsiderate behavior, they inevitably will be faced with repercussive Karma until they learn the Lesson.

◆ EVIL – ITS SOURCE, ITS WAYS, AND HOW TO AVOID IT ◆

> It is a man's own mind, not his enemy or foe,
> that lures him to evil ways.
> - Buddha

As discussed earlier, evil is separation from love, from God. When we're faced with evil, there's a message, a Lesson to be learned, as well as a Test to evaluate how we will react. Will we respond with hatred or anger, emotions that fuel evil? Or will we stay grounded, connected and loving?

♦ EXPERIENCE VARIETY OF EMOTIONS ♦

This chapter covers a large sampling of emotions and behavior we encounter with a crisis. Being exposed to these – and many more – feelings are important Lessons in and of themselves. To quote Jimmy Buffet, "How can you describe an ocean if you've never seen it?" The experience itself opens us up, so we can better relate to – and help – others.

♦ FAILURE ♦

Have you ever noticed how we learn more from our failures than we do from our successes? The following quotes say it all:

> You may encounter many defeats, but you must not be defeated. In fact, it may be necessary to encounter the defeats, so you can know who you are, what you can rise from, how you can still come out of it.
> - Maya Angelou

> I have not failed. I've just found 10,000 ways that won't work.
> - Thomas Alva Edison

> Only those who dare to fail greatly
> can ever achieve greatly.
> - Robert F. Kennedy

♦ FAITH ♦

What is faith to you? And how has your faith changed during hard times? Words used to define faith include belief, confidence, honesty and trust. It can involve the Divine or other human beings. During times of adversity, we're given a choice: to have faith or to succumb to despair and abandon all hope. Elie Wiesel, a survivor of the horrors of the holocaust, explains as follows:

> No faith is as pure as a wounded faith because it is faith
> with an open eye.
> I know all the Reasons Why I shouldn't have faith.
> I have better arguments against faith than for faith.
> Sure, it's a choice. And I choose faith.
> - Elie Wiesel

♦ FORGIVENESS ♦

Expressing Forgiveness

Forgiveness is such an important lesson; it warrants its own chapter! Too often we misunderstand what it means to forgive. One of my favorite definitions of forgiveness is "the release of resentment." It means we're able to accept the actions of the past, so we can find a way past anger and animosity and discover a way to heal.

Inherent in forgiveness is that we feel like someone has treated us badly or unfairly. However, it doesn't mean we have to condone or tolerate cruel or evil behavior; or that we have to let it continue. When someone asks for our forgiveness, we should be able to release our resentment toward them.

> To withhold forgiveness
> is to choose to continue to remain the victim.
> – Larry James

153

> To err is human; to forgive, Divine.
> - Alexander Pope

The following quote, from *The Gospel Today* by Rev. Dr. Robert Landrum encapsulates the challenges – and ways – of forgiveness: "Forgiveness is not easy. True forgiveness of the one who wronged us may take weeks, even months, of daily prayer. It means praying not only for the love and strength to forgive, but praying for the person who committed the act against us or our loved ones. Hardest of all is praying for the strength and grace to love that person, as a neighbor and brother or sister."

Forgiving Yourself

Maya Angelou said it best:

> It is very important for every human being to forgive herself or himself because if you live, you will make mistakes – it is inevitable. But once you do and you see the mistake, then you forgive yourself and say, 'well, if I'd known better I'd have done better,' that's all. So you say to people who you think you may have injured, 'I'm sorry,' and then you say to yourself, 'I'm sorry.' If we all hold on to the mistake, we can't see our own glory in the mirror because we have the mistake between our faces and the mirror; we can't see what we're capable of being. You can ask forgiveness of others, but in the end the real forgiveness is in one's own self.
> - Maya Angelou

♦ FORTITUDE ♦

> If you're going through hell, keep going.
> – Winston Churchill

The above quote is a great expression on fortitude in the face of disaster. Fortitude is a combination of patience and courage, with a willingness to proceed forward, no matter the obstacles.

♦ FREE WILL ♦

> Man is a being with free will;
> therefore, each man is potentially good or evil,
> and it's up to him and only him (through his reasoning
> mind) to decide which he wants to be.
> - Ayn Rand

Free will places an awesome responsibility on us. By giving us free will, the Divine gives us the choice to make mistakes — and learn from them.

When we acknowledge and accept the power of this responsibility, that it isn't some outside power that's influencing us, but the actions of humans against humans, and humans against the planet, we can no longer make excuses. It is our obligation to embrace our free will to improve our circumstances.

> The reason we are made to forget any pre-birth memories is so that we might more fully experience the physical things, be physically challenged, make choices out of free will, so we can make mistakes so that we can learn from them in ways that only a physical life can impart. If we retained these pre-birth memories, we might not bother to experience physical life for its fulfillment. We might decide to skip the pain and thus miss the pleasure.
> - Afterlife 101

◆ FRIENDSHIP ◆

> Friends are the gifts we give to ourselves.
> - Unknown

My friends are some of the most important blessings I have in my life. In fact, I've often told people that the thing I like about myself the most is the quality and variety of my friends.

> The real friend is he or she who can share
> all our sorrows and double our joys.

155

- Barry C. Forbes

When we go through troubling times, we find out who our true friends are. At the same time, we learn to accept others' limitations. When I went through my eight years of hell, I lost a lot of people in my life whom I thought were friends. I found out that many were not just "fair weather" friends, but treated me as if my problems were contagious. Through that experience, however, I've been blessed by the long-time friends who stuck by me. In addition, I've been much more aware of the real qualities I seek in a true friend: an ally, a supporter, a sympathizer.[41]

> Since it has been my lot to find, at every parting of the road, the helping hand of comrade kind to help me with my heavy load, And since I have no gold to give and love alone must make amends, my humble prayer is, while I live – God, make me worthy of my friends.
> - Unknown

♦ FUN ♦

Fun is one of life's greatest gifts. What do you do for fun? One tragedy-within-a-tragedy that distresses me is the feelings of guilt so many of us have when we break through the darkness and pain in the midst of a crisis or loss and smile, laugh or have fun. Somehow we feel like it's inappropriate, or disrespectful.

> "Laughter through tears in my favorite emotion."
> – Truvy Jones (Dolly Parton), in the movie Steel Magnolias

But the truth is, laughter, joy and fun are a healthy release that helps us heal.

As far as being disrespectful to the memory of those who have passed on, from everything I've read on the subject of death

---

[41] The definition of friend in Webster's Dictionary.

(and it's a lot) the best tribute we can give to our loved ones on the other side is when we can let go of our grief and enjoy life.

> Laughter is not at all a bad beginning for a friendship, and it is far the best ending for one.
> – Oscar Wilde

♦ GIVING UP AND LETTING GO ♦

> Some people believe that holding on and hanging in there are signs of great strength. However, there are times when it takes much more strength to know when to let go – and then do it.
> - Ann Landers

Giving up is considered to be negative. But what really is giving up? It doesn't mean quitting, but instead it is releasing control of the situation to a higher intelligence. When we "give up" we're turning over our problems to God. Similarly, letting go is another way to liberate attachment. Prayer to release your problems to the Divine helps us to give our problems to a power greater than ourselves – one that will always guide us to the most loving solution to any problem.

♦ GUILT ♦

> "Hold on to your power: don't let others squash it. Hold on to your courage: don't let others preach it out of you. Hold on to your independence: don't let others scare it out of you. Author your life without guilt or shame: do not live to please others. Refuse to surrender except to your truest self and your wisest voice."
> - Patricia Lynn Reilly

Writer Peter McWilliams has the best definition of guilt I've found: "Guilt is anger directed at ourselves." What good does that do? You already know how destructive anger can be. Since emotions comes from our Inner Self, the Lesson of guilt is that it shows a lack of love – for our Self.

Our society is filled with groups ready to instill shame and guilt on each of us. Governments, religions and clubs often use guilt as a motivating tool.

> The question we should ask ourselves when someone
> tries to make us feel guilty is,
> "Are they doing this to control us?"
> - Brownell

Guilt holds us tethered to the past, instead of making changes for the future. However, guilt is absolved when we do three things:

- Learn from our mistakes and end the destructive behavior
- Make amends for our actions, and
- Help others to learn from our experience

♦ HAPPINESS - FUNCTIONAL VS. CIRCUMSTANTIAL ♦

> As human beings we all want to be happy
> and free from misery... we have learned that the key to
> happiness is inner peace. The greatest obstacles to inner
> peace are disturbing emotions such as anger, attachment,
> fear and suspicion, while love and compassion
> and a sense of universal responsibility
> are the sources of peace and happiness.
> - Dalai Lama

Perhaps your Lesson in your crisis is to learn the difference between Functional Happiness (or Internal) and Circumstantial (External) Happiness.

Before you tell yourself "I'll be happy when..." or "If I get _____ I'll be happy" you should know that a study demonstrated that external, circumstantial factors make little difference in happiness. On a life satisfaction scale from 1 to 7,

Calcutta slum dwellers put themselves at 4.6, while *Forbes Magazine's* "richest Americans" rate themselves only a 5.8.

> Many people become so attached to their work or making money that they ignore the other people around them, or they use it as a way to avoid facing themselves at a deeper level. When they lose that job or lose their money they are devastated and have an identity crisis. Without these things they no longer know who they are! Loss of physical things is difficult, but it is an opportunity to get in touch with the needs of your soul, to go beyond the ego into the better part of yourself.
> – Carmen Harra

Functional Happiness means that you can find love, peace and joy, regardless of the outer circumstances of your life. You're able to appreciate what you have and find joy in the moment. Functional Happiness isn't just a positive attitude. I don't know about you, but it's annoying to me when people say, "Smile and you'll feel better" or Get a positive attitude." Functional Happiness comes from several Lessons discussed in this chapter: optimism, appreciation, faith, removal of fear, faith, openness, recognition of the Divine plan, the ability to enjoy pleasure, fun and humor and, above all, love.

> Happiness is a sign that we have accepted God's will.
> - Marianne Williamson

♦ HARM OF VICES ♦

> Sin is lack of love. An immature person is never able to love. Immaturity means separateness.
> Anyone in that condition is selfish, egocentric, blind and cannot understand others.
> - Pathwork lecture #102

The Seven Cardinal sins are: Pride, Covetousness (Greed), Lust, Anger, Gluttony, Envy and Sloth. Vices or sins all come from some form of harmful self over-indulgence, which happens as a result of not listening to the internal messages coming from an immature Inner Self.

♦ HELP YOU LIVE YOUR LIFE BETTER ♦

Suffering can give us clarity about what is truly important in life, thereby helping us find a better way to live our lives. Whether we learn to treasure and cultivate special relationships, to take better care of ourselves or to pursue our life's purpose, we're now in a position to live a better, more fulfilled life.

♦ HONESTY ♦

> Each time you are honest and conduct yourself with honesty, a success force will drive you toward greater success. Each time you lie, even with a little white lie, there are strong forces pushing you toward failure.
> -Joseph Sugarman

Honesty includes both truthfulness and opening up to others – each a valuable Lesson. Dishonesty is identified by Napoleon Hill as one of the thirty-one major causes of failure, probably because it's an action based in fear and breeds distrust.

Opening up is a gift – to us and to others. I have countless stories to tell about myself (as I'm sure you do as well) where special friendships were initiated because I was open about myself – even about those things that most people would keep private. I can think of one particular bond that developed because I was uninhibited about my hysterectomy, even to relative strangers in the workplace. A new friend came to me because she heard – and wanted some guidance to help her with her own problems, and we've been a close, loving support to each other ever since.

It takes courage to be open, to be vulnerable. But I've always said that I would rather have someone reject me because of who I am than because of someone I am pretending to be.

◆ HUMOR ◆

> Laugh at yourself and at life. Not in the spirit of derision
> or whining self-pity, but as a remedy, a miracle drug,
> that will ease your pain, cure your depression, and help
> you to put in perspective that seemingly terrible defeat
> and worry with laughter at your predicaments, thus
> freeing your mind to think clearly toward the solution
> that is certain to come.
> Never take yourself too seriously.
> - Og Mandino

Trey Parker and Matt Stone, the creators of the TV show "South Park" are also the geniuses behind the highly acclaimed, Tony award-winning musical "The Book of Mormon." (While I'll readily admit that Parker and Stone's humor isn't for everyone, I happened to think they're quite brilliant).. Anyway, there's a song in the musical called "Hasa Diga Eebowai." It's a (very crude but very funny) song that shows how you can take humor to express yourself. One of the lines says, "Raise your middle finger to the sky." I think you get the picture!

I love the following quote because it's so refreshing to hear the great, accomplished physicist express his sense of humor:

> Life would be tragic if it weren't funny.
> – Stephen Hawking

I've interspersed amusing quotes throughout this book for us – the reader as well as the writer – to have a reason to smile.

◆ IMMORTALITY ◆

> We do not believe in immortality
> because we can prove it, but we try to prove it
> because we cannot help believing it.
> - Harriet Martineau

Immortality has two connotations: life after death, and leaving a legacy on Earth. The Lesson of both come to clearer focus when faced with tragedy and death.

In the chapter on Basic Assumptions, I identified Life after death as one of our Basic Assumptions, but there's nothing like facing death to make us try to learn more about life's greatest mystery: where we go when we die. There are dozens of books and articles from a variety of sources that have helped me get clarity and formulate my own strong belief in the afterlife. None are proof in and of themselves, but because of the variety of sources and the commonality of experience, and because I've confirmed the knowledge with inner knowledge and higher guidance, collectively I've found the answer that has added tremendous value and meaning to my life.

> But he who has been earnest in the love of knowledge
> and of true wisdom, and has exercised his intellect more
> than any other part of him, must have thoughts immortal
> and Divine. If he attain truth, and in so far as human
> nature is capable of sharing in immortality,
> he must altogether be immortal.
> - Plato

Immortality also involves leaving a legacy behind when your physical body goes. How will you be remembered? How do you want to be remembered? Is there a difference?

> We all leave personal legacies
> for the people we know and love.
> - Christine Gregoire

♦ IMPERMANENCE ♦

> We need to surrender to the fact that all efforts at permanence are hopeless. No structure we can build will protect us from the contingencies of life. But in the midst of that impermanence is the incredible gift of life.
> - Ecclesiastes

Impermanence is one of the essential doctrines of Buddhism. Buddha taught that, because things are impermanent, attachment to them is futile, and leads to suffering. "The only thing permanent is change," said the I Ching. No one lives in our particular bodies forever, and we need to accept this and be prepared for change, and be prepared for the transitions in life, and in death.

The upside of this Lesson is we can recognize that our suffering is also impermanent. "This, too, shall pass." The next step is continued in Buddhist text, "Do not waste your life."

> Old friends pass away, new friends appear. It is just like the days. An old day passes, a new day arrives. The important thing is to make it meaningful: a meaningful friend - or a meaningful day.
> - Dalai Lama

♦ INDEPENDENCE ♦

Many of us stay in destructive relationships because we fear we can't make it on our own, meaning our Lesson is independence and self-reliance. There's nothing like standing on your own two feet. It gives you freedom to make your own choices, without others' approval. Conversely, co-dependence is recognizable as a psychological problem. It's also called "relationship addiction," because people with codependency are in relationships that are one-sided, emotionally destructive and/or abusive.

There's a big difference between needing and wanting. I remember a conversation where I told someone I didn't want him to need me. I told him he could accomplish whatever he wanted without me. Yes, the project might be more expansive with my help, but he didn't need me, and I encouraged him to move forward on his own. If he wanted my help, I would be there. I would rather be wanted than needed. And I would rather want than need something or someone. Need indicates a weakness. Want indicates healthy desire.

> The four cornerstones of character on which the structure of this nation was built are: Initiative, Imagination, Individuality and Independence.
> - Edward Vernon Rickenbacker

◆ INTUITION ◆

> Intuition is the highest sense perception
> a human can attain.
> - Pathwork Lecture #72

Intuition is a result of our connecting to all three of our Selves. The messages come from our Higher Self, but in order for our Conscious Self to listen to the message, our Inner Self needs to be comfortable and attended to.

It's kind of like a radio. The subconscious mind is the radio itself. The conscious mind turns the knob and listens to the message. The Superconscious is the actual message coming through.

Imprisonment, health issues and other forms of isolation are crises that put us in a position to have a lot of time to ourselves, and a lot of time to develop the power of intuition. Intuition is an amazing gift we all have the potential to acquire. With the facility of intuition, we can't only identify and learn other Lessons more quickly, but it can help us become "in tune" enough to avoid problems altogether.

◆ JOY ◆

> The greater your ecstasy and joy,
> the more you contribute to the world.
> - Pathwork lecture #177

Close your eyes right now and sense the feeling of joy inside you. See how it lifts you up? It makes your heart leap. Your facial muscles transform; your breathing changes. What a feeling!

Cultivating joy is a Lesson we all have the ability to learn, without assistance, without an external source. We can just feel it. When our life is in darkness it seems elusive – but we need to learn that it's right there all the time. Just feel it! (And if you need a friend, a funny movie, a special song or a walk in nature to feel it, no problem!) J.K. Rowling, author of the widely popular Harry Potter books, created Dementors, a being that "sucked out your soul." What was the only way to combat the dementors? The happiest of memories. In other words, joy.

> If you were all alone in the universe with no one to talk to, no one with which to share the beauty of the stars, to laugh with, to touch, what would be your purpose in life? It is other life, it is love, which gives your life meaning. This is harmony. We must discover the joy of each other, the joy of challenge, the joy of growth.
> - Mitsugi Saotome

◆ JUDGMENT ◆

> When you judge another, you do not define them,
> you define yourself.
> - Wayne Dyer

Have you ever noticed that the people who are the most likely to be judged by others are just as guilty for condemning someone else? That often the people who are victims of prejudice often display prejudicial behaviors themselves?

We're more likely to criticize others when we ourselves are feeling weak or vulnerable. This is the basis for Social Darwinism, defined as "competing for survival in a hostile world." When we feel threatened, we react in a number of ways: anger, fear, or subjugation of our supposed opponent.

> Before you criticize someone, walk a mile in their shoes.
> That way, when you criticize them,
> you're a mile away and you have their shoes.
> - Jack Handey

Judging others creates a karmic cycle. The more we criticize others, the more we invite criticism back at us, sabotaging both us and our perceived "opponent."

◆ KARMA ◆

> Karma is a process designed
> to ensure evolution of consciousness.
> - Dr. John Mumford

The purpose of Karma is to learn. In every karmic situation, there's a Lesson to be learned – that how we treat others will be reflected back on us.

Similarly, we should also look at every Lesson and ask, "Is this the result of past Karma? If so, how can I stop the karmic cycle? If not, is it possible I could create negative Karma from this situation – and how can I prevent it?"

LEARNING FROM MISTAKES

Many times we create our own problems. Either we don't listen to our Inner Self or we ignore the warning signs. Hindsight is 20-20 and it helps us learn from our mistakes. Understanding what has happened – and why – is an important Lesson, even if it means that we, ourselves, are responsible. Once we learn from our mistakes we can avoid making them in the future.

> Learn to get in touch with the silence within yourself,
> and know that everything in life has purpose.
> There are no mistakes, no coincidences,
> all events are blessings given to us to learn from.
> - Elisabeth Kubler-Ross

The good news is that we also can learn from the mistakes of others.

> Learn from the mistakes of others – you can never live
> long enough to make them all yourself.
> - John Luther

◆ LEARNING AND TEACHING ◆

> The real difficulty is to overcome how you think about
> yourself. If we don't have that we never grow, we never
> learn, and sure as hell we should never teach.
> - Maya Angelou

Most of the greatest teachers in history have experienced tragedies and failures. They learned from their experience and went on to help others learn as well. In every situation we should ask ourselves, "What am I learning? Is this something I can share with others?"

◆ LIFE GOES ON ◆

> We must let go of the life we have planned, so as to
> accept the one that is waiting for us.
> - Joseph Campbell

When faced with troubling times, an important Lesson to learn is that "the show must go on." No, I'm not saying to just "put on a happy face" and pretend that nothing happened. You do need to connect with the emotions. But we often hold on to guilt, blame, anger and feelings of revenge – having a "pity party" instead of moving on.

> Rolling in the muck is not the best way of getting clean.
> - Aldous Huxley

◆ LIFE IS PRECIOUS ◆

> Live life fully while you're here. Experience everything. Take care of yourself and your friends. Have fun, be crazy, be weird. Go out and screw up! You're going to anyway, so you might as well enjoy the process.
> Take the opportunity to learn from your mistakes: find the cause of your problem and eliminate it. Don't try to be perfect; just be an excellent example of being human.
> - Anthony Robbins

There's nothing like a terminal diagnosis or a brush with death to learn this Lesson: Life is precious. Every day is a gift.

◆ LOSS ◆

> When the desire is to let go and to be guided by the Higher Self, the human is unattached to the event and is happy in the feeling of freedom. He is satisfied even if it be the loss of everything, or the hardest fate.
> – Harold Percival

When a friend is confronted with the breakup of a relationship, my advice is always to "Remember, the other side of relationship is freedom."

This isn't to say that loss isn't painful, because undeniably it is. But the Lessons in loss include the importance of detachment and realizing that the opening left by loss provides an opportunity for something new. While we allow ourselves to heal, we should look for Divine Love to fill the opening.

♦ LOVE ♦

> Love is the only force capable of
> transforming an enemy into friend.
> – Dr. Martin Luther King. Jr.

The Beatles song "All You Need is Love" said it all. I learned one of the most powerful Lessons of all during my recent crisis: There's an endless supply of love available to all of us – all we have to do is ask for it. Every time I ask my spirit guide for love, I feel a shower of Divine Providence reign down on me, comforting me and lifting me up.

Where have you experienced love in your crisis? Love is all around. Love is the cure for all. If you don't love yourself, you can't love the Divine because the Divine created you. If you can't love someone else, you can't love God, because He created them, too. Look inside and all around for the beauty of God's creation.

> "Love is the ultimate reality. It is the only. The all. The feeling of love is your experience of God."
> – "God" (Neale Donald Walsh)

If there is only one Lesson, it is Love.

If there is only one Solution, it is Love.

♦ LUCK – GOOD AND BAD ♦

> Some luck lies in not getting what you thought you wanted but getting what you have, which once you have got it you may be smart enough to see is what you would have wanted had you known.
> - Garrison Keillor

Joshua Piven, best-selling author of *The Worst Case Scenario Survival Handbook,* wrote a book entitled *As Luck Would Have It,* which is full of examples of the ambiguity of luck. He tells of blessings that turn into curses and of seemingly bad luck that turns to good. It's a good book to read when you think you're faced with bad luck, because you'll learn from the stories that "every negative is simply a chance to create a positive."

◆ Make A Difference ◆

> Let everything you do be done
> as if it makes a difference.
> - William James

Tragedies often give us a chance to show our courage, demonstrate our strengths and make a difference. There are countless examples, throughout history, where a crisis inspired people to make a difference. Will you do the same?

> I truly believe that individuals can make a difference in society. It is up to each of us to make the best use of our time to help create a happier world.
> - Dalai Lama

◆ Make Amends ◆

> Classic remorse, as all the moralists are agreed, is a most undesirable sentiment. If you have behaved badly, repent, make what amends you can and address yourself to the task of behaving better next time.
> - Aldous Huxley

The easiest way to be forgiven is to offer to make amends – and then follow through. Can you envision the power in this? What if everyone, who did something wrong, admitted it, and then asked, "What would it take for me to make it up to you?" It would be difficult, even for horrible crimes, to hold onto resentment and anger, when someone is sincere in their desire to stop the behavior and make amends.

◆ Motivation for Positive Change ◆

> Some change their ways when they see the light, others
> when they feel the heat.
> - Caroline Schoeder

When we are blinded by darkness, we look for the light, knowing that change is the only answer.

Change isn't easy, but sometimes it's our only choice. Once we open our eyes, we can see the opportunities for changing the one thing we can influence – ourselves.

♦ OPEN MIND ♦

> I would rather have a mind opened by wonder
> than one closed by belief.
> - Gerry Spence

Tragedy can help us find a new way to be open, to change, to learn. There's nothing like a new experience to provide an opportunity to open our minds - to new ideas, new people, new solutions to problems and new ways of looking at life.

I went to a lecture on the value of diversity. The greater the variety of ideas, experiences, cultures and beliefs, the greater the creativity, growth and progress. The American melting pot is a significant factor in making it the great country it is.

To paraphrase Carl Sagan, "If you are too skeptical (close-minded), no new ideas can make it through." Many years ago a work colleague shared his insight about my character and personality that defines openness, "Brownell, you are an explorer. You will always be an explorer. You'll always be seeking more answers, more questions."

I wouldn't be able to write this book if my mind wasn't open. There's no way I would have gotten the Divine insight required. How else can God enter if there's not an opening in our consciousness?

You wouldn't be reading this, if you weren't seeking an explanation to something bad that has happened to you, which means your mind is already open, at least a little bit, to learning. This is a great time to become an explorer, too. All it takes is an open mind and a desire to evolve.

♦ OPTIMISM VS. PESSIMISM ♦

> A pessimist sees the difficulty in every opportunity; an optimist sees the opportunity in every difficulty.
> - Sir Winston Churchill

Optimism can only come from open-mindedness. The more limited someone's views are, the more likely they're to see fewer options, which leads to pessimism.

There are natural optimists who see the glass as half full. They automatically see the opportunities in every situation. These people are to be envied because they didn't need to face a challenge in order to receive the faith necessary for optimism – it just comes to them naturally.

However, optimism can be learned and cultivated by experience. In fact, true optimism can only come once you've faced your fears. (Pessimism comes from denying the feelings of your Inner Self). It's only then, that you're able to look through the darkness and see the light.

♦ PATIENCE ♦

> We could never learn to be brave and patient
> if there were only joy in the world.
> – Helen Keller

"Patience is a virtue" and "haste makes waste" seem to conflict with "the early bird gets the worm," but, in essence these words of wisdom are all important Lessons on patience vs. action.

Patience and action, although seemingly opposites, can co-exist magnificently, when aligned with higher guidance. When we're connected to Spirit, we can trust and wait for the rainbow after the storm.

But impatience usually creates frustration, doubt and distrust, resulting in misdirected action. However, our soul has infinite patience.

> Impatience arises when one doubts the desired result.
> Hence patience, doubt and anxiety are closely linked.
> Since the inner will knows no doubt,
> it can bide its time and ultimately prevail.
> - Pathwork lecture #64

♦ PEACE ♦

> When you find peace within yourself, you become the kind of person who can live at peace with others.
> - Mildred Lisette Norman

When turbulence is swirling all around us, the one of the most important Lessons of all is Peace. Peace comes in many forms: inner peace, peace between individuals, peace between competitors, and peace between nations. Peace is a feeling, an action and a way of life. Peace is comfort, harmony and cooperation. All, when manifest, are a reflection of the Divine in all of us.

Inner Peace

The following quote from Pathwork lecture #1 exemplifies the benefits in attaining inner peace: "If you can find the answer within you, you will experience a wonderful victory, a sense of relief, of liberation, of peace and truth and thus you will be a step nearer to God."

Peace Between Individuals

> If you want to make peace, you don't talk to your friends. You talk to your enemies.
> - Mother Teresa

Peace, like love, is a feeling that's instantly bestowed upon us by Spirit the moment we ask for it. It calms us, lowers our blood pressure, and prepares us to act lovingly and responsibly. All we have to do is ask. When we're in conflict with another, this serenity is available to guide us to a peaceful resolution.

When we're guided by Divine peace, we no longer feel separated from others and can find a Higher Ground on which we can resolve *any* conflict.

Peace Between Competitors

Many years ago, I worked for an amazing man, Warren Rosenthal, who made the following comment, which has stayed with me to this day. He said he'd "rather have competent competitors than incompetent competitors." He knew that when a competing business acted unfairly, or provided an inferior product, it brought down the entire industry, but a good, competent competitor was not only good for the consumer and the economy, but even good for his company. It kept us on our toes and, instead of trying to put down or bad-mouth the competition, we had to keep providing better products and services.

This is the kind of attitude and behavior that creates peace between competitors. Mud-slinging campaigns bring the energy down to a low level and create "war." In healthy competition everyone wins.

Peace Between Nations

No one could ever convince me that the only way to attain peace is with war. That's like saying the only way to win a game is to cheat. It's the coward's way to attack a problem. War creates negative Karma and makes the planet more divisive than ever.

> There was never a good war or a bad peace.
> - Benjamin Franklin

Peace is only possible when we attempt to understand and accept our differences – and our similarities. No matter where you live in the world or whom you do or don't worship, everyone in the world has the capacity for love, peace and joy. No country or religion controls the market on the ability to show affection for their children, desire for acceptance and capacity for love.

♦ PERSISTENCE ♦

Nothing in the world can take the place of persistence. Talent will not; nothing is more common than unsuccessful men with talent. Genius will not; unrewarded genius is almost a proverb. Education will not; the world is full of educated derelicts. Persistence and determination are omnipotent.
- Calvin Coolidge

Just as we need to know when to let go and "fold 'em," we also need to "know when to hold 'em" and keep trying. How can we learn the difference? When we ask for Divine Guidance, ask which choice is the most loving and positive, we can "feel" the difference. The path will be clear.

♦ PLEASURES ♦

When you die, God and the angels will hold you responsible for all the pleasures you were allowed in life that you denied yourself.
- Unknown

What was your reaction to the above quote?

If your reaction was surprise, even possibly amazement, that a book with spiritual messages should endorse pleasure, it tells us a lot about how our traditional society has brainwashed us against experiencing pleasure.

Certainly, there's a difference between self-indulgence, addictions and pleasure. As you learned in the previous chapter, self-indulgence and addictions are a destructive cry for attention from our Inner Self.

> Health and longevity result from the capacity for pleasure. Conversely, to the degree that you deny yourself pleasure – due to shames, fears, misconceptions, negativities, impurities – to that degree you cut off your body from the wellspring of the universal flow.
> - Pathwork lecture #177

Alternatively, pleasure, when combined with awareness, is a way we can show love toward all three of our selves.

In Michael Newton's book, *Destiny of Souls*, one of the souls in the afterlife explain why he loves coming to Earth: to eat an orange. In heaven, he said, you can "remember" the taste of an orange, but it's not the same as eating one.

When was the last time you really treasured eating an orange? Or taking a bath? Or walking in the woods? Or listening to the ocean? Or _____ (fill in the blank). When we're facing problems, we often cut ourselves (our Selves) off from experiencing pleasure, multiplying our unhappiness, when what we need most is to fully immerse ourselves in life's pleasures.

◆ POWER ◆

> We realize that these so called bad events and circumstances in our lives are necessary things that once again point to the power of our thoughts. They urge us not to get stuck in that event or circumstance but to accept full responsibility and to then dedicate ourselves to changing them…Our true motivation is to improve life for all of humanity by working on the one thing we know we can improve, ourselves. This is rooted in an unwavering respect for all beings and creatures great and small, and indeed for the planet itself.
> We realize that we are here to LOVE everyone and everything for what it is at that moment.

> For in this we know that we are manifesting
> The Divine that exists within everything.
> – Alan Marsh

The above quote eloquently describes the process of attaining true power. Power relates to several things: authority, influence and control. Power can be exerted internally (toward our own attitudes or behavior) or externally (toward others), but always flows from within.

♦ PRAYER ♦

> Pray till prayer makes you forget your own wish,
> and leave it or merge it in God's will.
> - Frederick William Robertson

Arguably the first response we have to tragedy is to pray, no matter what are our religious affiliations or spiritual beliefs. Prayer can take the form of negotiation, plea, request, or demand. We'll discuss prayer in much depth in a later chapter, including suggestions on the optimal way to pray. The important message here, though, is to recognize prayer as a valuable Lesson through a crisis.

♦ PREJUDICE ♦

> Prejudice is a burden that confuses the past, threatens
> the future and renders the present inaccessible.
> - Maya Angelou

Prejudice is pre-judging. How can we pre-judge someone we've never met? And what would happen if we spent a lifetime (or even a moment) pre-judging and condemning a group of people, and then we're faced with a situation where we need something from someone from that group? For example, what if we're trapped in a burning building and the only person who can save us is a member of the "other" group? What if our child needs a transplant? Would we reject their help because we think they're "beneath" us in some way? Of course not. But that's sometimes how Lessons are learned. We sometimes need a crisis to force us to see people in a different, more accepting light.

◆ PURPOSE FOR EVERYTHING ◆

> For everything there is a season, And a time for every matter under heaven: A time to break down, and a time to build up; A time to weep, and a time to laugh; A time to mourn, and a time to dance.
> - Ecclesiastes 3:1-8

Nothing said it better than the above famous passage from Ecclesiastes.

◆ PURPOSE OF PAIN ◆

Pain is an extreme way to get our attention, to wake us up, to make us listen. We need to face the pain in order to determine the Reasons Why it occurred. The only way to move past pain is to move through it.

> Pain is not something to be shunned at such high cost that the pain resulting from the avoidance becomes worse than the original pain would have been.
> - Pathwork lecture #57

◆ PURPOSE – YOUR LIFE'S PURPOSE ◆

> Blessed is he who has found his work; let him ask no other blessedness. He has a work, a life purpose. He has found it and he will follow it.
> - Thomas Carlyle

Tragedies have an interesting way of bringing out the best in us. The HBO television series, *Band of Brothers*,[42] illustrates the

---

[42] This extraordinary 10-part miniseries tells the true story of a company of American soldiers in Europe World War II.

extraordinary coping and leadership skills that emerge from seemingly average men, when faced with the horrors of war.

When we discover our strengths, there's no limit to what we can accomplish. Marcus Buckingham and Donald Clifton's book, *Now, Discover Your Strengths,*[43] explain how our brain develops synapses that determine our strengths. Your personal combination of the thirty-four strengths is what makes you unique and can thereby help you make your own personal contribution in the world.

From our strengths, we can find our purpose in life. There are many good books on the topic.

> For those who really fulfill themselves, even if the outside result is not immediately noticeable, inside there will be a deep and peaceful contentment, security and a sense of fulfillment.
> - Pathwork lecture #11

♦ RECOGNIZING BEHAVIOR PATTERNS ♦

> The test of one's behavior pattern is their relationship to society, relationship to work and relationship to sex.
> - Alfred Adler

The key to changing ourselves is awareness of our patterns of behavior and emotions, because if we can't see it, we can't change it. The solution is getting in touch with our subconscious, making friends with our Inner Self.

♦ RELATIONSHIPS ♦

> The relationships we have with the world are largely determined by the relationships we have with ourselves.
> – Greg Anderson

---

[43] A *great* book! I bought copies for all my employees when I had my business. When you buy the book you get a code to go online and do an assessment of your top five strengths (out of 34) – invaluable and insightful!

179

Relationships are simultaneously a fulfillment and a challenge. They're always an indicator of your inner state and a way for us to learn. How happy or unhappy you're in a relationship is always a way to reveal emotions.

The Lessons we learn, to make a relationship work, can help us with relationships throughout our life. But if we don't learn what we need to learn about ourselves we'll be faced again and again with the opportunity to learn in the future – with one person or another.

Lessons are inherent in any and all relationships, whether they're fleeting encounters, short-term associations or lifetime connections.

> A perfect relationship, I think, is one that delivers the lessons we have chosen to learn.
> Likely it won't always meet our definition of "bliss."
> Likely it will include the toughest, most difficult lessons two people can teach each other, lessons they would never abide from any other soul. But we humans are brilliant at choosing, with unerring precision, exactly the partners we need to learn what we must.
> – Richard Bach

♦ REMEMBRANCE ♦

> It is foolish and wrong to mourn the men who died.
> Rather we should thank God that such men lived.
> – General George S. Patton, Jr.

Remembrance is the appreciation of experiences in our past and is a tribute to everything and everyone that has enlightened and enriched our lives. Remembrance is the lighter, more loving, flip side of grief, because instead of feeling sorry for ourselves, we feel thankful that we had the experience.

Remembrance is also a form of gratitude, a way of thanking the Divine for the gifts in our life, which gives us hope and enriches our faith.

◆ REVENGE ◆

> Before you embark on a journey of revenge,
> dig two graves.
> - Confucius

We crave revenge because we feel wounded and want to lash out at the perpetrator of our pain. If our attacker doesn't make any attempt to make amends, we feel a need to "force" them to pay – to get revenge.

The more hurt and anger our Inner Self feels, the more unhealthy the reaction is, and the more this part of us craves revenge. "I'll show them!" "I'll make them pay!" and "They can't get away with this!" are all cries from a wounded Inner Self.

The Inner Self needs – and deserves - to be healed. If the perpetrator apologizes and offers to make amends, the healing can begin. But we can't count on that. Some people are too unhealthy and wounded themselves. Yes, these people need to learn a Lesson of their own. However, a course of revenge is a path "to the dark side," also known as a mutually destructive karmic cycle. The good thing about Karma is that it isn't our responsibility to teach anyone a Lesson. We can be free from the karmic cycle by releasing our perpetrators to their own path of higher learning, where they'll face the repercussions of their actions, without our help.

◆ REWARD ◆

We'll talk about Reward as the fifth Reason Why in another chapter. We need to remember that looking for Reward is an important lesson. The lyrics of the classic Cat Steven's song, *Moonshadow,* delivers a gentle message that even what we might consider the worst tragedies can be looked at as a positive. He sings that if he should lose his legs, he wouldn't have to walk, if he lost his eyes, he wouldn't have to cry.

◆ RISK ◆

181

> To live is to risk dying. To do is to risk failure. To laugh is to risk appearing a fool. To love is to risk not being loved in return. To cry is to risk appearing soft and sentimental. To reach out to another is to risk involvement or rejection. To place your ideas, dreams, and desires before people is to risk ridicule. The greatest omission in life is to risk nothing. The person who risks nothing, gets nothing, has nothing, is nothing. He may avoid suffering, pain and sorrow, but he does not learn, grow, live, or love. He is only a slave - chained by safety - locked away by fear. Only a person who is willing to risk, not knowing the results, is alive.
>
> - Anonymous

The gift in tragedy is that sometimes when we have nothing more to lose, we're willing to take a risk. I know, when I lost everything – my business, my home and many of my possessions – I found the freedom to do anything I wanted. No longer bound by ego or pride, I could pursue my future with a renewed sense of adventure.

Life itself is a risk. But if we play it too safe and don't take a chance aren't we also risking by missing an opportunity available only to those who go out on a limb?

◆ SECURITY ◆

> If money is your hope for independence
> you will never have it.
> The only real security that a man will have in this world
> is a reserve of knowledge, experience, and ability.
> - Henry Ford

The compulsion for security comes from insecurity and a lack of faith, both in yourself and in your Higher Power. Money lasts only so long. Relationships can end. Jobs are lost. The only real security is in knowing that you can, with Divine help, get through anything.

◆ SELF-ACCEPTANCE AND SELF-LOVE ◆

> To love one's self
> is the beginning of a life-long romance.
> - Oscar Wilde

I was talking with a friend, who is beautiful, talented, compassionate, giving and kind. But she still puts herself down. Or should I say her "Self" down. Because she's so self-less, she can't justify loving her self. I told her I would love for her to name her Inner Self, because I thought it would open up her self-love in an extraordinary way. Once she names her "little sister" or Inner Self, she will be able to love "her" with the same kind of love she shows others. She will be able to look in the mirror and say, "I love you _____" – something that's unfathomable now.

How do I know this will happen to her – and to you? Because I lived it. I know I'm not the most beautiful woman alive, with a perfect body. But I truly and honestly love my Inner Self – which means loving my body (in spite of obvious shortcomings), my physical drive, my emotions, my looks – all of it.

Have you ever noticed how, when you fall in love with someone, you love their faults? It may be their cute little belly paunch, the way she snorts when she laughs, or his weird birthmark, but you love the things that make her unique, even if the attribute may be traditionally considered a flaw. We need to learn to love our "Self" the same way. Not in spite of our faults, but perhaps *because* of them.

Self-love is not arrogance. Arrogance is a result of acting or feeling superior to others. Self-love is just loving yourself as you are.

> "You must be really flexible...
> to be able to kiss your own ass that way."
> - Will (Eric McCormack) in the TV show Will & Grace

183

The following quote from *The Afterlife of Billy Fingers* by Annie Kagan is a lovely way to look at self-love: "If there's one thing worth doing on your planet, it's discovering self-love. I say "discovering" instead of "learning" because learning implies you're starting from zero; but the truth is, you already love yourself. When you're born, when the amnesia happens, you forget your magnificence, and think you have to earn the right to be loved. How can you earn what already belongs to you?"

◆ SELF-CONTROL ◆

> He who lives with his senses well controlled, moderate
> in his food and drink, he won't be overthrown, any more
> than the wind throws down a rocky mountain.
> - Gautama Buddha

The Lesson of Self Control really means the ability to gain control of the emotions of your Inner (shadow) Self. Self-control is nearly impossible, without identifying and connecting with your three selves. Once you make friends with your Inner Self, it will become easier and easier – even effortless.

For example, I have conversations all the time with my Inner Self, especially when I'm feeling some form of discomfort. She will tell me that she's tired, or wants to exercise and, if I don't listen, she will speak louder and louder (I'll get more and more tired or agitated) until I'm forced to listen. So now I ask "her" what she wants to do – and then pay attention. As a consequence, she rewards me with a happier disposition and more self-control.

◆ SELF-FULFILLMENT ◆

> For those who really fulfill themselves, even if the
> outside result is not immediately noticeable,
> inside there will be a deep and peaceful contentment,
> security and a sense of fulfillment.
> - Pathwork lecture #11

"You complete me" is a famous movie quote. It may be a romantic thought for the big screen, but the only true way anyone can find completion is within themselves. In fact, you can only offer yourself fully to a relationship if you're a complete, whole person yourself, as fully complete as you can possibly be.

The more experiences you have in your life, the more complete – and self-fulfilled – you become, because you find out what you're really made of.

♦ SELF-RELIANCE AND SELF-SUFFICIENCY ♦

> To character and success, two things,
> contradictory as they may seem, must go together.
> Humble dependence on God and manly reliance on self.
> - William Wordsworth

Many kinds of crises teach about self-sufficiency and self-reliance, proving you have everything you need to make it through on your own. There's nothing more empowering than finding out you can accomplish you never thought you could do.

> I learned that the richness of life is found in adventure.
> It develops self-reliance and independence.
> Life then teems with excitement.
> There is stagnation only in security.
> - William Orville Douglas

♦ SHARING ♦

> Happiness is like a kiss. You must share it to enjoy it.
> -- Bernard Meltzer

Sharing is never a one-sided experience. It's a process where two people are mutually and simultaneously giving and receiving. The Lesson of sharing can be in learning how to give – to receive. Either way, it's a gift, and a valuable Lesson.

Some of us let pride get in the way of receiving another's charity, but sharing is a gift for both the recipient and the giver.

Learning how to receive graciously and without a feeling of guilt or self-reproach is an art. It's an important Lesson, often learned only when we're in times of significant need, when Bad Things are happening to us.

Taking, without being authorized to do so, is a function of Social Darwinism, where one person has to exert superiority over another —a sign of a frightened being. Sharing, however, is a function of Spiritual Darwinism, when both giver and receiver are connected with a higher source, the source of Infinite Divinity.

Giving freely of ourselves, whether we give our time, finances or possessions is much easier and more likely when we become functionally happy and spiritually connected.

◆ STRENGTH ◆

> The world breaks everyone, and afterward,
> some are strong at the broken places.
> - Ernest Hemingway

The above quote is absolutely true, in both psychology and physiology. We never know how strong we can be, until we have faced – and survived – a tragic event. After a bone has been broken, it heals stronger than before the accident. The same is true of our psyches. Tragedy has a way of making us stronger once we have given ourselves a chance to heal.

◆ SUFFERING ◆

> Disease and want are among the chief means
> of learning from experience.
> – Richard Matheson

What could be the Lesson in suffering? Perhaps the result is realizing we are a survivor. Perhaps it's so we can be more compassionate, and therefore helpful, toward others who are suffering. Or perhaps it's to find out that we didn't need to suffer as long as we did – if at all. Often, some time after a catastrophic event, we look back and ask ourselves, "Why did I let that bother me so much?" or "Why did I suffer so long?"

Yes, the pain happens for a reason, and we need to capture that reason, to be able to move forward to healing. But it doesn't have to go on and on. In subsequent chapters I'll give you tools to learn how to "suffer" consciously. And then to end it quickly.

In the book, *The Afterlife of Billy Fingers*, one of the messages delivered from "the other side" related to a concept called "Divine Suffering." It sounds like an oxymoron – how can there be divinity in suffering? -

The following is an excerpt from one of my books in the DUET stories series:

> Despair is a cruel companion. It robs you of everything; especially the choices that still lie within your control.
>
> Life is a continuum; neither black nor white,
> but a series of shades from light to dark.
> When the shadow is in front of you,
> all you see is the darkness
> and forget the sun is at your back.
>
> Always remember, my child:
> There is no shadow without the sun.
> No suffering without divinity.
> No fear without love.
> No despair without desire.
> No hopelessness without faith.

Anthony de Mello offered the following insight on suffering: "If you're suffering, you're asleep. Do you want a sign that you're asleep? Here it is: You're suffering. Suffering is a sign that you're out of touch with the truth. Suffering is given to you that you might open your eyes to the truth, that you might understand that there's falsehood somewhere, just as physical pain is given to you so you will understand that there is disease or illness somewhere. Suffering points out that there is falsehood somewhere. Suffering occurs when you clash with reality. When your illusions clash with reality, when your falsehoods clash with truth, then you have suffering. Otherwise there is no suffering.

◆ TAKING CARE OF YOURSELF ◆

> Learn the skills needed to nurture you. Ask yourself:
> 'How do I nurture others?' and apply that to yourself.
> - Luke De Sadeleer

Many of us need to nurture ourselves better. We "put off" our own pleasure in order to get the report finished, do something for someone else, or complete something else on our "to-do list."

When our Inner Self isn't listened-to, he/she will do whatever they can to get our attention – including emotional bursts, disease and more. Why do you think people get so many colds? So they can take time off from work. Not that a lot of them do this, of course. They come to work anyway, further ignoring their bodies' messages. It's unnecessary to get sick from a cold virus.[44]. I've proven this many times. But you have to listen and take care of yourself.

> "Animals in zoos are bored, obese, and have lost their
> sense of meaning. The American dream."
> – Homer Simpson, The Simpsons

◆ TALENT ◆

> We are all born with God-given, unique traits and skills.
> But, as with all possibilities they will remain unrealized
> unless they are developed, nurtured, and put into
> practice. You may have the "capacity" to love, but if left
> undeveloped, you will never gain the "ability."
> - Leo Buscalia

Our talents are our gifts from God. Talents can only be fulfilled – and fulfilling – when we're working in concert with

---

[44] This is discussed in a little more depth the chapter on prevention.

our spiritual connections. Talents can only be fully expressed when they're used to make a difference in the lives of others, whether to give pleasure or to offer comfort and support.

Sometimes it takes a force of great change – a crisis – to unearth our true talents. Many writers, artists, composers, filmmakers and other artistic talents found their talents come to the surface during times of strife. The important Lesson here, though is to continue your talent after the dust has cleared and the sun is shining again.

♦ TRUST AND EASE ♦

> Develop trust in your capacity to adjust and incorporate the surprises and mysteries of life toward a deeper understanding and greater fulfillment in your life. That comes from deep communion with your Inner Self,
> not from relying on externals
> – Deepak Chopra

The following paraphrased excerpt from Harold Percival's *Thinking & Destiny* does an amazing job of describing trust, and its subsequent goal, ease. It changed my life to read this passage, because then I understood what is perhaps the biggest Lesson of all to comprehend during a crisis. The goal is ease:

> "Trust is a natural feeling that one can depend upon life, that one won't be harmed, that one can get along and find its way, that whatever the conditions are he or she will be borne over them, that he or she will swim and not sink.

> "Trust may be evidence that the person has had a wide, deep, lasting experience and they can be depended upon by other people. Trust is a reward for duties well performed, for goodwill, generosity and helpfulness. Trust is an expression of fundamental inclination to

honesty. Even if this quality of trust seems at times out of place and without foundation, when the human feels forsaken or cast down, it will bear him or her up and carry them along. The person's periods of dejection, if any, will be very short and it will never entertain bitterness or doubt. There will be always an underlying feeling that there's something to rely on, something that is beyond vicissitudes and all changes.

"Ease is a further development of trust. Only a developed person can feel at ease in riches or in poverty, in sickness or in health. Ease comes to a person only after he or she has been the victor in many battles and difficulties and has learned their ways and how to live with them. Ease does not depend on easy circumstances, but the person maintains their ease notwithstanding any outward conditions, favorable or adverse. Ease is a feeling of confidence that the person will find its way through life."

♦ Unhappiness ♦

> Unhappiness is aggravated
> by comparing yourself to others.
> - Brownell

Now you know the difference between functional (inner) happiness and circumstantial (outer-focused) happiness. What about *un*happiness?

When we're functionally *un*happy, the slightest – or remotest – setback or difficulty can affect us deeply. Functional unhappiness comes from not connecting with our shadow emotions.

On the other hand, circumstantial unhappiness is fleeting. We can lose something or face a difficulty, but when we're in touch with our emotions, we adapt quickly. It doesn't mean we don't hurt – problems *are* painful. But once we can face, feel and free our problems, we can't only survive, but perhaps thrive.

When a friend has a happy event – a job promotion or a new romance, we can be happy for her even when we're circumstantially happy or unhappy, as long as we're happy on the inside. But when we aren't functionally happy, we would be jealous or critical. We would see her gain as our loss.

When my problems were in their darkest period and a friend would ask me how I was, I would joke and sing a song from the South Park movie entitled, "I'm Super" which said, "The whole world's gone to hell…– but how are you?" It was a way to show that I could acknowledge that, even though my life was falling apart around me, I would be fine.

◆ UNIQUENESS ◆

A wonderful realization will be the day you realize that you are unique in all the world.
There is nothing that is an accident.
You are a special combination for a purpose—so that you can do what is essential for you to do. Don't ever believe that you have nothing to contribute.
The world is an incredible unfulfilled tapestry.
And only you can fulfill that tiny space that is yours.
- Leo Buscalia

An exceptionally popular writer and lecturer, said if you want to be successful, all you have to do is find a successful person and do what he or she does.

Sorry. It doesn't work that way. You are unique, and your Karma is unique. To me, it's another way of looking at the issue of cloning. If, for some reason, humans are able to perfect cloning and pursue it with a loved one, we'll be sorely disappointed. Not that I can't understand the motivation. When I

191

lost my precious dog, years ago, I was so desperate to have her back that I pursued finding an identical dog through the same remote breeder. The problem is, even if it could've had the same exact DNA, but it wouldn't have had the same dog-personality, the same dog-soul.

The merging of our three-part being makes each of us unique. If another soul had chosen your body, a different being would have been created. I talked with a friend about this a few months ago. I explained it simply: if his soul had chosen the body of another man we both knew, that body would have been more physically fit and stronger for sure. But selecting that body – with the parents, lifestyle, family and circumstances that goes with it - may not have given him the Lessons he needed to learn. Our uniqueness is a valuable Lesson. It means that although we can learn from others, our ability to respond to our crisis is unique – and extraordinary.

♦ VIOLENCE ♦

Who better to explain the Lesson of violence than Martin Luther King, Jr.?

> The ultimate weakness of violence is that it is a descending spiral, begetting the very thing it seeks to destroy. Instead of diminishing evil, it multiplies it. In fact, violence merely increases hate. Returning violence for violence multiplies violence, adding deeper darkness to a night already devoid of stars. Darkness cannot drive out darkness: only light can do that. Hate cannot drive out hate: only love can do that. Hate multiplies hate, violence multiplies violence, and toughness multiplies toughness in a descending spiral of destruction....
> The chain reaction of evil — hate begetting hate, wars producing more wars — must be broken, or we shall be plunged into the dark abyss of annihilation.
> – Rev. Martin Luther King, Jr.

♦ VIRTUES AND VALUES ♦

> The greatest virtues are those which
> are most useful to other persons.
> - Aristotle

A virtue is defined as "moral excellence" or a strong character. Each of the Seven Cardinal Sins are sins against a virtue: Pride is a sin against humility; Avarice or greed is a sin against generosity; Envy is a sin against love; Wrath or Anger is a sin against kindness; Lust is a sin against self-control; Gluttony is a sin against faith and temperance and Sloth is a sin against zeal.

Essentially, all virtues, whether they're trust, self-respect, or charity come from some form of love – love for yourself, love for others, love for the planet.

What are your virtues and values? Are they the same? Have any hidden virtues come to the surface, as a result of your crisis? Did you find out you were more considerate of others than you thought you could be? Have you learned to take better care of yourself? Or have you been able to release your judgment of others? Are you more peaceful and loving?

♦ WAR ISN'T THE ANSWER...EVER ♦

> "Dad, how do soldiers killing each other
> solve the world's problems?"
> - Calvin & Hobbes (Bill Watterson)

By now you should realize that the cause of war is a dysfunctional group collective unconscious caused by the inflammation of Social Darwinism – where insecure people and societies feel the need to subjugate and overpower another group in order to feel temporary power.

What is the solution? When each of us, one by one, do our personal jobs in getting in touch with our Inner Self, we can then love ourselves, God, and then God's creatures, including and especially other human beings.

> All war must be just the killing of strangers against
> whom you feel no personal animosity; strangers whom,
> in other circumstances, you would help
> if you found them in trouble, and who would
> help you if you needed it.
> - Mark Twain

◆ WHAT'S IN YOUR CONTROL AND WHAT ISN'T ◆

"You Create Your Own Reality" is a buzz phrase common in society today. What does it really mean and is it really true?

Most of our life is in our control, but some is conscious and some is unconscious/subconscious. This is where it gets tricky. Even though our subconscious takes direction from our conscious, he/she often rules our lives because we don't listen to them. If we did a better job of listening, "we" would have much more under our control.

Most of the remainder of the things that are not in our conscious control are the creation of our Higher Self in conjunction with the Divine.

There are some random events we can't control, but we do have the ability to prevent them from affecting us, as you'll learn in the chapter on Spiritual Darwinism.

The things we *can* control – or at least influence - include:

- Personal Predictable Surprises – These are the things we do that are bad for us without regard for the predictable consequences. This includes smoking cigarettes, drinking and driving, eating dangerously unhealthy foods, a sedentary lifestyle, etc.
- The Lessons you're here to learn in this lifetime – and if, when and how we learn them (the easy way or the hard way)
- How we respond to tragedy
- The problems resulting from Subconscious Sabotage and not listening to our Inner Self.
- Whether we perpetuate negative Karma or rise above it.

- You create additional problems – and Lessons (and Karma) when you perpetuate negative emotions and behavior.

The collective "we" – the humans on the planet – can influence the following:

- The health – or destruction of the planet
- Peace – or War on Earth
- Calm – or Environmental disasters
- Tranquility – or Crime

The problem with the way most people believe that "You Create Your Own Reality" is that it can create enormous guilt – or self-righteousness. Neither is effective, unless it stimulates change and improvement.

> Believing in something beyond yourself can provide a profound sense of comfort and purpose and can enrich every aspect of your life. People who are spiritually fulfilled have a greater sense of confidence and control. They feel peaceful, stable, and grounded.
> Regardless of what you believe, the rewards are finding more joy and meaning in everything you do.
> So live your values: trust, integrity, compassion, align them with your actions, find ways to express them in what you say and do.
> - CIGNA MCC Behavioral Care

◆ WHY? ◆

One of the most powerful Lessons to learn is to ask – and keep on asking – Why? What are the Reasons Why this happened? And when you get an answer, keep on digging for the deeper answers to "why." Include in our prayers the plea, "Please, Higher Power, help me understand why this happened." And then listen.

> The most beautiful thing we can experience is the
> mysterious It is the source of all art and science.
> - Albert Einstein

◆ WILL TO LIVE/SURVIVAL ◆

> We shall draw from the heart of suffering itself the
> means of inspiration and survival.
> - Winston Churchill

There's nothing like the risk of losing something – or someone - to make us fight for keeping it/them, and there's nowhere that this is more true than facing a threat to our own mortality. People who have experienced the dying process, through a near-death experience, realize there's nothing to fear and therefore maintain a strong will to live. They know, perhaps more than most of us, that we are here for a reason and our purpose can only be fulfilled in our physical form – by living.

There was a quote from Morgan Freeman's character, "Red," in the movie, *The Shawshank Redemption,* where he said, "Get busy living or get busy dying." It's a good Lesson, and something worth continuously reminding ourselves.

OTHER LESSONS?

Have you learned other lessons through your crisis? Please visit the Reasons Why website (www.ReasonsWhy.com) and let me know! And, if you're open to sharing with others, you could help make a difference in their lives.

WHY WE NEED LESSONS

Now that we know what we need to learn, the next question is, "Why?"

Lessons are the reason we're here. It's like we have all enrolled in "Earth School." Some of us take more challenging classes than others. Many of us have to repeat courses again and again – but we're all here to learn. The kinds of Lessons are different for everyone. But why do we want the "Earth School" degree? There are seven reasons:

1. To change – to be better people, to make a difference, to love.
2. To redirect us when we're off course – when we're not living our best lives, when we're not loving enough, when we're too judgmental or have too many harmful emotions, actions and behavior.
3. To keep us from getting too complacent. We're faced with Lessons when we aren't trying very hard. The Divine wants us all to make a contribution, not to just "hang out."
4. To prepare us for the future – Lessons come to us to help us be ready for upcoming events.
5. To help and care for others.
6. To make us more interesting (compassionate, loving, accepting, etc.)
7. To get to "ease." The more we experience, the more we learn. The more we learn the closer we get to "ease" – the ability to know that, no matter what happens, we'll survive and thrive.

All Lessons are design to help each of us become a more positive, accepting, loving person.

> I refuse to let a failure go
> without squeezing out an answer from it.
> - Greg Behrendt

CAN WE "FAIL" EARTH SCHOOL?

In a word, yes. I've had debate after debate with people who say that everything is happening just as it should be, that even criminals or absentee parents or dishonest people are acting in accordance with the Divine plan – with Divine will.

I say, "Hogwash." Not everyone is doing the best they can. Many of us – including myself, to be perfectly honest – are not doing our best all the time. This is a difficult planet, with a lot of distractions, temptations and challenges. Earth School is a combination of Harvard, Cal-Tech, Divinity School, Boot Camp and Clown College, all rolled into one, and some of us are taking the hardest classes and going for advanced degrees.

The following quote from Dr. Brian L. Weiss' book, *Same Soul, Many Bodies* is a good explanation of souls who have "failed."

> "True, some souls chose to come back as Saddam Hussein, another as Osama bin Laden. I believe they came back to maximize their learning opportunities, the same as you and me. They did not choose to come back initially to do harm, to cause violence and blow up other people and become terrorists. They came back to resist that urge, probably because they had succumbed to it in previous lifetimes. They came back for a kind of field test in this school we live in, and they failed miserably."

Okay, failure is a strong word. It could be argued that only a select few are truly failing Earth School. The preceding quote identifies a few. We can all list more, I'm sure.

But, remember, it isn't up to us to judge. I've read stories of "angels in disguise," where Divine beings or very enlightened humans come to Earth masquerading as all kinds of simple folk, including panhandlers, janitors, landscapers, etc., and we all know of the example of a particular carpenter…

THE ROLE OF THE DIVINE

We all have Lessons to learn, and our Spirit guides are here to help us in that endeavor, but they won't interfere with our free will. So unless we ask for help, all they can do is to provide the opportunities to learn. The rest is up to us.

A few months ago, I was talking to a friend in crisis and he kept saying, "I need help! Why won't Spirit help me?" My answer, out of total love and respect for my friend, was, "What help do you want? You have everything you need."

All we have to do is ask, "What is the Lesson here?" They'll help us with the answer. If we pray, "Please help me learn the Lesson," we'll be shown the way. It's as if we have a built-in tutor who can help us with the classes. We just have to ask for the assistance.

Our Higher Power wants us to learn. He or She wants us to make our planet more loving, more peaceful, more pleasant. We have been given an awesomely beautiful place to live. We have been given each other for companionship. And we have been given a twenty-four-hour hotline for whatever support we need, to become more caring. What else do we need?

> When one door of happiness closes, another opens; but often we look so long at the closed door that we do not see the one which has been opened for us.
> - Alexander Graham Bell

HOW LESSONS COULD EXPLAIN VARIOUS EXAMPLES OF BAD THINGS

There's always an opportunity to learn through any crisis. The following is a look at a few tragic events and what Lessons could be involved:

Someone close to you is in an accident or diagnosed with a serious illness

- You realize how much you love him/her.
- You learn how to take care of someone.
- You learn how you can help him/her with their faith/trust.
- You find out that life isn't over when your body is injured.
- You learn about preparing for death.
- If terminal, you help him/her make the most peaceful transition possible.

Lessons

Your car is stolen

- You learn detachment from possessions.
- You recognize the potential for Reward.
- You're reminded to take better care of your stuff.
- You appreciate what you have.

You're fired from your job

- You learn that you really didn't like your job/company.
- You didn't appreciate what you had and admit that you created the event.
- You learn not to compromise your ethics in the future.

Your home is broken into and you are raped

- You develop compassion and understanding for rape victims.
- You realize where your responsibility begins and ends.
- You learn how to defend yourself without hostility.
- You're able to take action without anger or resentment.

Your home is destroyed by fire/flood/hurricane/ tornado

- You learn what's really important in life – and it's not possessions.
- You start to appreciate and take better care of your possessions.
- You look for the Reward – an opportunity to move to a safer area, with family, etc.

You hate the way you look

- You learn to accept and love yourself the way you are.
- You learn to take better care of yourself.

COULD THERE BE A LESSON INVOLVED IN YOUR CRISIS?

Questions to ask yourself:

1. What have you learned through your crisis?
2. Are you looking at your experience as an adventure or as something to fear?
3. Has your tragedy made you experience (and learn) any of the lessons in this chapter?

> Our problem is within ourselves. We have found the means to blow the world physically apart. Spiritually, we have yet to find the means to put the world's pieces back together again.
> - Thomas E. Dewey

CHAPTER 10: THE FOURTH REASON WHY: TESTS

> This life is a test. It is only a test.
> Had it been an actual life you would have received
> further instructions on where to go and what to do!
> - Anonymous

For many people, the title of this chapter may sound the most ominous – we can't stand the idea of being tested. It takes us back to exams in school where we got nervous and scared, second-guessing every choice we made.

Well, Earth School has Tests, too. But once you know the curriculum and material – and how you're being graded – there's no reason to be nervous. It's more like an open-book exam. The answers are everywhere and easy to access. And, the most important fact is that there isn't any stern, threatening professor waiting to judge you. Instead, you'll be evaluating yourself.

> Life on Earth is a test. God continually tests people's character, faith, obedience, love, integrity, and loyalty. Words like trials, temptations, refining and testing occur more than 200 times in the bible. God constantly watches your response to people, problems, success, conflict, illness, disappointment and even the weather!

> ...When you realize that life is a test, you realize that
> nothing is insignificant in your life.
> - Rick Warren

As I was working on this chapter, my computer completely crashed. I lost all the work I'd done for two days. Since the work on this book is often "channeled" in a way, it's difficult to re-create the thoughts I'd put into it. It was a distressing time, to be sure. I tried and tried to diagnose the problem, but it just seemed to get worse and worse. At one point in the process, I felt myself "pull back" and look at the situation. It became clear to me it was a classic Test situation, with the exam question: "How are you handling it?"

When my computer failed, I could've become angry, frustrated, distressed, or succumbed to any number of ways of getting upset. I could have let it ruin precious time: an hour, a minute, an evening or longer. But I didn't.

First, I was grateful that I had backed-up two days earlier. And the past two days' work had only been a total of about five hours, compared to the usual two-day workload of twenty hours. Second, I recognized it as at least one Reason Why: A Test. Third, I was open to looking at the potential explanation from other Reasons Why. Maybe the situation also included a Lesson, or perhaps a Reward. Maybe, in re-writing, I would have better ideas come to me. Or perhaps there could be some serendipity in getting the machine fixed.

It turns out it was probably just a Test, to see how I would react. To see if I was, indeed, becoming more accepting of challenges that come my way.

In essence, all Tests are ways to see how we're managing a situation. If life is too simple and uncomplicated, it means one of two things. Either our Earth School classes are too easy, which means that, like in other types of schooling, we won't be as rewarded in the end from choosing simpler classes.

Or, it could mean that we have learned how to pass even the most difficult Tests. Sometimes this happens as a result of being tested before on the subject. For example, if I had been through a computer crashing many times and had known how to handle the situation, then the Test wouldn't have been so difficult. Alternatively, though, it could mean that I've learned the tricks on how to pass a Test – any kind of Test.

In this chapter we'll discuss the ways you're being tested, the purpose of Tests, and what happens if you "pass" or "fail."

WHAT MATTERS MUCH MORE...

In the children's book I wrote called, "Sometimes I Wonder," I here are a couple of verses related to tests:

So we set up our challenges
And mountains so high
To test our endurance
And reach for the sky

It doesn't much matter
If we get to the top
What matters much more is
What we do when we stop
© 2016 Brownell Landrum

CHARACTERISTICS OF EARTH SCHOOL TESTS

Earth School Tests have several characteristics. First, the curriculum and class schedule are pre-determined. Second, the "exams" are all open book, with answers everywhere. Third, we all have access to great teachers. Fourth, all the Tests are self-administered and self-graded. Fifth, the Tests are important and happen for a reason.

Curriculum and Class Schedule

As discussed in the chapter on Lessons, we each choose most of the classes we want to take before we're born. The same is true of Tests we'll face.

The difference between Lessons and Tests is kind of like school. When we take a class – learn a Lesson – we're tested to determine whether we learned the material. The more thoroughly we learn the Lesson, the easier the Test.

> Experience is the hardest kind of teacher. It gives you the test first, and the lesson afterward.
> - Anonymous

We're born with natural talents and abilities. Some are genetically handed down through the DNA in our physical bodies, from our ancestors and others through our soul's individuality. But we may need to be tested in this particular body in its current circumstances "to be sure."

Sometimes we're just randomly tested, to see if we need to learn or re-learn a Lesson. Sometimes we face Tests on their own. The biblical story of Job is a good example. By all accounts, Job was a respectful, faithful, loving and understanding man before he experienced his tragedy. But he was tested under extreme circumstances to measure the strength of his trust and love of God and others. I'll discuss his story later in this chapter.

So, the curriculum and class schedule for Tests in Earth School are like the Lessons we face: predetermined before we're born. But, like the Lessons, there's a list of kinds of Earth School Tests that we face – and this chapter provides the "cheat sheet."

Open Book

All of the Tests we face in Earth School are open book Tests. This means that we have access to all the answers we need. In addition to this book, there are dozens, if not hundreds, of books, articles and other study materials available to help us pass the Tests we face.

Teachers

Even though we "grade" ourselves on how well we do, Teachers, coaches, and learned scholars are also all around us, ready to help us with answers to our Test questions. They can take the form of friends, work colleagues, parents, children, lovers, bosses, professors, spouses, casual acquaintances and mentors, as well as those of leaders, celebrities, clergy and inspirational guides.

We all also have Higher Guidance, which is accessible at all times. All we have to do is close our eyes, focus and connect.

Self-Testing and Grading

All Earth School Tests are self-administered and self-graded. This means that, at the end of our lives, we'll be evaluating ourselves on how we've done. In the Life Review, we re-experience everything from our lifetimes – every feeling and every action – not only from our own perspective but from the perspective of everyone we've ever encountered. From this point, we have absolute clarity and zero deception or rationalization, which means that we become our own most discerning judges.

If you have difficulty accepting the fact that each of us tests ands evaluates ourselves, it could be because you've not experienced the Divine in yourself. This heavenly, loving, understanding and purely objective part of each of us is not only our connection to Spirit, it's our own personal manifestation of God.

The Purpose of Testing

In regular school, what is the purpose of Tests? It's to determine if we learned the course material. The same is true of Earth School. Before we know if we need to take a class again, we take a Test. If we pass with flying colors, we move on to other Lessons. If not, we'll likely face the same course, and sometimes the next class we take is more difficult. So Tests are significant and necessary to move along in Earth School. How else can we tell if we learned the Lesson and, consequently, have changed, or if we need to have a refresher course?

The Basic Test Question

> There's no such thing as a problem
> without a gift for you in its hands.
> You seek problems because you need their gifts.
> – Richard Bach

All Tests are in the form of a question, and the underlying basic question in all Earth School Tests is, "How are you handling it?" The answer depends on the situation you're facing, but here's a tip. It always has to do with a form of love: love of others, love of yourself, love of the Divine, love of the planet.

The following analysis of the Book of Job, from the Old Testament, illustrates a classic story of a man being faced with a series of Tests.[45] Although it isn't up to any of us to judge, it seems clear Job's story is told to us to establish the standard for passing the Tests we all face.

THE BOOK OF JOB

The book of Job in the Old Testament of the Bible, is a classic story about the Test of faith. Whether you believe the story as written or learn from it as a parable isn't important. Either way, it's a powerful example of Tests.

Simply summarized, Job was a man with everything one would hope for in life. He had a thriving and loving family, wealth and property and good health, love, faith, devotion, integrity and respect. However, in the course of the story, Job is tested by gradually having all of the external factors of happiness taken away. His family is killed, his riches stripped and his own health is withdrawn into painful disease.

Throughout his ordeal, several people near him suggest that he should either curse God or end his life. While he did

---

[45] I would like to point out that I do not use this example to demonstrate that a personalized God – or Satan, for that matter, is the instigator of the Tests that we face. In fact, I believe those two "characters" are used to define the choice each of us must make – whether to act in good and love or to act in evil.

experience the excruciating pain and overwhelming grief one would expect, and although he questioned God and even reached the point where he wished he hadn't been born, Job showed great courage.

- When his clothing was destroyed, Job said "Naked came I out of my mother's womb, and naked shall I return thither: the LORD gave, and the LORD hath taken away; blessed be the name of the LORD."

- When stricken with an agonizing ailment, Job's response was, "Shall we receive good at the hand of God, and shall we not receive evil?"

- He asked for guidance. "Teach me, and I will hold my tongue: and cause me to understand wherein I have erred."

- He refused to give in to the advice of friends: "My lips shall not speak wickedness, nor my tongue utter deceit."

- He showed humility. "If I justify myself, mine own mouth shall condemn me: *if I say*, I *am* perfect, it shall also prove me perverse."

- He exhibited wisdom. "For wrath killeth the foolish man, and envy slayeth the silly one."

- He refused to condemn or lie. "My lips shall not speak wickedness, nor my tongue utter deceit."

- He expressed hope. "For there is hope of a tree, if it be cut down, that it will sprout again, and that the tender branch thereof won't cease."

- And he held onto his faith. "My righteousness I hold fast, and won't let it go: my heart shall not reproach *me* so long as I live."

Another interesting quote from The Book of Job is the following, "For the thing which I greatly feared is come upon me, and that which I was afraid of is come unto me." It suggests the harm of fear and the potential for Subconscious Sabotage in explaining the Reason Why Job was faced with experiencing his fear.

We can learn a lot from Job's response to being tested:

- The Impermanent Nature of Possessions
- Understanding That Both Good and Evil Exist In Our Lives
- Ask for Guidance
- Not to Give in to Temptation
- Show Humility
- The Folly and Destructiveness of Wrath and The Silliness of Envy
- Holding onto Dignity and Honor
- The Power of Hope
- Steadfastness in Faith
- The Ability of Fear to Create That Which You Fear

In researching this book, I read a story about someone going through a crisis, who was dumfounded. She had lived an exemplary life, she had great faith, had resolved any negative Karma and was building a lot of positive Karma. She was connected with her three selves and was dedicated to learning Lessons and open to change. She kept asking, "Why did this happen to me?" Her parallels to Job were apparent, which meant the answer seemed clear: she was facing a Test. How else can we determine if we really do have great faith? How else can we be sure we wouldn't return negative Karma? How else are we going to validate that we have learned our Lessons? Job passed his Tests with flying colors. I hope the woman in the story did as well, in getting through her crisis.

LARGE DISASTERS

Large disasters are a unique opportunity for being tested. As a response to Hurricane Andrew, the American Psychological Association created the Disaster-Response Network, to help victims of disaster. The psychologists identify two phases of trauma, each with opportunities for us to demonstrate both the worst and the best in ourselves.

209

The initial phase, called the Impact Phase, lasts a few weeks to possibly months and is characterized by feelings of shock, anger and frustration. However, also in the first phase, people can show the best of themselves by helping each other, even demonstrating heroic acts.

The second phase, the Recoil Phase, is when the day-to-day reality of the disaster takes its toll, and people become exhausted and frustrated and often angry. With the case of a natural disaster, the target of the anger is elusive, leading people to curse the Divine or the government. When neither of these "authorities" responds to their resentment, people often turn their rage either to their families or inward toward themselves.

Yes, anger is a natural response to any crisis, and, as you'll learn in the chapter on resolving your Reason Why, emotions like anger need to be faced, felt and then freed. The problem with anger is that it can evolve into its own worst enemy. When you express anger in times of crisis, either toward others (resentment) or toward yourself (guilt), you create more problems with negative Karma and additional Subconscious Sabotage.

Large disasters also provide an opportunity for the expression of great love, charity, appreciation, and heroism. Not only does responding this way create positive Karma and increases your opportunity for Reward, but it also helps you maintain a feeling of responsibility and control.

INTERRUPTION IN EXPECTATION
OF FUTURE DIRECTION

In the chapter titled Understanding Your Crisis, you were asked to review the areas of your life that were affected, and to what degree. One of the areas of life in that evaluation, which identified internal and emotional problems, included "Future Direction Expectation." When in the midst of a crisis, one of the most significant Tests we face is the often abrupt halt in our expectations for the future. If our business fails, what will we do next? If we lose our ability to walk, we'll probably never be able to climb Mount Everest. If we lose our spouse, the trip we planned with him or her won't take place as planned.

Every year, I have a Kentucky Derby party and I continued the tradition this year. Several people came up to me weeks before and said, "I guess you won't be having the party next year, since you're losing your house." What was my response? "I have no idea what will happen. Maybe I'll have next year's party in a mansion."

Albert, a good friend of mine, told me he never gets upset when life throws curve balls at him. If he's caught in traffic, he figures he's delayed for a reason, potentially avoiding an accident, for example. He'd done exhaustive research, when buying a motorcycle, and then the deal fell through. But his expectations in life led him to look for the opportunity, instead of the problem, and he ended up with a better bike for a better price.

Our success is measured by how we face uncertainty. Do we over-inflate our pessimism of the future? When a relationship ends, are we "certain" we'll never meet anyone else? If we lose our house, do we fear we'll have to live with a friend forever? If someone gets a five to ten-year jail sentence, do we say, "his life is over"?

Of course, things will be different, but they won't necessarily be worse. In fact, how we view the situation – passing the optimism Test - will determine if we discover the Blessing in Disguise.

> This polarization between optimism and pessimism creates a crossroads – which means that humanity is at a point of choice. When one has choice, one has power.
> - James Redfield and Carol Adrienne

CHANGE IN DAY TO DAY ACTIVITY

When our daily activity changes, we're tested on our ability to adapt. Will we embrace change or will we hold onto the past? Will we live in regret or fear, or will we look for the opportunity in each new day?

> Life is a storm …you will bask in the sunlight one moment be shattered on the rocks the next. What makes you a man is what you do when that storm comes.
> - Alexandre Dumas, The Count of Monte Cristo

THE TEST OF TERRORISM AND WAR: ASKING WHY?

Writer Katie Elliot reflects on her trip to Bali:

"Before my trip, when I told people that I was going to Bali they were shocked. 'You're going there!? Haven't you been watching the news? Don't you know what's going on over there right now? Well, you'd better be very careful, that's for sure.' But for all those terrible warnings, I found that Bali and the Balinese people were wonderful. It is a place with such loving and peaceful people. In fact, when all the bombings happened in Bali a few years ago, and this peaceful, beautiful place was targeted, no one could understand it. But here's the great thing about the Balinese people - when all this occurred, the Balinese asked themselves, 'What did *we* do to have this happen to us?' For them it wasn't a matter of "How dare you do this to us? You will pay!" Rather, they looked within, to discover what was it that *they* did. Very interesting way to look at it don't you think? What if Americans, as a whole, had asked the same question when September 11th occurred? Maybe we'd be closer to understanding what we've done to be the target of hatred and attack. Maybe we'd be closer to changing that."

> Hatred is the worst possible basis for human relations, especially hatred between nations. It is our contention that hatred dehumanizes everyone and makes problems more intractable. Hatred is never simply one-way traffic. It is a relational reactive condition.
> It affects how judgments are made about what actions are permissible, appropriate and warranted on both sides of a mutual divide of distrust. It can become a mutually sustained cycle of defensive reaction, a self-fulfilling and self-perpetuating prophesy.
> - Ziauddin Sardar and Merryl Wyn Davies

A REMARKABLE TEST STORY

The story of Ashley Smith is an impressive example of being tested. Ms. Smith is the Atlanta woman, who was held captive in her apartment for seven hours by Brian Nichols, the man the media called "The Courthouse Killer." After allegedly killing several people that fateful day, Nichols forced his way into Smith's apartment and threatened to kill her. Although clearly terrified, instead of trying to fight Nichols with aggression, Smith instead exhibited compassion and understanding, treating Nichols as a fellow human being.

She talked with him about faith and read to him a passage entitled "Using What God Gave You," from Rick Warren's book, *The Purpose Driven Life*. Her encouragement for him to think about how he might serve the Divine convinced Nichols to surrender, which undoubtedly saved lives – including Nichols' own.

Smith said to Nichols, "Do you believe in miracles? Because...you are here for a reason. You're here in my apartment for some reason. You got out of that courthouse with police everywhere, and you don't think that's a miracle? You don't think you're supposed to be sitting here right in front of me listening to me tell you, you know, your reason here? You know, your miracle could be that you need to be caught for this. You need to go to prison and you need to share the word of God with them, with all the prisoners there."

Ashley Smith's story is one of faith, courage, perception, restraint and consideration, when faced with an extreme circumstance. The result inspired Nichols to call her "an angel sent from God" and allowed Smith to turn her own life around and follow a higher, much more rewarding path.

> The ultimate measure of a man is not where he stands in moments of comfort and convenience, but where he stands at times of challenge and controversy.
> - Martin Luther King, Jr.

TEST CATEGORIES AND QUESTIONS

There are six basic Test categories:

1. Higher Path
2. Responsibility
3. Inner Self and Outer Self Reactions
4. Appreciation and Silver Lining
5. Make a Difference
6. Preparation

A Higher Path

Which course will you take – the higher path or the lower one?

Faith

- Will you curse God or get closer to your Higher Power?
- Will you show faith, either in a Higher Power or in other humans?
- Will you trust your Higher Power, believing this happened for a reason?
- Will you keep faith?

Seek Guidance

- Will you look for guidance for what actions to take – from others, from God, from your Inner Self, from your higher self?

Connection

- Will you use the time to get connected to your Higher Self?
- Will you take the time to find out what you really want – and what's best for you?

Social Darwinism or Spiritual Darwinism?

- Survival of The Fittest – Are you guilty of Social Darwinism (putting others down in order to feel stronger) or are you pursuing the Higher path?
- Will you accept others' help?
- Have you been able to see the benefits in a higher Spiritual Connection? If so, have you thanked God?

Responsibility

- Will you take responsibility for your role in what happened?
- Will you learn from your mistakes?
- Will you take responsibility? Will you apologize?
- Will you explain why you did what you did?
- Will you show regret?
- Will you get bitter and angry or will you look for the Reasons Why?
- Will you accept your role in what happened?
- Will you make the best of the situation and learn?
- Will you look into yourself and your life and look for what's missing? Why have you been living someone else's life?

Find out why

- Will you dig deep inside yourself to find out why it happened?
- Will you relentlessly pursue the Reasons Why?

Will you change?

- Are you willing to see how your actions contributed and then change?

- Are you willing to change?
- Will you get therapy to learn why you let this happen?
- Will you learn to detach from money and possessions?
- Will you learn the real purpose of money?
- Will you take better care of yourself?
- Will you change your self-sabotage?
- Can you figure out a way to stop the abusive behavior?
- Will you join a victim support group?
- Will you keep going?

> If you don't like what you're doing, you can always pick
> up your needle and move to another groove.
> – Timothy Leary

Inner Self and Outer Self Reactions

How are your Inner Self and your Outer Self reacting to your event? What are your emotions and feelings? What are your actions and reactions?

Emotional reactions

- Will you seek revenge?
- Are you angry or resentful?
- Will you become vicious and vengeful or will you learn acceptance and forgiveness?
- Will you release your hate and find ways to love instead?
- Will you face the challenge with courage?
- Will you look for the bright side?
- Will you become better or bitter?
- Will you let the thoughts control you, or will you control the thoughts?
- Will you use the emotions as motivators?
- How will you handle despair?
- Are you consciously aware of your emotional reactions?

> Pain is temporary. It may last a minute, or an hour, or a
> day, or a year, but eventually it will subside and
> something else will take its place.
> If I quit, however, it lasts forever.
> – Lance Armstrong

Outward reaction

- Will you seek revenge or will you learn a new, peaceful way to "fight" for what you believe?
- Will you learn to compromise to get people to see your side?
- Will you confess and make amends to those you've harmed?
- Are you ashamed of anything you've done? Have you tried to reverse the mistake?

Appreciation and Silver Linings

Will you be able to remember to appreciate the gifts in your life, and look for a blessing in disguise or an opportunity to make a difference?

- Will you find ways to be happy?
- Will you give thanks for what you still have?
- Will you consider that it could be a Blessing in Disguise and you might have been spared a bigger problem??
- Will you look for the potential Reward?
- Will you use the opportunity to learn about yourself and what would make you happy?
- Will the experience bring you closer to your friend/companion/family member?
- Will you find out that you have strength and resourcefulness that you didn't realize you had?

Make a Difference

- Can your experience allow you to make a difference in the lives of others? If so, will you do so?

Help Others, Show Understanding and Be Compassionate

- Will you take care of others?

- Will you show understanding, during your friend's time of need?
- Will you get your life back together?
- Will you help your others learn from your experience?
- Will you stand by your loved ones – without judgment, but still loving them?
- Can you help a group or country learn the effects of group Karma?
- Will you ultimately become a cautionary tale or an inspirational story?
- Will you label yourself as a failure and let it define who you are for your lifetime?
- Or will you find your own way to succeed in life?
- Will you let this event poison the rest of your life and relationships/jobs/ business?

> "My father never believed in me! I'm not gonna make the same mistake. From now on I'm gonna be kinder to my son and meaner to my dad."
> – Homer Simpson, The Simpsons TV Show

Preparation

Has your crisis helped you become better prepared for life – and death?

- Will you – and your loved one - be better prepared for death?
- Are you now ready for change?
- What has your experience made you more prepared for?
- What are your thoughts about death?
- What is your will to live?
- Are you ready to face your feelings?
- Are you ready to face others?

ROLE OF THE DIVINE

If we're being tested and we essentially "grade" ourselves, what is the role of the Divine? First of all, our Higher Power and personal spirit guides are always available to us to help and support us throughout our lives, and especially while we're facing challenges and Tests. We can connect with them at all times to access love, guidance, and insight. There are only two obstacles: not trying and possible interference through not attending to our Inner Self.

Second, the Divine genuinely cares about how we do on our Tests. We're a reflection of Him/Her, when we embody a loving, peaceful, divine attitude. When we act in anger, hatred, fear or violence, we act in separation from God. So the Divine wants us to "pass the Tests" and has given us everything we need to do so. We just have to know how to ask.

EVIL EXPLAINED BY TESTS

As communicated, we establish and administer our own Tests. They're not dispensed by an outside force, either Divine or evil. However, both forces influence our Tests. Evil, as defined in the Basic Assumptions, is a human creation, generated from our harmful and destructive thoughts and action. *Whether or not we pass the Test is up to us.* We can ask for and follow Divine guidance or we can react with anger, vengeance, bitterness, abuse, dishonesty or fear, all manifestations of evil.

THE WHY OF TESTS

Simply put:

Failure	Tests Your	Resilience
Loss	Tests Your	Appreciation for What You Have
Rejection	Tests Your	Love for Yourself
Deception	Tests Your	Honesty

Pain	Tests Your	Ability to Take Care of Yourself
Fear	Tests Your	Faith
Abuse and Violence	Tests You	Compassion
Betrayal	Tests Your	Capability to Forgive
Loss in Future Direction	Tests Your	Ability to Look for Alternatives
Isolation	Tests Your	Connection with Your Selves and the Divine
Problems Faced by Those Close to You	Tests Your	Selflessness
Delay	Tests Your	Patience
Death	Tests Your	Beliefs
All Challenges	Test Your	Ability to Love Capacity to Change

> I believe life is constantly testing us for our level of commitment, and life's greatest rewards are reserved for those who demonstrate a never-ending commitment to act until they achieve. This level of resolve can move mountains, but it must be constant and consistent.
> As simplistic as this may sound, it is still the common denominator separating those who live their dreams from those who live in regret.
> - Anthony Robbins

HOW TESTS COULD EXPLAIN VARIOUS EXAMPLES OF BAD THINGS

It's likely in any traumatic situation, that we're feeling tested in one way or another, even if it's only "How will we handle the crisis?" The following lists a few of our Bad Things and some of the possible Tests involved:

Your child is abducted
- How will you handle it? Will you become vicious and angry or will you learn forgiveness?
- How will your child handle it?

You're fired from your job
- Will you accept your role in what happened?
- Will you take a rest or will you go out and get the same kind of job?
- Will you use the opportunity to learn about yourself and what would make you happy?

Your car is stolen
- Are you going to get angry?
- Are you going to figure out *why* it happened?
- Are you willing to change?
- Will you look for guidance for what actions to take?
- Will you look for the potential Reward?
- Will you trust your Higher Power that it happened for a reason?
- Will you consider that it could be a Blessing in Disguise – that your car could've broken down and you were spared a bigger problem?

Someone close to you is in an accident or diagnosed with a serious illness
- Will you take care of him/her?
- Will you learn more about the handicapped, the disease or other prevention/support groups?
- Will he/she explore the benefits in her situation (more time for reflection, opportunity to write/dictate her novel, come up with ideas, etc.?)
- Will you both find ways to be happy despite his/her plight?

- Will you both explore the Reasons Why this may have happened and make changes in your life?
- Will you both face the challenge with courage?
- Will you both be better prepared for death?

A country is the victim of a terrorist attack or war

- Will this nation learn the effects of group Karma?
- How will this country react to what happened?

COULD TESTS BE INVOLVED IN YOUR CRISIS?

Questions to ask yourself:

1. How could you have been tested with your ordeal?
2. Do you think you're passing the Test?
   - If so, why?
   - If not, why not?
   - (Don't worry – we haven't gotten to the Diagnosis, Elimination and Prevention chapters!)

> Here is the test to find whether your mission on Earth
> is finished: If you're alive, it isn't.
> - Richard Bach

CHAPTER 11: THE FIFTH REASON WHY: REWARD

We all know stories of people's lives have changed significantly for the better, following times of crisis. Perhaps they found their true purpose in life. Perhaps they developed a strength they never knew they were capable of. Or perhaps they found one of the greatest gifts of all – inner peace.

- Would Steven Hawking have discovered his breakthrough theories and achieved such acclaimed recognition if he hadn't become quadriplegic?
- Would Oprah Winfrey have been as warm and relatable to her guests if she hadn't endured her childhood tragedies and her on-and-off struggles with her weight?
- Would Franklin D. Roosevelt have become the memorable, compassionate leader if he hadn't been stricken with polio?
- Would Sir Walter Scott or Florence Nightingale have accomplished what they did if they hadn't been crippled?
- Would John Bunyan or Susan B. Anthony have had their resolve if they hadn't been locked in prison?
- Would George Washington or Joan of Arc have accomplished such remarkable feats if they hadn't faced such tremendous odds?

- Would Abraham Lincoln or Mother Theresa have been as understanding if they hadn't faced poverty themselves?
- Would Kurt Vonnegut, Jr. have achieved his literary status, if he hadn't been captured and imprisoned by the Germans in WWII?

> There's no disaster that can't be a blessing, and no blessing that can't be a disaster.
> - Richard Bach

WAS IT WORTH IT? ARE THEY HAPPIER?

I can't tell you if any of these people feel like "it was worth it." I can't tell you if any of these people are happier now than before they had to face their problems, if they feel that their lives are richer and more fulfilling from having gone through these experiences. But it's certain that each was able to make the best of a bad situation, learn from it, and provide a significant, positive impact on the lives of others.

No one can judge anyone else's Reasons Why; therefore, no one can say whether anyone's Reward was worth the trauma that someone went through. Only they can say that. In the big picture, however, one could argue that at least some level of Reward was attained by each of these souls, whether it was notoriety, contribution to the lives of others, the ability to instigate history-altering change, or peace of mind.

WHAT IS REWARD IN A CRISIS?

We have a lot of phrases in our language which convey Reward found in tragedy. Silver Linings. Blessings in Disguise, the Light at the End of the Tunnel and even Serendipity explain a form of Divine Providence that comes seemingly out of nowhere.

But the truth is, it doesn't come out of nowhere and it often comes as a result of a tragic event. In fact, Reward could be the sole Reason Why your crisis occurred. Your crisis could be just the preparation or change needed for you to become a much more satisfied, peaceful, thoughtful and loving contributor to the planet.

Psychologists who study psychotraumatology, the reaction to crises and traumatic circumstances, have recognized a phenomenon called Posttraumatic Growth, where trauma survivors report positive life changes following a catastrophe. In fact, according to numerous studies, this Reward is considerably more common *and far outnumbers* the experiences of other posttraumatic disorders.

The kinds of positive changes reported include "improved relationships, new possibilities for one's life, a greater appreciation for life, a greater sense of personal strength and spiritual development...Reports of posttraumatic growth have been found in people who have experienced bereavement, rheumatoid arthritis, HIV infection, cancer, bone marrow transplantation, heart attacks, coping with the medical problems of children, transportation accidents, house fires, sexual assault and sexual abuse, combat, refugee experiences, and being taken hostage.[46]"

There is the potential for Reward in every catastrophe. But not everyone in every situation attains it. Why? Perhaps it's because they haven't ended the karmic cycle, eliminated the Subconscious Sabotage, learned the Lesson or passed the Test. Sometimes the Reward isn't recognized and other times it isn't appreciated.

> "Each circumstance is a gift, and in each experience is hidden a treasure."
> – "God" (Neale Donald Walsh)

Finally, Reward can also be a way of looking at things differently. Once you come out of a fog and the air is clear, your perspective changes. When you wake up from a nightmare and realize the horror is over, you see the world in a new light.

---

[46] Richard Tedeshi, PhD. and Lawrence Calhoun, Ph.D., in *Psychiatric Times* magazine.

> Intense distress after a sudden crisis is normal, and does not prohibit people from ultimately getting some benefit from the experience. Recovering and growing doesn't mean suppressing these responses but instead gradually incorporating them into a new perspective on life.
> - *Psychology Today* magazine staff writers

CANCER AS A GIFT?

Multiple Tour de France champion, Lance Armstrong, describes his cancer as a gift:

> "The most interesting thing about cancer is that it can be one of the most positive, life-affirming, incredible experiences ever. When somebody is in that position, he starts to really focus on his life, on his friends and family, and what's really important. You experience a different emotion and feeling than the guy who's woken up for thirty years in perfect health and gone to work or school and never had to worry about anything. That guy forgets that every day, when you wake up, it's really a gift."

Any situation we experience that forces us to face our mortality has the potential to make us appreciate life even more. We can learn to take better care of ourselves, to appreciate the people and pleasures in our lives, and to be grateful for the preciousness of time. We also find ourselves looking in the mirror and asking the question, "Why am I here?" and "Have I accomplished my purpose?"

In the website, Afterlife101.com, they provide guidance to cancer patients: Do Not Fear (death is painless); Be Honest (do not hide what you're going through – allow yourself to feel the emotions); Embrace It (do a life review and see what you've learned); Allow Quality Time and Ask for Spiritual Support. The underlying message is similar to that of Lance Armstrong: that there are Lessons and gifts in the experience of cancer and other life-threatening diseases.

Their advice: "You are being given an opportunity that many, many people do not get to experience. It is so often looked at as to be tragic, but you are the fortunate few. We all know that someday we're going to cross over. Many of us just are not given the opportunity ahead of time to embrace it."

A WEIGHT PROBLEM AS A GIFT?

I've struggled with my weight all my life, a problem that's a source of mystery and frustration for millions of people. But a number of years ago I realized something: my weight problem has been an invaluable gift in many ways. First of all, it's a handy defense mechanism that eliminates the superficial people from my life. Also, because it's something I've always had to attend to, I have healthier eating and exercise habits than many people who never had my "problem," which means I'm more likely to live a healthier life. But mainly, I've realized the biggest gift of all. My Inner Self loves to exercise and, when I give her what she really loves, she opens up my communication to my Higher Self in a powerful and beautiful way. I get my most brilliant, exciting and unique breakthrough ideas when I'm exercising, whether it's at the gym or hiking in the woods. Would I have preferred to have a naturally leaner physique? Yes – but I wouldn't trade the gifts I have for it. No way.

PAIN AS A GIFT?

> Pain nourishes courage. You can't be brave if you've only had wonderful things happen to you.
> - Mary Tyler Moore

Have you ever considered that pain could be a good thing? Many of us would do anything to live a pain-free life. But pain is a gift. It's a warning to pay attention.

In researching this book, I found out something fascinating about the disease of leprosy. I had thought that the disease was characterized by limbs becoming atrophied and falling off. What I learned is more profound. Leprous people live a virtually pain-free existence. The absence of pain is the greatest enemy of the leper. As the blood flow is cut off from key parts of their body, their nerve endings die. With the death of their nerve endings comes the death of their ability to sense danger to their bodies. Because pain is absent, leprosy victims are more vulnerable to accidents, more likely to burn themselves, tear ligaments, break bones, and more.

> There is no coming to consciousness without pain.
> - Carl Jung

Pain carries many important messages. Are you listening?

DEATH AS A GIFT?

Once you learn everything you can about "life" on the other side, you'll know the existence after this earthly life is its own gift. Except in rare cases of extreme wrongdoing, it's a positive experience for everyone. (And even in these cases, the "guilty" face their own punishment of remorse, which is usually self-imposed isolation, once they see what they've done. It isn't hell, fire and brimstone.) Either way, when someone says, "They're in a better place," it is always true. So, death to the one who's passed over is a gift to them, even if it isn't embraced until the last breath.

If you want a great story that confirms this, the book, *The Afterlife of Billy Fingers: How My Bad-Boy Brother Proved to Me There's Life After Death,* is a beautiful, profound story about how even someone so-called "bad" can have an awe-inspiring life "after."

But what about death of a loved one? How can that possibly be a gift? First of all, you now know that it isn't an ending, that you'll see them again. Secondly, even though it's possible to communicate to the other side, there's a break in the communication. Even though they can "hear" us talking to them and praying for them we have difficulty on our side tuning into the right frequencies to be able to hear from them. Even when we do, the information is choppy and hard to decipher. But it is possible and there are tools to cultivate that potential.

Thirdly, when we have someone close to us on the other side, we now have an advocate, someone to guide us, who knows us and our challenges in life. I've heard many people say that when a close relative passes away, their lives improved significantly. They felt as if they had a new, relatable "guardian angel."

BUSINESS FAILURE AS A GIFT?

In a memorable episode of the classic TV series, *The Love Boat*[47], a rich and powerful businessman had rented the cruise ship for his daughter's wedding. In the beginning of the episode, the businessman didn't show much energy or emotion. He just seemed to be going through the motions of life. Then, in the middle of the cruise, he received a phone call: his financial advisor had stolen all his money – he was penniless!

As soon as the word got out, several of his family members and wedding guests came up to him to console him. However, what they saw in him surprised them very much! He was energetic and happy! When they asked him why he was so happy, he replied, "I'm not worried! I'm excited about the challenge! I built a multi-million-dollar business from nothing before, and I can do it again! I can't wait to get started!" What a great story about motivation and optimism!!

That's what learning is, after all; not whether

> we lose the game, but how we lose and how we've changed because of it and what we take away from it that we never had before, to apply to other games.
> Losing, in a curious way, is winning.
> - Richard Bach

---

[47] I don't know who the writer or writers of this episode were, but I would like to acknowledge them in future printings of this book and on the www.ReasonsWhy.com website. So if anyone knows who should get credit for this great story, please let me know!

JOB LOSS AS A GIFT?

I worked for a company that had major layoffs every six months for years. The energy in the office was one of constant trepidation and resentment. You could cut the tension with a knife. People had put their hearts and souls into their careers at that company, some for much of their lives, and they never knew if their name would be on the chopping block the next go-around.

The weird thing is, the people who were happiest in their jobs were the ones more likely to go out looking for a new one, while the more vulnerable employees were immobilized by their fear and just waited to see their fate. Why is this? Because the happier people were more confident in their abilities, perhaps due to the fact they were less likely to be laid off, which was in direct contrast to their more peers in a weaker position.

It's very rare for someone who is truly happy in his or her job to be laid off. It's almost always a sign that the job and/or company weren't a good fit, but the situation evolves into creating a lack of self-assurance that leads to self-destruction. If the people who were fired were able to learn from the experience in order to find what they really wanted and where they'd make a greater contribution, they usually found a career that was much more satisfying. But some took longer to learn, and some may have changed jobs and companies, but are still fighting the same fear-based battles. The "Good or Bad" story later in this chapter illustrates the path one of my peers took.

If you're unhappy, or if you've been laid off from your job, it's a sign that you'd be happier elsewhere. Yes, we need to learn the Reasons Why we're in the wrong job (or relationship, for that matter). The following is a quote from a good book on the subject , *When Smart People Fail* by Carole Hyatt and Linda Gottleib:

> Outright failure is one of the most liberating things that can happen. It possesses a clarity that hidden failure lacks. If before you thought, Maybe I should leave but there are good reasons why I should stay, or I'll just keep on trying this a little longer – rejoice, you have had

> a cosmic kick in the pants. Visible failure has this
> enormous virtue: It gets you unstuck.
> You are free now to reinvent yourself.
> - Carole Hyatt and Linda Gottleib

If you don't recognize the gift, you're probably still facing a Fear of the Unknown, which I'll discuss in the chapter on resolving your Reason Why.

ANGST AS A GIFT?

A few years ago I was having a conversation with a friend about happiness and Abraham Maslow's Hierarchy of Needs.[48] She was wondering if society would every become fully happy, once the basic needs are met and our sole focus is on self-actualization. My response was that not only is universal happiness not likely, it probably isn't for the best. So-called negative emotions are powerful motivators for change. Most of the progress in the world has been the byproduct of anger, frustration, fear, and discontent.

If everyone was happy one hundred years ago, we would never have some of the things that we "can't live without," like air travel, the Internet, cures for polio and other diseases, and thousands of examples of inventions and cures that have enhanced our quality of life.

NOT GETTING WHAT YOU WANT
AS A GIFT?

> Remember that not getting what you want
> is sometimes a wonderful stroke of luck.
> - Dalai Lama

---

[48] Maslow's hierarchy of needs is often depicted as a pyramid consisting of five levels: the four lower levels are grouped together as *deficiency needs* associated with physiological needs, while the top level is termed *growth needs* associated with psychological needs. More information on Maslow's acclaimed findings is available on www.Wikipedia.com.

Garth Brooks' song, *Unanswered Prayers*, tells a beautiful story of how not getting what we think we want can be the best thing that happens to us. He sings of running into his high school flame, whom he had prayed and prayed would be his forever. But, as he looks at his wife, he "thanked the good Lord for the gifts" in his life.

Can you look back at some of the things you hoped and prayed for and now be thankful that they didn't happen? Perhaps it was a job you really wanted. Or a relationship with someone. Or perhaps another kind of opportunity.

> I may not have gone where I intended to go,
> but I think I have ended up where I needed to be.
> - Douglas Adams

STRUGGLE AS A GIFT?

> Where there is no struggle, there is no strength.
> – Oprah Winfrey

It's a fact of nature that struggle creates great strength. Trees and bones are good examples. When you break a bone, it heals back stronger than it was before the break. And a tree's roots grow deeper and stronger following a drought or when forced to withstand intense winds.

The same is often true of humans. Nietzsche's famous quote below is used frequently in movies and books, either as a motivation to persevere, or as a description of another's determination. If you had been through every possible crisis and not only survived but thrived, you'd be armed with a wealth of tools and information for coping with anything life throws at you – the ultimate security.

> What does not destroy me makes me strong.
> - Friedrich Nietzsche

FACING DEATH AS A GIFT?

I've read dozens of accounts of near-death experiences. In every one, the person who got a glimpse of the other side talks about the occurrence as a life-affirming, extraordinary gift. Even if they emerge from the situation with an excruciatingly painful recovery, they learn perhaps the most valuable Lesson of all: the evidence of the life that continues after death. Once the fear that "this is all there is" is eliminated, we can all live much more fulfilling, spirited and peaceful lives. This is because most fears in life are based in the fear of death. Think about it. If you peel the layers of your fears, at the core is often a fear of death.

> He who has felt the deepest grief
> is best able to experience supreme happiness.
> We must have felt what it is to die,
> that we may appreciate the enjoyments of life.
> - Alexandre Dumas

LOSS IN FUTURE DIRECTION AS A GIFT?

How can an interruption in plans be a gift? It's just disruption and confusion, right?

If we're going down the wrong path (wrong being defined as not being in our highest good, not beneficial to ourselves and the planet, etc.) then we'll be nudged (and sometimes shoved!) to change our direction. Although we have free will, our Higher Self can step in to make sure we follow the course we set out to achieve, which is our alignment with Divine Will.

It does feel unsettling, though, to be shoved. It's as if we're going through a maze and then are abruptly picked up and put in another place. Even if our new path gives us the opportunity to proceed on a more rewarding course, it might not be clear to us at first, which makes us disoriented. This is because our Inner Self works like a heat-seeking missile that focuses on the target ahead of us. When the target is removed, he/she no longer has a focal point, which makes them frustrated.

The gift is that your Inner Self will pester you for instructions, since he/she needs your guidance to know what to look forward to. You'll feel restless until you decide what you want, which gives you the freedom to choose a new life for yourself. What kind of life do you want?

> Change has a considerable psychological impact on the human mind. To the fearful, it is threatening because it means that things may get worse.
> To the hopeful, it is encouraging
> because things may get better.
> To the confident, it is inspiring because
> the challenge exists to make things better.
> - King Whitney, Jr.

FREEDOM AS A RESULT OF FAILURE OR LOSS?

> "It's only after we've lost everything
> that we're free to do anything."
> - Tyler Durden (Brad Pitt) Fight Club

Although the above quote is from an atypical source, it's nonetheless true. When talk with friends in the midst of a breakup, I'll usually say, "The opposite of relationship is freedom." And it's true. It doesn't mean that relationships can't be valuable and rewarding, but it does mean that failure and loss create an opening for great change and happiness.

When there's a place missing inside us, it creates a void. It's up to us to decide if we fill the space with excitement or fear, with adventure or apprehension, with or hope or despair.

What does freedom mean to you? And, if you lost it, what would you do to get it back?

> We who lived in concentration camps can remember the men who walked through the huts comforting others, giving away their last piece of bread. They may have been few in number, but they offer sufficient proof that

> everything can be taken from a man but one thing: the last of human freedoms – to choose one's attitude in any given set of circumstances – to choose one's own way.
> - Viktor Frankl

MAKING LEMONS FROM LEMONADE

The real heroes in life are the ones who are able to take their tragic experiences and make the best of them, turning lemons into lemonade. They're the ones who start foundations and discover cures, who not only learn everything they can, but also become teachers as well. They're the ones who channel their outrage at injustice and take action to instill change in the world.

> I believe if life gives you lemons make lemonade…then find someone that life gave vodka to and have a party.
> - Ron White

Helping Others

Our world is full of people who have been able to significantly improve our planet as a result of their own tragedies. The Elizabeth Glaser Pediatric AIDS Foundation, Christopher Reeve's efforts toward spinal cord research, Candy Lightner, founder of MADD, the Susan G. Komen Breast Cancer Foundation and dozens, perhaps hundreds more, are well-known examples. And there are perhaps thousands of additional examples of lesser-known heroes and heroines..[49]

Disease, disaster, accident, loss, suicide of a loved one, betrayal, abuse, and even self-instigated crises like being convicted of a crime, causing an accident or succumbing to self-created addictions and diseases, are all opportunities to make a difference and help others.

---

[49] Do you know some such examples? Please go to the ReasonsWhy.com website and tell us!

235

Learning and Teaching

I went through dozens of opportunities to learn through a crisis. Once we learn our own Lessons, we're in a position to help others learn as well. If we can all tell enough people not to touch a hot stove, perhaps no one in the future will get burned. In fact, if we learn an undeniable truth that can save the lives of others, it is our moral obligation to spread the word. Certainly, we might run against obstacles. Either people will put their heads in the sand and continue to live in denial or someone will try to refute what you say. Either way, it's usually because they're demonstrating the destructive side of Survival of the Fittest, clawing for their own greed.

> Great spirits have always encountered violent opposition
> from mediocre minds.
> - Albert Einstein

But even against obstacles and opposition – or perhaps because of them – we need to spread the word. Throughout history, naysayers have tried to prevent progress, but, thankfully, courageous leaders continue to fight to teach and inform. Columbus proved the world wasn't flat, and other passionate pioneers are committed to warning us of the dangers produced by the impending climate crisis (increased frequency and intensity of storms like hurricanes and tornadoes, floods and drought), as well as the warning for the future (massive death and significant destruction of the planet).

After gaining clarity on the Five Reasons Why, I became compelled to write this book. Nothing could stop me. Even if no one reads it and I have spent months in research and writing, when I could've been doing something more profitable, it's something I just had to do.

Maybe It's How You Look At It

Have you considered the ways your tragic event could turn out to be a blessing in some way, no matter how disguised it may be?

Whether it's freedom, an opening to find something – or someone – more meaningful or valuable, an opening to resolve negative Karma, an opportunity to face your fears, or a chance to make a difference, if you look for it, there is the potential for a gift in your tragedy.

> The happiest people don't necessarily have the best of everything. They just make the best of everything.
> - John Rockefeller, Jr.

I have a friend who looks for Reward in every setback he encounters. When he gets caught in traffic, he assumes it is to avoid an accident ahead. When he gets loses something, he believes that something better is around the corner. When he lost his job, he started his own thriving business.

Even when he faces a problem without a Reward, he sees the benefit for others in the situation. For example, he told me a story about driving down a busy street and seeing a piece of 2x4 in his path. He couldn't swerve to miss it, because there was traffic on his right and more cars coming toward him to his left. He buckled down and concentrated and ran over the board. It took out his tire, but he was able to control his car until he could pull over. Even though it happened at a time when finances were extremely tight, he still thinks of the experience as a gift. He figures his awareness and strength were able to remove the obstruction from the path. If someone else had hit it, perhaps a woman with children in her car talking on her cell phone, there would have been multiple casualties. How's that for a positive attitude?

Do you know anyone with this outlook? What makes someone have this glass-half-full way of thinking? Is it something you're born with or is it how you were raised? Is it something you can develop? The good news is that anyone can develop it. It just takes some work with your Inner Self and faith.

WANT TO SUCCEED? LOSE A
LITTLE

Every great success story occurs when someone succeeds, despite overwhelming odds. Many of these stories are preceded by failure – sometimes significant. Consider the following examples:

- Babe Ruth held the home run record for years, but he also struck out 1,330 times, leading the American League in Strikeouts five times.
- Thomas Edison failed 10,000 times before succeeding in inventing the incandescent light bulb.
- Albert Einstein didn't speak until he was four years old. His teacher described him as "mentally slow, unsociable, and adrift forever in foolish dreams." Einstein was Time Magazine's "Person of the 20th Century."
- Katie Couric was banned from on-air reports by CNN, because they didn't like her voice
- The Beatles were turned down by ten recording companies, before Capitol signed them.
- Marilyn Monroe was dropped from her contract with Twentieth Century Fox because they thought she was "unattractive."
- Dr. Seuss's first book was rejected by twenty-seven publishing houses.
- Walt Disney went bankrupt several times before he built Disneyland.
- Barbara Walters was told to "stay out of television" in 1957 by an executive producer.
- Henry Ford was broke at the age of 40.
- IBM did a study in the 1980s and found the managers who accomplished the most also had the longest history of mistakes.
- The original best-selling *Chicken Soup for the Soul* book was rejected by one hundred and forty publishers.

And there are thousands of other examples throughout history.

> Many of life's failures are people who did not realize how close they were to success when they gave up.
> - Thomas Alva Edison

By going through Bad Things and making it through, you learn a lot about yourself – and what it takes to overcome failure and loss.

BLESSINGS IN DISGUISE

We all know the phrases "blessing in disguise" and "silver lining." They denote the potential for a Reward, hidden within a perceived tragedy. Sometimes the rewards are obvious. Rain is necessary before the flowers can grow, for example. Some are the results of Lessons, like finding out how strong we are, when we're forced to lift ourselves up. And sometimes the rewards are truly hidden deep and we might not find out what they're until much later (if ever).

Some of the blessings are global. For example, high gas prices might be the stimulus we need to pursue alternative sources of fuel, and recent storms might be the wake-up call we need to stop global warming. Others are individual and personal.

Many of us were captivated by some of the blessings in disguise on September 11, 2001. A man lost his job at the World Trade Center two days prior to the attack. There were many who were late to work that morning. There were a lot of people who missed flights that would have crashed.

I've heard that, statistically, two-thirds of passengers miss a flight that crashes. Why does this happen? When asked, some of the people had been frustrated and angry that they'd been held up "against their will." They weren't consciously aware of the Reason Why they were delayed, but nonetheless they were spared. Others got a premonition that they shouldn't get on the flight, and heeded the "advice."

Either way, we feel as if our lives were spared for a reason by some Divine source, whether we call this help our Guardian Angel or Spirit Guide. In a more subtle way, Traffic Angels.[50] help us along our paths in life to get where we need to go. All are significant examples of Spiritual Darwinism: to become connected to the Source of all that is Divine, to help us fulfill our life's purpose.

Blessings in disguise are often recognized after the fact. The trick is to recognize them *before* the fact and have faith that things could work out better in the midst of change. For example, as I write this I'm facing the potential loss of everything I own. The "pre-Five Reasons Why" me was fearful and desperate. I didn't know where to turn or what to do. Now, however, I feel free and alive. I've faced my fears and am now ready for the adventure of life: the unknown. Therefore, my crisis has been a blessing in disguise because if I hadn't learned what I now understand about WHY, I wouldn't now be happier than I ever have been in my life, despite the turmoil around me.

> Not many people are willing to give failure a second opportunity. They fail once and it's all over. The bitter pill of failure is often more than most people can handle. If you're willing to accept failure and learn from it, if you're willing to consider failure as a blessing in disguise and bounce back, you've got the potential of harnessing one of the most powerful success forces.
> - Joseph Sugarman

---

[50] Introduced in the Basic Assumptions, "Traffic Angels" are Divine Beings whose "job" is to assist and connect us, showing the paths that will lead us to each other and to our highest destiny.

SERENDIPITY, SYNCHRONICITY AND COINCIDENCES

Serendipity

Serendipity is defined by Webster's as "an apparent aptitude for making accidental fortunate discoveries" and is often referred as "happy accidents." Common examples of serendipity include the discoveries and inventions of penicillin, Post-it notes, Viagra and Silly Putty, to name a few. Who would have thought that mold growing in Fleming's messy lab could cure infections? Who would have foreseen that a potential treatment for angina could have, err, unusual reactions in men? Who would have predicted that researching products to be used in warfare would have become an enduringly popular children's toy?

> There is an art to wandering. If I have a destination, a plan – an objective – I've lost the ability to find serendipity. I am on a quest, not a ramble.
> I search for the Holy Grail of particularity and miss the chalice freely offered, filled and overflowing.
> - Cathy Johnson

Serendipity is a hidden Reward that's found when we're looking for something else. Have you ever lost your keys, only to find something else you had lost? Have you ever taken the wrong road, only to meet someone you'd have never met, if you'd gone the "right" way? Have you ever been delayed in traffic, only to find out that, if you had been on time, you could've been involved in the accident? Or have you ever done an internet search for one subject and found something else that helped your project?

Where does Serendipity come from? And how do we find it? Was it always there? Did we just need to get centered and connect to it? Was it placed by the Divine? The above quote is true – but it's because it's our efforts that allow us to find serendipity!

> Serendipity is God's way of remaining anonymous.
> - Unknown

Serendipity is Reward that was always there, hidden beneath the surface. All we had to do was stop, look and pay attention, which happens when our Outer Self, Inner Self and Higher Self are connected and communicating. Discovering serendipity is like opening a gift! It is my wish for everyone reading this book to learn to cultivate the excitement and joy that comes from uncovering the hidden gifts in life.

Synchronicity and Coincidences

Closely related to Serendipity is Synchronicity. James Redfield, in his breakthrough best-selling inspirational novel, *The Celestine Prophecy*[51] identifies Synchronicity or Coincidences as the first of nine "insights," "Coincidences are happening more and more frequently and that, when they do, they strike us as beyond what would be expected by pure chance. They feel destined, as though our lives had been guided by some unexplained force. The experience induces a feeling of mystery and excitement, and as a result, we feel more alive."

Synchronicity is a term coined by psychologist Carl Jung to describe the "meaningful coincidences" with an "underlying pattern or dynamic that's being expressed through meaningful relationships or events…Jung believed that many experiences perceived as coincidence were due not merely to chance, but instead, suggested the manifestation of parallel events or circumstances reflecting this governing dynamic."[52]

So, you may be asking, is anything a true coincidence, or is everything happening "on purpose?" And if so, how much is pre-determined? The answer depends on your point of view and, your connections to your Higher Power. Apophenia is a word defined as "the spontaneous perception of connections and meaningfulness of unrelated phenomena." Is this real or

---

[51] A must-read!
[52] Source: Wikipedia; www.wikipedia.com

imagined? Is it Divinely inspired or illusion? If you can find, as the Edie Brickell song said, philosophy on a cereal box, and it helps you find more meaning in your life and live your life better, then who can argue its value?

THE ROLE OF THE DIVINE

First and foremost, the Divine (Spirit, our Higher Power, etc.) wants us to be happy and an expression of His/Her love. He doesn't want us to suffer. Suffering only happens as a result of separating ourselves from the Divine. The Divine wants us to look through the storm to find the pot of gold at the end of the rainbow. All we have to do is open our eyes and ask to see the Big Picture.

> The mark of your ignorance is the depth of your belief in injustice and tragedy. What the caterpillar calls the end of the world the master calls a butterfly.
> - Richard Bach

HOW REWARD COULD EXPLAIN VARIOUS EXAMPLES OF BAD THINGS

The following lists a few of our Bad Things and potentially rewarding consequences:

Your business fails and you lose everything
- You write a book on your experience and help other people. ☺
- You join the Peace Corps and help others.
- You get closer to God.
- You find a business or lifestyle that fits better.
- Once you learn the Lessons and pass the Tests, you find a buyer for the business.

Reward

Your wife gets breast cancer
- You learn to love her on a deeper level.
- She becomes healed and you both are an inspiration to others.
- She gets a double mastectomy and reconstructive surgery and *loves* her new breasts!

Your home is destroyed by fire/flood/hurricane/tornado
- You get to rebuild the house as you want it.
- You enjoy living with a friend or family member while your home is rebuilt.
- You move somewhere you enjoy more.

Someone close to you is in an accident or diagnosed with a serious illness
- You get closer to him/her and heal past hurts.
- You become an activist for the disease/cause and help save the lives of others.
- You learn about healing.
- You become a hospice or hospital volunteer and help others.
- You earn karmic brownie points.
- You appreciate the people in your life more.

A country is the victim of a terrorist attack
- The country learns WHY they were attacked and finds a way to find common interests and a long-term peaceful solution.

You were born without the ability to see
- You become an accomplished musician, sculptor, etc.
- You aren't superficial and connect with people beyond their physical appearance.

You hate the way you look
- You learn to love your soul and let the light within shine.

CHAPTER 12: THE BIG REASON WHY: CHANGE

> Change is inevitable, except from vending machines.
> - Robert G. Gallagher

What do all the Five Reasons Why have in common? They're all a motivation to *change*, to learn, to improve ourselves and this planet.

The purpose of Karma is to help us learn the repercussions of our actions, both positive and negative, so we'll know how to be more conscientious and understanding.

Subconscious Sabotage is interference generated by the force of our own inner thoughts and feelings, and those of others. Like Karma, once we recognize and understand Subconscious Sabotage, we can harness this power to accomplish constructive goals.

The intention of the Lessons in Earth School is to help us gain knowledge that will guide us toward improving our lives.

Similarly, Tests are conducted to make sure we're on the right track, or to steer us toward it.

> "If you want to be like me I will help you, knowing that
> we are alike. If you want to be different,
> I will wait until you change your mind."
> – Jesus, *A Course in Miracles*

Reward is the result of having improved ourselves – of having changed from the inside and then making a difference to the outside world.

THE WHY OF CHANGE

It's pretty obvious why our Higher Power wants us to change: He/She wants us to be happy – individually and collectively. It might not feel that way when we're in the midst of catastrophe, but sometimes we need an impetus to change. We get stuck in our ruts and need something significant to get our attention.

It's up to us whether we change for the better or not. We can become bitter or better.

> To change and to change for the better
> are two different things.
> - German Proverb

THE BENEFITS OF CHANGE

Change can produce enormous and extensive benefits, for us as individuals and for the planet as a whole. As discussed in previous chapters, we become stronger after enduring a crisis.

Benefits in Evolution

The objective of Survival of the Fittest is to encourage evolution, or progress. The physically, intellectually or emotionally strong endure over those with lesser abilities.

The problem, as discussed in the Basic Assumptions, is that it can lead to Social Darwinism, which is when an individual or group feels the need to subjugate another person or group in order to ensure its own survival.

But now we have the opportunity to realize that our crises have a purpose: to direct us to pursue a new form of advancement. Spiritual Darwinism affirms that those with more highly evolved spiritual connections and enlightenment will be the ones who not only survive in the evolving world, but also thrive.

> It is not the strongest of the species that survive,
> nor the most intelligent, but the one that
> proves itself the most responsive to change.
> - Charles Darwin

Benefits in Relationships

In the Pathwork lecture #44, entitled *Love, Eros and Sex*, they define the driving force behind lasting relationships as Eros, or continuous discovery. This is the "spark" that often dies when we've been with someone for a while, because we think we know all there is to know about him or her. Eros, "the adventure, the search for knowledge of the other soul," can only happen when the partners are unguarded with each other, and open to changing and evolving.

"Eros strengthens the curiosity to know the other being, as long as there's something new to find. The moment you believe you've found all there is to find in the other soul, and as long as you reveal yourself, Eros will live. Without Eros, many people would never experience the great feeling and beauty that is contained in real love."[53]

> Eros = Discovery = Change = Evolvement

Benefits in Illness

Barbara Brennan, in her book, *Hands of Light,* talks about the life-changing benefits of illness. When change is forced upon you by illness, it's "...simply a message from your body to you that says, 'Wait a minute: something is wrong. You're not

[53] http://www.pathwork.org/lectures/P044.PDF

listening to your whole self; you're ignoring something that's very important to you'..." So listen to what your body is saying. It could save your life.

> The truth is that our finest moments are most likely to occur when we are feeling deeply uncomfortable, unhappy, or unfulfilled.
> For it is only in such moments, propelled by our discomfort, that we are likely to step out of our ruts and start searching for different ways or truer answers.
> – M. Scott Peck

HOW HAVE YOU CHANGED?

How has your crisis changed you? I've always said the most important thing in any relationship is to find someone who brings out the best in you. The same is true of a crisis. Has it brought out the best – or the worst in you?

> I can be changed by what happens to me.
> but I refuse to be reduced by it.
> - Maya Angelou

It's not only okay to admit that you've had angry, damaging or even self-destructive thoughts. It's healthy and a step toward healing – as long as you know how to process these feelings (which you will learn to do in the chapter on Resolving).

How Have You Changed?

Start thinking of all the ways you've changed since your crisis began, both positive and negative, and enter answers to the following questions in your journal:

- Have you experienced any unfamiliar emotions?
- Have you done anything you'd never done before?
- Do you do something more now than you did before your crisis, like sleep, eat, cry, etc.?
- Has anyone told you that you seem different?
- Have you changed physically at all?

- Do you sometimes not recognize yourself?
- Have you met anyone new?
- Have you seen a different side of the people close to you?
- Has anything surprised you?

Remember that real change can take time, and the only real change we can experience is internal change.

HOW DO YOU WANT TO CHANGE?

Look at the areas of your life that are being affected as you identified them in the chapter on Understanding Your Crisis:

- Relationships
- Financial/Career
- Home
- Job/Career
- Self-Image/ Reputation/ Credibility
- Physical/Health Problems

These are the areas that are subject to change. It's up to you, whether you embrace change or fight it.

> Life is change. Growth is optional. Choose wisely.
> - Karen Kaiser Clark

How Do You Want to Change?

Ask yourself these questions.

- What feelings do you want transformed – into what?
- What activities do you want to stop?
- What activities that stopped when your crisis happened would you like to bring back into your life?
- What beliefs do you have that you want to change, if you could?
- What internal things do you want to change?

- If you could change something about your body, what would you change?
- What external things?

Imaginary Lives

Julia Cameron, in her innovative book, *The Artist's Way – A Spiritual Path to Higher Creativity,* challenges us to ask ourselves, "If you had five other lives to lead, what would you do in each of them?"

If you could live the same life multiple lives, how many lives can you imagine?

> Man cannot discover new oceans
> until he has courage to lose sight of the shore.
> - Andre Gide

Some choices might exclude others. For example, one choice involves being in a relationship and another is being single. Or you could find a conflict, if one choice is job security and another is an entrepreneurial venture. But, for now, think of all the alternative lives you could lead from this moment forward.

Now think of how your recent experience might be the stimulus that puts you on the new road that could make it happen.

> Change takes but an instant. It's the resistance to
> change that can take a lifetime.
> - Hebrew Proverb

Self-Pity and Victim Mentality

If you find any resistance to the material and concepts throughout this book, you may be embracing a victim mentality. That's because sometimes it can be easier to be a victim than to change. Everyone wants sympathy or understanding, but when you blame your problems on someone else, you become a perpetual victim. A victim, because you fail to take any responsibility for your plight, and perpetual because you're unlikely to change. After all, if it's someone else's fault, then there's no room for you to change, so the problems will continue and continue. That is, until you recognize that there are Reasons Why that can explain your problem – and that you have complete responsibility and control over making the changes necessary to overcome them.

Yes – it takes work. But it's a lot more fun to embrace change than it is to avoid it, believe me!

Understanding in Self Pity

Honestly answer the following questions, using both your analytical, Outer Self and emotional Inner Self:

- Have you ever known anyone who seems to be a victim?
- Can you see any similarities between you and them?
- What could be the benefits in staying a victim?
- How is self-pity helpful?
- What are the downsides in self-pity?
- What could be the benefits in changing?
- What would you have to do to change?

> Love of our fellow man can ensue only when we stop condemning, fearing and hating each other.
> Such radical change, however, can be disorienting; the courage to endure the temporary discomfort of growth is required, and the mind tends to resist change
> as a matter of pride.
> – David R. Hawkins

ARE YOU READY to embrace change?

The Big Reason Why

CHAPTER 13: DIAGNOSIS: WHAT IS THE CAUSE OF YOUR CRISIS?

The purpose of this chapter is to help you consider which of the Five Reasons Why apply in your situation.

The Reasons Why Workbook contains a wealth of exercises, including left-brain (analytical) and right-brain (creative) tactics to discover your truth. I'll suggest some traditional and obvious methods and some unusual approaches as well. You made a commitment to be open-minded – this is the time to remember that.

WHICH OF THE FIVE REASONS WHY EXPLAINS YOUR SITUATION?

By now you should have read all the chapters and understand each of the Five Reasons Why and how they explain all kinds of traumatic events. You've also learned that the "big reason why" is to instill change. In the preceding chapters, you were given a whole host of problems people encounter and the possible explanations of Karma, Subconscious Sabotage, Lessons, Tests, and Rewards that could've created that particular kind of crisis.

253

ANALYTICAL APPROACH: WHAT DO *YOU* THINK?

We often have a feeling, at least on some level, of why things happen to us. I asked this question in the chapter on Understanding Your Crisis. Now, ask yourself again: Why do you think this happened to you? This is an instantaneous response question – what are the first thoughts that come into your mind?

Which of the Five Reasons Why Applies to You? Do you have a gut feeling on which of the Five Reasons Why are causing your crisis?

- Karma?
- Subconscious Sabotage? By you toward yourself or by others toward you? Or was it part of a group event?
- What is the Lesson (or Lessons)?
- Has there been a Test?
- Can you see a Reward? Is there the potential for a Reward or gift?

Or could it be a combination of more than one Reason Why?

TECHNIQUES FOR DETERMINING YOUR REASON(S) WHY

Our Three Selves are the key to diagnosing and comprehending our crisis on the deepest and highest levels. As you now know, our Inner Self is not only our connection to the Collective Unconscious, but also to our Higher Self, and our Higher Self is our link to the Divine.

If our Inner Self is satisfied, we'll be more creative, fun-loving, playful, and even intuitive, because if our Inner Self isn't attended to, all connections to our Superconscious or Higher Self is blocked.

> When our Basic (Inner) Self is troubled
> by a deep sense of guilt and unworthiness,
> it punishes us through illness, accidents, failures
> (big, dramatic ones, or strings of little ones)
> or other forms of self-sabotage (such as selecting a
> business partner who robs us, choosing an
> incompatible marriage partner, and so on.)
> We make these "choices" on a subconscious level.
> - Dan Millman

CONNECTING WITH YOUR THREE SELVES

In Chapter Eight, you were asked to name your Inner Self. Did you do that? If not, please stop now and do so. Because of the strong role the Inner Self plays in diagnosing the cause of your crises and in the prevention of future crises, he/she must be recognized. While it's beneficial to name each of your three Selves, it's critical to do so with the Inner Self, in order to connect with our Self and our Higher Power.

Naming Your Selves

The best way to get in touch with your Inner Self is to unearth his or her own unique name, which is separate from yours. It's very helpful to identify a name for each of your three Selves. It may sound like New Age nonsense to name your Inner Self, but it's extremely helpful, and even critical to identifying the ways you might be creating Subconscious Sabotage in your life. By coming up with a separate name, you can give that part of you its own identity, its own motivations, its own talents and opportunities.

If you didn't do this in the chapter on Subconscious Sabotage, please perform this exercise now. The Reasons Why Workbook has a lot of great ideas to help if you get stuck!

One of the characteristics of your Inner Self is that "they' will be much more likely to communicate with you when their basic needs are met – when you're fed, comfortable and rested. My

Inner Self loves to exercise and she opens the channels of communication frequently when I'm at the gym doing cardio or on a hike.

Now you need to pay attention.

Be prepared: once you acknowledge your Inner Self, "they" will want your attention – be ready to listen! I have a friend who quickly identified the name of her Inner Self (it was what she called her imaginary childhood friend) but afterward didn't give it much more thought, so she didn't do the exercise I had recommended. She called about two weeks later and said she thought she was going crazy, that the weirdest things had been happening to her: She was sure she had locked the door, but found it open. She was sure she had set the alarm, but it was turned off. Plus, things were missing. I told her, "It's your Inner Self trying to get to notice her!" She had "awakened the giant within" and now "it" wanted her attention! Once she asked the questions below, the unexplained things stopped happening.

> Ending the war inside yourself means bringing the conflict among all your personalities to an end.
> You can relieve the shadow self of its burden of held energies from the past and thus create a condition for inner peace, since it is fear of being hurt that makes your inner voices mistrust one another.
> But you can't begin to resolve these inner tensions until you know what your inner personalities are made of.
> – Deepak Chopra

Some questions to ask your Inner Self:

- Will you confirm to me that you are my Inner Self, my body, my subconscious?[54]
- I'm sorry I haven't known how to contact you before. What would you like to talk about?
- How are you feeling?

---

[54] It's important to get confirmation that the "voice" you communicate with is indeed your Inner Self, and not an outside force.

- How can I help?
- How do you feel about this communication?
- Will you help me open up communication with our Higher Self?
- Can you help me diagnose which of the Five Reasons Why are influencing my current situation?
- (If yes,) What do you think is the Reason Why this happened to us?
- Do you think it was Karma?
- Do you think Subconscious Sabotage was involved?
- Are there any Lessons I need to learn?
- Am I being tested in any way?
- Can you see if there's any Reward or Blessing in Disguise in this situation?

ADDITIONAL TOOLS FOR IDENTIFYING YOUR REASONS WHY

Meditation

What is meditation – and how does it differ from prayer? Many of us confuse the difference between praying and meditating. In essence, prayer is talking to God, and meditation is listening to God.

Just as in human conversation, effective communication requires both talking and listening. Meditation allows us to clear our minds and become open to listening to our Higher Power, while prayer gives us the opportunity to express our desires.

> Many kinds of meditation exist; their tradition in both East and West is guided by the principle that you have a core of Being or essence that can be entered.
> Access comes not by thinking or feeling. Rather, to meditate is to go directly to the silent region within.
> – Deepak Chopra

257

As Deepak Chopra suggests, there are several kinds of meditation, each using a different technique. Extensive research has been conducted on the physiological and psychological benefits of meditation, including stress reduction, lower cholesterol, self-realization, decreased depression, more restful sleep, improved integration between brain hemispheres, enhanced creativity, increased immunity, better grades in students, better job performance in workers, and even a reduction in crime rate and attainment of world peace!

The three primary kinds of meditation are Mind-Clearing or Transcendental Meditation, Sitting or Directed Meditation, and Guided Mediation.

Mind-Clearing or Transcendental Meditation

Transcendental Meditation, or TM, is a form of meditation where the goal is to reach Nirvana or Universal Peace. The pathway for this and similar forms of meditation is to become very still, either repeating a mantra, focusing on breathing or visualizing a color and then allowing the brain to release all thought.

A few years ago my (then) 17-year-old nephew asked me my thoughts about drugs and alcohol. I suggested meditation and told him that reaching Nirvana is better than any drug. It's a high with no downside – only positive repercussions. Essentially it is connecting to Spirit, the Divine or God.

> The way to assess ourselves and others is through relaxed spiritual contemplation and meditation, and the time to start is in the present. Contemplation means concentrating on a specific subject or object – the idea of loving kindness, for example, or the beauty of a butterfly. Meditation requires keeping the mind completely blank, in a state of mindfulness or awareness, free to accept whatever feelings, ideas, images or visions enter it and letting associations flow to all aspects of the object or thought – to understand its

> form, shape, color, essence. It is the art of observing
> without thought, without mental comment.
> - Brian L. Weiss

Mind-Clearing Meditation [55]

To do a mind-clearing meditation: Start by praying for protection and guidance. Then, decide what you'd like to "focus" on: a color, your breathing, a single word or feeling (like peace), or even just looking at the inside of your eyelids.[56]Sit comfortably. There are many types of poses you could do, but the primary goal is to be comfortable, without your arms or legs crossed, yet not so comfortable you'll fall asleep. Relax, breathe normally, and think of what you've chosen to focus on. When a thought enters your head, gently release it and come back to your focus point. Your breathing will slow down considerably the more you relax. Your mind may go completely blank, like you're in a kind of void. This is good! It might be fleeting, but it's the sign of Nirvana – the ultimate goal.

When you come-to, you'll feel more peaceful and refreshed – which will open a pathway for both your Inner Self and your Higher Self to communicate to you.

Directed Meditations or "Sitting"

Sitting, or Directed Meditations are designed to help you receive specific information or guidance from your Inner Self, Higher Self, or Higher Power. Think of a specific question you want answered, and ask it out loud. Then sit comfortably, relax, clear your mind and wait for the answer to come to you. When the answer does come, ask, "Is this from the Highest Source?" You should get a "yes" answer right away. If you don't, and especially if you feel uncomfortable at all with the answer,

---

[55] TM is a specific type of meditation taught exclusively through instructors. There are several books on alternative Mind-Clearing mediations; some are listed in the Bibliography.

[56] I did this for the first time on a whim a few months ago and loved it. It was kind of a psychedelic experience. It is best done when there is at least some natural light in the room or nearby. Just allow your mind to enjoy the swirling of colors.

disregard it and ask again. The information should be completely peaceful and loving. Make a note of the information you receive.

Guided Meditations

Guided meditations come in a few forms. Some just direct the listener toward a path, without requiring a response or thought. Another kind of guided meditation prompts the listener to react in certain ways, through breathing or relaxation. A third kind of meditation is intended to help the participant connect and open communication with their Inner Self, their Higher Self, their Spirit Guides or all three.

Guided meditations usually have a purpose, it could be relaxation, reprogramming the subconscious, gaining information or reaching enlightenment.

Dreams

> It is a common experience that a problem difficult at night is resolved in the morning after the committee of sleep has worked on it.
> - John Steinbeck

You can get a lot of information and assistance through dreams, especially if you know how to interpret them. I've been getting prophetic dreams for most of my life. I use *The Dreamer's Dictionary,* by Lady Stearn Robinson and Tom Corbett to help me analyze them. I feel like this particular tool works for me because my Inner Self knows that this is the book I'll reference when I wake up. Any dream analysis book can work for you, but I recommend you stick with just one. (You don't want to confuse your Inner Self). I've found it beneficial to dissect my dream symbols, whether it's a caution of jealousy nearby, a sign that success is on the way, or that I'm being protected.

There are basically three kinds of dreams:

Electrical impulses

- These dreams are just the release of the day's electrical impulses. They're easily recognizable, because they contain symbols, sights and thoughts you had that day. These happen the most when you're very stressed, but they're preventable, if you do a Mind-Clearing mediation.

Communication from your Inner Self and/or Higher Self

- These are the majority of your dreams if you meditate regularly or do other stress-reduction exercises, and are the ones worth analyzing.

Communication from the Collective Unconscious, including the Inner Self of others

- These are very rare, but sometimes someone else's Inner Self will come to visit you in your dreams. It's difficult to explain how you can tell the difference between these and the second type, but it "feels" different. It's always someone close to you – they may be consciously aware of thinking of you, or it may be solely their subconscious (Inner Self).

- These kinds of dreams can also come from the souls of people "on the other side," who like this method of visitation because it's the easiest for us to accept.

To get information from your Inner Self and/or Higher Self about your Reasons Why, all you have to do is ask the question aloud before you go to bed, and ask for the answer to come to you in your dreams. When you awaken, don't rise too soon. Keep your eyes closed and try to remember every detail you can. Then write it down as soon as you can!

Astrology

I've had people ask me about astrology. Is it bunk or is it valid? My answer is that it can be a very helpful way to get insight into yourself and others. I'm not sure if it has been "proven" scientifically, although I do own a complicated book on the physics of astrology. I say, "There are a lot of ways that the Divine can talk to you. It just depends on how you're listening."

I'm not saying every astrologer is acting in accordance with Divine Will, just like not every clairvoyant or even every psychologist is aligned with Spirit. You'll have to decide for yourself if it's meaningful, loving and associated with your Higher Power.

Empirically, there seems to be some merit to astrology. I have a book called *The Birthday Book,* by Gary Goldschneider and Joost Elffers, that I've brought out at birthday parties and work occasions. The writers break down sun-sign astrology into birth date (not just birth month). In the dozens of people I've shown it to, it's usually uncannily accurate. (On occasion, however, it's totally off…)

Astrology may explain the destiny we chose before we were born, which means it could indicate some of the key challenges and obstacles we're likely to face – including, potentially, some Karma, Lessons, Tests and Reward.

If you follow astrology (or numerology), look at your resources. Check books, articles, and your chart (if you have one) to see if there are any signs or patterns. If you go to an astrologer, ask him or her to point out anything that might help you diagnose your Reasons Why.

Morning Pages (Free Flowing Writing) and Automatic Writing

Julia Cameron, in her extraordinary book, *The Artist's Way*, introduces us to a device designed to help writers and other artists get the creative juices flowing.

My interpretation of the technique is that it's a way to release the thoughts from our Inner (and sometimes Higher) Self. It's a free-form way of writing, with no purpose other than the release of thoughts, emotions and ideas. The reason it's suggested as a morning activity is that our Inner Self is most open to us when he/she is comfortable and relaxed.

Another similar method of accessing information from our Inner Self and Higher Self is called Automatic Writing. In this case, you (your Outer Self) isn't aware of what is being written.

It can be done in either with your eyes closed and you "block out" what you're writing, or in a trance state. It's a tool used in Freudian psychology and other studies of self-exploration.

Mind Mapping

Mind Mapping is a brainstorming and problem-solving tool that helps you access your creative right brain. Defined by Wikipedia[57], "A mind map is a diagram used for linking words and ideas to a central key word or idea. It's used to visualize, classify, structure, and generate ideas, as well as an aid in study, problem solving and decision making."

Mind mapping has been used since the Third century, but it has been contemporized by authors Tony Buzan (*The Mind Map Book: How To Use Radiant Thinking To Maximize Your Brain's Untapped Potential*, and *Mind Maps At Work: How To Be The Best At Your Job And Still Have Time To Play*) and Michael J. Gelb (How to Think Like Leonardo da Vinci and *Mind Mapping: How to Liberate Your Natural Genius*).

I used a form of Mind Mapping to outline this book, when the concept was really rough. All I knew at the time were the 5 Reasons, but I had no idea how to organize my thoughts. I started with one page and put the title of the book in the middle, and from there drew spokes or legs outward, naming each chapter and other ideas. Then I took each of the Five Reasons Why and created a separate Mind Map for each. I am by no means an expert, so if you're interested in this technique, you'll want to do your own exploration and training. (Who knows, once this book is published I might become an expert! I know my Inner Self would like that!)

Mind Mapping is a fun way for you and your Inner Self to play together. I don't recommend the mind mapping software because it's too linear – too left brain – which isn't the best way to release your Inner Self. But there are a lot of good books and information on the internet that can help you.

---

[57] www.wikipedia.com

Kinesiology

Kinesiology,[58] also called Applied Kinesiology, Diagnostic Kinesiology or simply Muscle Testing, is a way for your body to "talk" to you.

According to the International College of Applied Kinesiology, it "AK is a system that evaluates structural, chemical and mental aspects of health, using manual muscle testing with other standard methods of diagnosis."

AK uses what they call the Triad of Health, which asserts that the underlying cause of a problem can be attributed to one of three areas: Mental/Emotional, Chemical, or Structural. AK, or Muscle Testing, uses your body (which is actually your Inner Self) to "tell" you what's wrong with you.

AK is most commonly used by chiropractors or other health practitioners in order to diagnose allergies, spinal misalignment, and other physical maladies. However, it can also be used as a tool for psychologists and therapists to retrieve information from our Inner Self, which was my experience.

Hypnosis

Hypnosis is a close cousin to Guided Meditations, although it's usually used in person by someone who is a licensed practitioner. You could find someone to guide you to discovering your Reasons Why though several approaches. You could investigate present-life memories, do a past-life regression or even explore your "between" life or pre-birth planning session. You could also ask your hypnotist to help you connect with your Subconscious or Superconscious.

> What if you went back to a past life
> and saw yourself dressed up for Halloween?
> Would you think you had really been a vampire?

---

[58] I introduced the concept on Kinesiology in the chapter on Subconscious Sabotage, including a brief description of my phenomenally helpful experience with its use.

Tarot and Palm Reading

If you're knowledgeable and experienced with reading Tarot cards, you could go this route in diagnosing your crisis. Alternatively, you could get a reading by a respected clairvoyant or psychic.

Psychic/Clairvoyant Reading

If you know of a good psychic or clairvoyant, you might consider going to have a reading. There are many with excellent talent for connecting with guides, who can give you advice and suggestions on your Reasons Why.

There is also some whose connection may be questionable. If you go this route, I suggest you consider the following recommendations.

- Get a good reference before you go. Make sure he/she is understanding and enlightened.
- Don't take anyone's advice or direction without meditating and asking for validation from your own Higher Self.
- The information could be beneficial if it's loving and peaceful and in alignment with your three selves.

STILL NOT SURE? HERE'S WHAT TO DO

If all this hasn't helped, and you still don't know your Reasons Why, don't worry too much. In the next chapter we'll go through all five of the Reasons Why, so just to be sure you can resolve all five areas!

Diagnosis: What is the Cause of Your Crisis?

CHAPTER 14: THE REMEDY: RESOLVING THE REASONS WHY

> Resolve and thou art free.
> - Henry Wadsworth Longfellow

By now you probably have a good idea what the Reasons are for your Crisis. This chapter will discuss ways to remove the causes, so you can move past your problem and move toward long-term healing.

The Reasons Why Workbook has dozens of exercises and activities to help you resolve your Reasons Why.

> "Inquire within, rather than without, asking:
> 'What part of my Self do I wish to experience now in the face of this calamity?
> What aspect of being do I choose to call forth?'
> For all of life exists as a tool of your own creation,
> and all of it events merely present themselves as
> opportunities for you to decide, and be, Who You Are"
> – "God" (Neale Donald Walsh)

No, this isn't a promise that your difficulties will disappear overnight. Depending on your troubles, you'll still likely be dealing with the specifics of your predicament, and you'll always have the experience of your crisis "with" you, just as I always know I went bankrupt. But once you identify and resolve the cause, you gain more control over your situation and improve your emotional responses. You'll find your outlook and attitude significantly improved and will be able to achieve Functional Happiness, even in the midst of circumstantial unhappiness. You'll become more than a survivor – you'll turn into a Thriver.

The following entry in my journal demonstrates the internal peace that has come to me from this understanding:

> I'm writing this book as I'm about to lose my home to imminent foreclosure. I sit out on my deck and listen to the waterfall in the pond I dug and built. I enjoy the landscaping I carefully designed and managed. I've lived in this home longer than anywhere in my life – just over seven years. Yet, soon it will all be gone. Thankfully I have a friend who's lovingly and generously offered me her extra bedroom to move into. Yes, I can – and do – allow myself to mourn the loss. But what I won't allow myself to do again (now that I've learned what I write about in this book) is to fear what may come. Not only because I know that my thoughts create, and that any thoughts of fear could produce the very thing I fear, but also because I know that change – even loss – can lead to many wonderful, beautiful things. Who knows where I'll be living a year from now? Many, many extraordinary experiences could be over the horizon. I won't even focus and try to visualize a specific outcome because I know that God's vision of my future may be vastly more beautiful than any I can conjure. So, instead, I give thanks for what I have, now, today. I have a beautiful

spring day in a lovely environment that I designed – with Divine help. Right now, today, I have food in my refrigerator, a number of friends on speed dial, loving parents, and a healthy body which may not be perfect but which I appreciate and treasure nonetheless.

Dr. David R. Hawkins, in his book, *Power vs. Force*, distinguishes the difference between treating and healing, describing healing as "to bring about an absolute removal of the cause of the condition, rather than mere recovery from its symptoms." Dr. Hawkins uses the following analogy, "It's one thing to prescribe an anti-hypertensive medication for high blood pressure; it's quite another to expand the patients' context of life, so that he stops being angry and repressive."

The goal in this chapter is to heal you, so you can reach this place of internal peace and joy, of functional happiness. To do that, we will:

- Address the areas of your life affected which were identified in the chapter on Understanding Your Crisis and provide suggestions for understanding and clearing.
- Establish the connection between the Outer Self (conscious mind) and Inner Self (subconscious).
- Connect with your Inner Self, to help you face, feel and free feelings that may be holding you back from happiness.
- Help you confront and put an end to your fears.
- Resolve the Reasons Why, to help you improve your life circumstances.

UNDERSTANDING YOUR CRISIS

In the chapter on Understanding Your Crisis you went through a review of your crisis to help you gain clarity on what you're going through. Now I'll briefly revisit this information and discuss what actions to take, to help you resolve the issues in your analysis.

Events and Potential Elements

Has your perspective changed in any way on the five events and potential elements? Revisit the following:

Role

It's unlikely you'll have changed your answer about your role, but you may now realize that even if the crisis isn't happening to you directly, there's still a Reason Why it continues to be affecting you. Therefore, it's still a sign there's something you need to recognize and resolve.

If the crisis is happening to someone not close to you, but still affecting you, you'll probably need to dig deeper and figure out why it's bothering you. It's likely to be caused either by something in your past that you haven't healed, or by some kind of fear. Either way, it's a strong signal that something in your life needs to change.

Cause

Has your answer changed? Are you now more aware of the effects of Karma or Subconscious Sabotage? It's healthy to take more responsibility for your own actions, because this gives you more control in order to be able to establish changes in your life. First, you need to forgive and love yourself, because you may have had some guilt or remorse, even some self-reproach. But now you should realize that there are a lot of factors, conscious and subconscious, that contributed, but which can also be cleared.

Time perspective

If you chose the first answer, that you fear the event may happen, you're in a unique spot, not that it's easy. Often worrying about something is actually worse than it happening. It's because you probably fear the unknown, and aren't sure you'll get the support (internal or external) that you need to endure.

© 2006, 2016 Brownell Landrum

If you know what's coming, and it's unavoidable, or it's something that's in process, then you'll need to align your three selves, process your emotions and prepare a new plan for your future.

Finally, if it's something from your past, you'll need to face and free the emotions that evolve from unresolved feelings, such as guilt, remorse, anger and resentment.

Area of Life Affected and Degree

It will be interesting to see if your answers have changed in this section, either in looking at the areas of life affected, or perhaps the degree has changed a bit. Maybe you now know that it's not so bad, since you have learned more about the Lessons or perhaps Reward involved. Even if nothing has changed in this section, this chapter will provide the tools to enrich the areas of your life that are affected.

Length of Impact

Of course, it depends on your situation as to whether you can completely eliminate your problem, especially if you expect it to affect you for the rest of your life. For example, if you had to have a limb amputated, it won't grow back. But you'll be able to move past your malady and adjust to discover a genuinely fulfilling life.

However, for other problems that are expected to last a lifetime, anything is possible – especially once you've recognized and resolved your Reasons Why.

Repeat Patterns and Downward Spiraling

Repeat patterns and downward spiraling are now much easier to understand: they stem from unresolved emotions from your Inner Self.

Characteristics of Crises

Change in Future Direction and Change in Day-to-Day Activity

To help you process the changes you're going through, you'll be taken through training, to help you in re-planning your future. In addition, you'll be guided through daily meditation.

Reduction/Elimination of Pleasurable Activities

One of the Lessons we need to learn in life is to enjoy its pleasures. Sometimes we punish ourselves by withholding things we enjoy. By resolving the darkness, you will be able to move toward the lighter, more enjoyable side of life.

Change in Relationships

Relationships will change, when we go through difficult times. While we cannot change anyone else, we *can* change ourselves. When you connect with our Inner Self and Higher Self, and once you process and release negative emotions, you'll be able to restore (or at least improve) nearly all of your relationships.

Separation from Others

Sometimes we're separated physically from others because of a significant loss or even death. And sometimes we just feel isolated. This chapter will help you integrate your selves and merge with the Divine, helping you reestablish your connection to others and the planet and even restoring your faith that you can spiritually connect with loved ones who have passed on.

Challenge of Faith or Trust

If you haven't already, it's my wish for you that by the time you've completed this book, you've reached a new level of faith and trust, and know with your entire being that your Higher Power is an endless supply of love.

You now have a better understanding of the motivations of other individuals, and that they're often driven by a misguided Inner Self. I'll help you heal the trust in the relationships that can be healed, and release with love the ones that cannot.

Harmful Habits

A disregarded, immature or hurt Inner Self causes all harmful habits and addictions. This is good news, because he/she really wants your love and attention and, when you provide it, you can gain control over harmful habits.

Responsibility and Burden

An overwhelming sense of responsibility and burden is common through a crisis, but it can be resolved by understanding your emotions and connect with your Inner Self. In addition, asking for – and receiving – help and guidance, whether from your Higher Power or from others, is very therapeutic and helps relieve the pressure of taking on all the responsibility yourself.

THE CONNECTION BETWEEN THE OUTER SELF AND THE INNER SELF

No matter what the reason is for your tragic event, this section is crucial. If your Reason Why was Karma, then this is the only way to stop the karmic cycle and react in the higher way. If your Reason Why was Subconscious Sabotage, then you already know the power of the subconscious mind, either your own or that of others. If the purpose of your crisis was to learn a Lesson or pass a Test, you'll have a difficult time resolving these, if you're not connected on all three levels. If your Reason Why was to achieve a Reward, it may mean you're already aligned. But if you have any residual negative or destructive emotions, you'll benefit from this learning.

You should now have a name for both your Outer Self and your Inner Self. (The name for your Outer Self is your given name, and you discovered the name for your Inner Self in the last chapter. If you don't have a name for your Inner Self yet, you need to have one before reading further, because it will be nearly impossible to resolve your Reasons Why without this important information).

As you now know, our Outer Self is our conscious self – the one we're aware of when we're paying attention. This is the "self" that makes decisions and is usually in control. However, our Inner Self will take the driver's seat in one of three circumstances:

1. When we feel threatened. This is the flight or fight mechanism to help us deal with a perceived danger, and it could result either in physical or emotional responses.
2. When our bodies have needs. Since our Inner Self is our physical being, he/she will do what they can to get us to become aware of their needs. This can be when "they" are hungry or thirsty. It can also be when it craves sunshine and fresh air, or when they need physical exercise.
3. When they're giving us messages from our Higher Self – cautions, as well as helpful information. This can happen to help us avoid an accident or threatening situation or to help us find guidance and solace when we need it.

The problem is that our Inner Self can become "difficult," if we don't listen to him or her. They can scream or cry in inappropriate situations. If they're emotionally or physically tired, they will make us sick to get us to rest. If we don't exercise, it will manifest in dangerous ways like high blood pressure or overweight.

There are also times when we don't recognize that our Inner Self is following our instructions. Because they take things literally, it can look like they're "against" us. For example, we might stub our toes when we abruptly change direction, without thinking about it. Or, we may search and search for an object, only to find something else we'd been looking for. This can happen in extreme ways. If we say we "hate our lives" or "would rather die," they can create what we're asking. Or if we say "I need a break" they will accommodate – either "helping" us lose our jobs or getting sick in order to rest.

There are other times when our Inner Self is working in accordance with our Higher Self to help us meet our Divine goals, but we don't recognize it, so it looks to us like they're sabotaging us.

The good news is it's quite easy to have a healthy communication with your Inner Self. Techniques include expressing emotions (in a safe environment), having journaling dialogues, doing free-flowing writing, affirmations, Neuro-linguistic programming, dream analysis, "checking in" with your Inner Self on a regular basis, and more. Left-brain and right-brain exercises are both helpful, individually or combined.

> "You have to let it all go, Neo. Fear, doubt and disbelief. Free your mind."
> - Morpheus (Laurence Fishburne) in the film The Matrix

EMOTIONS AND FEARS

Emotions and fears are created when our Inner Self senses threats that our Outer Self either doesn't understand or hasn't processed. Before we can understand emotions, we need to express the residual feelings we have from our past.

> Feelings are the means through which we can discern the parts of itself the soul seeks to heal, and through which we come to see the action of the soul in physical matter. The road to the soul is through your heart.
> - Gary Zukav

Expressing Emotions

Emotions and fears are energy that builds up until it's released. The longer it's held inside, the more the pressure increases. We need to learn how to safely and effectively release the emotional valve, because once we liberate our Inner Self, to channel his or her feelings, we feel amazing relief and peace.

Crying, kicking and screaming, wallowing, throwing a tantrum, being a brat, even acting ridiculous or silly, all come from our Inner Self. These actions can be damaging, when expressed at inappropriate times and unfitting places, especially in public. Neither men nor women want to be seen crying in a work situation and, although we might feel justified, it's embarrassing to scream at someone else, even while driving.

The reason our society frowns on public displays of emotion is that they usually come when our Conscious Self lets our Inner Self take over, which means that it's usually immature and unproductive. But, when consciously directed, the expressing of our emotions can be a beneficial and healthy release. So how do we "consciously direct" our feelings?

Crying is one of the best things we can do. It releases toxins, as well as pent-up energy, which is why we usually feel better following a good cry. Crying is analogous to rain: rain is necessary in order for flowers and crops to grow. Too much and there's a flood; too little and there's drought.

> There was no need to be ashamed of tears, for tears bore witness that a man had the greatest of courage, the courage to suffer.
> – Viktor E. Frankl on his experiences in a WWII concentration camp

> Life's disappointments are harder to take when you don't know any swear words.
> - Calvin & Hobbes (Bill Watterson)

> Crying washes the soul clean.
> - George Anderson

Resolving Emotions

Our emotions come from the deepest part of us, our subconscious or Inner Self, and, unless they are resolved, stay with us for our entire lives. In the chapter on Understanding Your Crisis you looked at a list of emotions and identified whether they applied in your situation – either as feelings generated by you, from others toward you, or by those around you. As discussed in the chapter on Subconscious Sabotage, emotions manifest as energy in our physical bodies, which can cause diseases and other physical and behavioral maladies.

Positive Intent of Negative Emotions

Believe it or not, there's usually a positive intent or message hidden inside a "negative" emotion. For example, aggression usually comes from fear, which means you don't feel loved or protected enough, so the positive purpose could be that it's a sign that you need more love from others or to love yourself. Although destructive (to yourself and others), it could be a way to "survive" or protect your body from harm. Another example is despair, which can mean a cry for help and hope.

> When you strip down the layers and get to your soul,
> there is nothing that can be taken away.
> This is the essence of freedom.
> - Brownell

> Do what you fear and fear disappears.
> - David Joseph Schwartz

RESOLVING FEARS

> You gain strength, courage and confidence by every experience in which you really stop to look fear in the face. You are able to say to yourself, 'I have lived through this horror. I can take the next thing that comes along.' You must do the thing you think you cannot do.
> - Eleanor Roosevelt

One of the beneficial side effects of understanding your Reasons Why is that now you realize everything happens for a reason and you have some degree of influence on not only what happens to you, but how you handle the problems thrown your way. Fear works two ways. First, the more we fear something, the more we draw it to us. But it also interferes with our desires. If we aspire to something, because we fear its opposite, then we not only don't attain the goal, but we bring forth that which we fear. For example, if we fear loss of love, and therefore hold onto

277

love too tightly, the relationship deteriorates. Or, if we fear failure, we cannot achieve success because of our fears.

Therefore, there's a lot to learn through our fears. In fact, this is the reason we experience the things we fear – to help us eliminate the fear itself. Once you experience something you've feared, and truly learn from it, you no longer have the fear of it. For example, fear of water is a reasonable fear, but once you learn to swim, you no longer need the fear.

> As long as you have fear, it is sometimes inevitable that you experience what you fear in order to lose the fear.
> If fear can be shed by realizing the truth that there is no reason to fear, then it is not necessary to experience it.
> – Pathwork Lecture #130

Fear carries powerful emotions – often as bad as going through the actual experience. This has, in fact, been proven with research using brain scans. For some people, anticipating pain is truly as bad as experiencing it. Have you ever noticed that worrying about something is worse than it happening? When you were a child, you may have been afraid of school, but once you went, you weren't so afraid. Can you remember something you worried about that wasn't so bad in hindsight? For me, worrying about losing my possessions was much worse than the actual experience. In fact, releasing the attachment to my possessions turned out to be a freeing experience.

In Daniel Gilbert's book, *Stumbling on Happiness*, he sites research proving this point, explaining that the anticipation of potentially tragic events is consistently worse than the experience of that event.

Reading this far may have already helped you alleviate some of the fears identified in the chapter on Understanding Your Crisis. Just in case, however, let's go through each of the kinds of fear and discuss ways to eliminate them – so that you can put an end to the Karma, Subconscious Sabotage, Lesson or Test that was the purpose for your tragedy.

> Nothing in life is to be feared.
> It is only to be understood.
> - Marie Curie

Fear of Death

Fear of death is arguably the most common and pervasive fear of all. It influences people from every demographic group, regardless of age, background, financial, religious, and education level. It's the one thing we all have in common, a fact that we will all face at one point of our lives.

But fearing death can affect our ability to live happy lives. As with any fear, we'll draw to us what we're afraid of. This is the purpose for many illnesses – to face death, so we remember to find meaning in *life*.

> It is impossible to truly love life
> as long as one fears death.
> - Pathwork Lecture #130

As established earlier, one of the basic assumptions of this book is that there is life before and after death, which means you should have some level of belief in the hereafter. But if you have a fear of death, it means either you still have some doubt, or you're afraid of what it will bring.

The more I read and learned about death, the less afraid I became. I've read just about everything I could put my hands on, from a variety of sources. I've read stories from Hospice volunteers, working with terminal patients, and first-hand accounts of people who have legally died and been resuscitated (called Near Death Experiences, or NDEs). I've delved into religious and spiritual texts, as well as research on hypnotic regression into "life between lives." And I've poured through articles and internet sources. The more I read, the more similarities I found between the sources.

> As death, when we come to consider it closely, is the true goal of our existence, I have formed during the last few years such close relations with this best and truest friend of mankind, that his image is not only no longer terrifying to me, but is very soothing and consoling! I thank my God for graciously granting me the opportunity of learning that death is the key which unlocks the door to our true happiness.
> - Wolfgang Amadeus Mozart

When facing a fear, I ask myself, "What's the worst thing that can happen?" and then, "Can I deal with it?" For example, the time I received notice of an irregular mammogram, I asked myself those questions. What was the worst thing that could happen? I would need a biopsy. Could I deal with it? Yes. Next: surgery. Could I deal with it? Yes. Next: radiation. Could I deal with it? Yes. Next, death. Could I deal with it? Yes.

Once I went through all the fear-based scenarios and realized I could handle anything that came my way, the fear held no power over me.

> Millions long for immortality who do not know what to do with themselves on a rainy Sunday afternoon.
> - Susan Ertz

We may fear death, but do we really want to live forever? In the movie, *The Green Mile*, based on the Stephen King story, Tom Hanks' character is punished for doing his job in facilitating the execution of an extraordinary prisoner, as he said, "killin' a miracle of God." His curse? He has an extremely long life, seeing everyone he cares about die before him. "And you, Elaine. You'll die, too. And my curse… is knowing that I'll be there to see it. It's my torment, you see…. I will have wished for death… long before death finds me. In truth, I wish for it already."

We can agree that we don't want to live forever, but most of us are still afraid to die. So what is fear of death? Fear of the unknown. Fear of how we'll die. Fear that we'll be punished in the afterlife.

If we have any of these fears, it's a sign that we need to be more prepared for the inevitable.

If the best way to reduce the fear of anything is to face what you fear, then how do you diminish a fear of death? The answer is to learn more about it and be prepared.

> Never knock on Death's door.
> Ring the bell and run like hell. He hates that!
> - Will Rogers

Learn about Life after Death

> In time of trouble, I had been trained since childhood,
> read, learn, work it up, go to the literature.
> - Joan Didion

The more you learn about something – especially death – the less you fear it. There are numerous resources on the subject.[59]. A search on Amazon.com showed over six thousand results! Choose the one that resonates with you the most. Here are a few suggestions:

- There are several books by Raymond Moody, who pioneered the study of Life after Life.
- For a first-hand account of NDEs, *Saved by the Light* by Dannion Brinkley was a bestseller.
- I also really like *Journey of Souls* by Michael Newton.
- Pathwork Lecture #130: *Finding Abundance Through Fear* (www.pathwork.org/ lectures /P130.pdf)
- The website www.Afterlife101.com is exceptional, and I recommend it highly.

---

[59] There's even a *Complete Idiot's Guide*, believe it or not!

Talk about Life after Death

Get together with friends or family members and talk about what they think they'll encounter on the Other Side. Some of the questions you could ask each other are:

- Is there anything you're afraid of?
- Who do you think will meet you when you transition?
- What do you think _____ (someone who's passed over) is doing now?
- Do you believe in reincarnation? If so, why? If not, why not?
- Are there any questions about life after death that you'd like to have answered that your church/synagogue/faith doesn't answer?
- Who do you think is in your immediate soul group?
- If you could see anyone you want, who would you like to see when you get there?
- Have you ever thought about your life review?

Or…better yet…read my book, *Sometimes I Wonder* to them and discuss! Yes, it's officially a "children's book," but it's much more than that! Because of the simple, lyrical writing and to-the-point messages, it can help facilitate a lot of valuable discussion!

> Everything science has taught me strengthens my belief in the continuity of our spiritual existence after death.
> I believe in an immortal soul. Science has proved that nothing disintegrates into nothingness.
> Life and soul, therefore, cannot disintegrate into nothingness, and so are immortal.
> - Werner Von Braun

How Do You Want to Die?

Contrary to popular opinion, I believe most people have some influence over how they'll die, based on my years as a hospice volunteer. Most people prefer to die peacefully at home, not in a hospital or nursing home, hooked up to tubes and monitors. Many people choose to die quickly, while others hang on to life, for various reason, not always fear.

When my uncle was diagnosed with cancer, he was determined to attend a reunion of his Royal Air Force flying unit from WWII. Once he accomplished his goal, he passed away peacefully shortly thereafter.

One of my patients was cared for lovingly and tenderly by her daughter and lived a year longer than the doctors predicted. Conversely, another patient had a relative who reversed their "Do not resuscitate" order request and the patient endured a miserable existence.

Most of us remember the Florida case where dozens of people debated on the fate of a woman with severe brain damage. No matter on which side of the debate someone found themselves, no one would have wanted to be in her place.[60] Exploring your feelings about death and your preferences surrounding your own can do a great deal to reduce and even eliminate the fear of dying.

> When you learn how to die, you learn how to live.
> - Mitch Albom

Deciding how you want to die is a very personal matter, and should not be judged by anyone. But preparing for the experience is imperative.

> I want to die at a hundred years old with an American
> flag on my back and the star of Texas on my helmet,
> after screaming down an Alpine descent on a bicycle
> at 75 miles per hour. I want to cross one last finish line
> as my stud wife and my ten children applaud,
> and then I want to lie down in a field of those famous
> French sunflowers and gracefully expire,

---

[60] I think this case also demonstrated two other interesting things. First, many people seemed to be exhibiting their fear of life after death in order to take the position that they did. Second, it sent a message to the public of the importance of making your end-of-life care decisions in advance by having a Living Will.

> the perfect contradiction
> to my once anticipated poignant early demise.
> – Lance Armstrong

How Do You Want to Be Remembered?

Write your obituary. What are the final words you see being spoken about you, if you had lived the kind of life you want to live? What is unique about you? What will people remember? Start with basics: When, how, where and with whom you died. Include your surviving family and career accomplishments.

> Too often we underestimate the power of a touch, a smile, a kind word, a listening ear, an honest compliment, or the smallest act of caring, all of which have the potential to turn a life around.
> - Leo Buscaglia

Feel better? I hope so! Now, the fun part. Like Jimmy Stewart's character George Bailey in the film *It's a Wonderful Life*, we have all probably made a difference in the lives of others, some without realizing it.

- People you helped
- People who you helped find purpose or direction in life
- People you made smile or laugh
- People you made feel important or special
- People you comforted through difficult times
- People you love or loved
- People you taught or helped learn something
- People who you mentored or for whom you set an example
- People who helped you
- People who helped you find purpose or direction in life
- People who made you smile or laugh
- People who made you feel important or special
- People who comforted you through difficult times
- People who love or loved you

- People who you learned from

Actions to take:

For the people you helped:

- Thank them for the opportunity to make a difference and give thanks to all three of your selves, because you wouldn't have been able to do it without their assistance and integration.
- Give thanks to the Divine for the gifts you have, which you were allowed to share.
- Ask to be shown more opportunities to make a difference in others' lives.

For the people who helped you:

- Thank them for their love and assistance – preferably in person. Send them light and love. If possible, ask them how you can help them in return.

Remember their gifts and ask the Divine for opportunities to be a help to others.

> If you love someone, hurry up and show it.
> – Rose Zadra, Age 6

When we pass over to the other side, we all experience a review of the life we just lived. The following excerpt from Dannion Brinkley's *Saved by the Light* is a good description of the life review he encountered during his near-death experience:

> "As my body lay dead, I was reliving every moment of my life, including my emotions, attitudes, and motivations. The depth of emotion I experienced during this life review was astonishing. Not only could I feel the way both I and the other person had felt when an incident took place, I could also feel the feelings of the next person they reacted to. I was in a chain

reaction of emotion, one that showed how deeply we affect one another."

By going through this profound experience, Dannion Brinkley's life was forever changed. The good news is that you can go through the life review before you die, and without a NDE.

Fear of God

One of the key messages in this book is that the Divine is pure love, and not vengeful, angry or to be feared. I've often wondered about the phrase "God-fearing," used as a human attribute. Why would someone fear God? How can you fear love? I guess it's easy to understand people fearing God, prior to understanding the Five Reasons Why. They may blame tornadoes, hurricanes and other natural disasters as "acts of God." They might think of God as being vengeful. To me, the worst thing you can say about the Divine is that He/She gave us this beautiful, magnificent planet, but also gave us the ability to destroy it – and ourselves.

We need to remember that our Higher Power loves us – our souls are a reflection of this Power. When we hate each other, we're saying we hate God. When we harm each other, we harm God. And when we disrespect and destroy our planet, we destroy God's creation.

Fear of Lack of Love

Fear of lack of love comes from the inability to love yourself. There are two solutions to this fear. First, you need to connect with your Inner Self and resolve any painful emotions. He/she needs your love and support.

Second, you need to realize you are lovable – everyone is lovable. You're lovable, even if your history may establish a pattern of lost love or abandonment. How do I know you're lovable? Because you are a child of God. Because everyone has something lovable about them. The following quote from

Marianne Williamson's book *A Return to Love.*[61], is one of the most beautiful, extraordinary collections of words ever written:

> Our deepest fear is not that we are inadequate. Our deepest fear is that we are powerful beyond measure. It is our light, our darkness that frightens us. We ask ourselves, Who am I to be brilliant, gorgeous, talented, fabulous? Actually, who are you not to be? You are a child of God. Your playing small doesn't serve the world. There's nothing enlightened about shrinking so that other people won't feel insecure around you. We are all meant to shine. We were born to manifest the glory of God that is within us. It's not just in some of us; it's in everyone. As we let our own light shine, we unconsciously give other people permission to do the same. As we're liberated from our own fear, our presence automatically liberates others.

As discussed above, the Divine is love and since the Divine is omnipresent, we're never, ever without an endless source of love. All we have to do is ask for it. Simple! Sadly, I went through most of my life without knowing this fact and just learned it about six months ago. But better late than never!

Now, whenever I want, I can ask my Spirit Guide for love and I'm showered with the most powerful love. No matter who you are, no matter what your belief, the same love is available to you 24 hours a day, 7 days a week, 365 days a year – 366 on leap year! Don't believe me? Try it! It works any time, any place. It's especially helpful when you're depressed or fearful, and the results are amazing, when you ask for it when you're angry or upset.

---

[61] This quote is often falsely attributed to Nelson Mandela, who used it in one of his speeches.

> Beloved, let us love one another: for love is of God; and every one that loveth is born of God, and knoweth God. He that loveth not knoweth not God; for God is love. Beloved, if God so loved us, we ought also to love one another. There is no fear in love; but perfect love casteth out fear: because fear hath torment. He that feareth is not made perfect in love.
> - 1 John 4

The first time I did this, I couldn't believe how easy it was — especially for something so incredible!

Loving Your Selves

The second source of love that has an endless supply is your ability to love yourself. Or, I should say, your Selves.

Do you love your body? Your face? Your emotions? Or do you put yourself (your Self) down? If you can't love your Inner Self, you'll never be able to give or receive love from someone else.

I used to hate to look in the mirror. I avoided it as much as I could. And I would beat my Self up in other ways, like putting my Self down and complaining about my self-sabotage behavior. But once I became friends with my Inner Self, amazing things started to happen. Not only could I look in the mirror, but I could also look my Self straight in the eye and say, "I love you." When I physically feel good, I tell "her" that I love my body. And I'm a good friend to her, as well. I listen to her, asking her what she would like to do especially when I feel conflicted or confused about something.

This doesn't mean that you should become arrogant. Arrogance and attitudes of superiority come from Social Darwinism and Survival of the Fittest – the need to put someone else beneath you in order to feel strong. Remember the piano keys analogy: no one note is superior to any other.

For many of us, we feel as if there's something wrong with us, if we love ourselves. But the beauty of separating and naming your Inner Self is that now you can love "him" or "her." Instead of saying "I'm tired" you can think, "_____ (my Inner Self name) is tired" and you can take care of them – even if you wouldn't take care of yourself.

Look in the mirror, directly in your own eyes, and say, "I love you." Watch how he/she will smile back. Do every time you look in the mirror – especially those times when you catch your reflection. If you notice something you don't like – some stress or fear or other emotion – then look at your Self and ask, "What's wrong? How can I help?"

If you've been deprecating your Self for a long time, you may face some overwhelming emotions. Allow yourself to feel them and work on reducing them.

Loving and Being Loved by Others

If our fear is lack of love by another person, the Beatles summed it up nicely:

> As wise men once said, what matters in the end
> Does the love you receive match the love you spend?
> - From *Sometimes I Wonder* by Brownell Landrum

What if you don't feel like this applies to you? If you feel like you've given someone else all your love, but he hasn't reciprocated? There are a few things you can do. First, you have to really love your Inner Self.

Second, you have to look at the degree and characteristics of your attachment to receiving his love. If you have any fear associated with losing his love, if you feel you "need" them, then it's a sign something is missing from inside of you and this "hole" can never be filled by someone else. It can only be filled by the Divine or within yourself.

The movie quote, "You complete me," is romantic nonsense. No one should look outside themselves to be completed – you need to already be complete within yourself before you can be in a healthy relationship. I've heard the phrase, "You'll meet someone when you least expect it," but I think it should be changed to, "You'll meet someone when you least need it." This is the only way to have a healthy relationship.

The third thing you can do when you seek another's love, is to ask yourself, "Do all three of my Selves love all three of their Selves?" I asked this of a friend once and her reaction was memorably profound. She was instantly clear that, no, she didn't love all three of the other person's selves. She knew she loved his Higher Self – the best of him – but she also knew that she could never love his tortured and torturing Inner Self.

Fear of Not Being Good Enough

If you identified this fear, the question I would ask is, "What are you not good enough for – and why?"

The next question is: "What ARE you good enough for and how can you use those skills to resolve this fear?"

Fear of Rejection

Many of us have a fear of rejection. Somehow we worry if someone "really knew us," she'd reject us. This fear comes from a wounded, isolated Inner Self and the result can be manifested in several ways. Some of us cover the fear by exhibiting an aura of superiority, which allows us to reject others, before they reject us. Others of us hide or distract ourselves behind our jobs, our physical flaws, or even in an unhealthy relationship or job. And some of us just isolate ourselves and give up trying for a new (or better) relationship, job or achievement.

I have a close friend who's been avoiding finding a new relationship because of a fear of rejection. I told her to face the fear and ask herself, "What if you met someone who rejected you for that reason?" I said it would be an instant sign that they weren't right for you – which would be a blessing!

Fear of Loss

If you recognize you have a fear of losing something or someone, I commend you, because recognizing the fear is critical to releasing it. The following quote from *Star Wars'* Yoda is valuable advice:

> "The fear of loss is a path to the Dark Side. Train yourself to let go of everything you fear to lose."
> - Yoda, (Frank Oz) Star Wars: Episode III—Revenge of the Sith

Fear of Loss of Money/Property

Have you ever noticed that when you're happy, you don't care as much about possessions but when you're unhappy or under a lot of stress, you tend to collect stuff – clothes and other possessions? Or that when you're unhappy, you dream of material things?

We aren't really looking for possessions. We're looking for feelings. We don't want a new car as much as we want status or luxury or safety. We don't want a vacation home; we want to go somewhere to relax. We don't want more money in the bank, we want security.

Fear of Loss of Mental or Physical Abilities

If your greatest fear is of losing your mental or physical abilities, it's the same as any fear of loss. Not only can fearing something bring it to you, but it can be relieved by facing the fear and releasing it.

Many years ago, my father discovered the magic of being able to videotape his favorite shows. When he got a little obsessive with making nearly one hundred tapes (each with three to six movies or shows), I asked him, "Why are you making so many tapes?"

His response floored me. He told me he was making videotapes of movies to watch, if he ever became incapacitated. What a great exercise in facing your fear! Not only was he preparing for something that most of us fear, but he was actually creating the opportunity to look forward to it! [62]

---

[62] He is still around, and so are the unwatched tapes. He's 84, and hasn't started watching the videos. He wishes now that the movies he has were DVDs, because he believes he'll outlive the videotape technology.

Fear of Being Trapped

> What we don't let out traps us.
> - Sabrina Ward Harrison

The fear of being trapped may have several underlying fears. We may fear being blocked physically (in an elevator, in a car, or in a body that doesn't work optimally), or confined in a particular situation (relationship, job, financial crisis, etc.)

As discussed in the Lesson on Choice, the remedy for a fear of being trapped is to reclaim your power for looking for alternatives and having the freedom to make a choice – not only in what direction you will take, but also in how you will handle the situation. For example, if you found yourself physically trapped in solitary confinement in a jail, or on a deserted island, you would still have things you could do. You could pray and meditate and find a closer relationship with your Higher Power, you could conjure up solutions to life's problems, etc.

Going through a crisis can free us from the traps of destructive situations. The quote, "It is only after we have lost everything, we are free to do anything" symbolizes the message here. We are able to start from scratch.

Fear of the Unknown

> The main element of fear is not a particular undesirable factor or event, but the unknown quality about it.
> - Pathwork Lecture #130

Like the other fears, Fear of the Unknown is alleviated when you anticipate all the options and potential outcomes and know that you can handle whatever life throws your way. But it also requires another important personality attribute: a sense of adventure.

Would you really want to know everything that's going to happen in your life? What fun is that? It would be like watching the same movie over and over, knowing how it will end every time. How boring!

Sure, it's comforting to know some of the things that will happen, so you can be prepared. I'll go over these in the next chapter. For now, however, you need to see whether your fear of the unknown has brought on (or is a part of) your crisis, and, if so, alleviate it. Since your fears come from your Inner Self, you'll need to go to him or her to unearth your unknown fears.

> When you have come to the edge of all light that you know and are about to drop off into the darkness of the unknown, Faith is knowing one of two things will happen: There will be something solid to stand on
> or you will be taught to fly.
> - Patrick Overton

The antidote to a Fear of the Unknown is to discover a sense of adventure.

> A man practices the art of adventure when he breaks the chain of routine and renews his life through reading new books, traveling to new places, making new friends, taking up new hobbies and adopting new viewpoints
> - Wilfred Peterson

Fear of the Future

Fear of the future could include fear of an impending event, fear of old age, or fear of the unknown.

Think back on something that you were afraid of at one time in your past. It could've been a fear of drowning, when you were learning to swim, or a fear of first grade that memorable first day, or some other "first." Remember how you weren't sure how you could make it through? But you did, somehow. You're still here.

All of us can think of examples of things we feared. Yet, by facing those fears and taking action, you learned you could get through a lot of things you initially believed impossible. In many instances, you became more than a survivor. You became a thriver.

Fear of Pain and/or Ill Health

No one wants to be in pain or suffer ill health, but so often we're so terrified by our fear that we live in denial. In the next chapter, you'll learn ways to prevent ill health, but first you need to remove the fear of pain associated with your current tragedy.

There are many kinds of healing out there, from traditional medical to holistic approaches to faith healing to new treatments and technology. Most, if not all, have the potential to be effective. However, it has been my experience that none can be fully effective, unless you identify the purpose and resolve the reason for the pain or illness. Even if one ailment is relieved, another will often appear to teach the Lesson.

The following quote from Pathwork lecture #58 describes the purpose of pain.

> "Pain is allowed (by the Divine) to serve a constructive purpose. When the purpose is fulfilled, there ceases to be pain. Instead of wallowing in the feeling that suffering is senseless…you will soon come to the point where the painful occurrence gives you an important new recognition about yourself, freeing you forevermore. The moment this recognition is reached, the pain ceases, even though the outer connection that created the pain still prevails. The very incident that has caused you acute pain before the recognition now becomes a source of joy."

Fear of Betrayal/ Misplaced Trust

Fear of betrayal or misplaced trust comes from a past experience of being cheated or lied to. Before you can remove the fear, you will need to heal the past. First, you'll need to release and forgive the person who treated you badly by forgiving him or her, apologizing for any questionable part you may have played. This is important, because you may have some responsibility in the reason she betrayed you. If you expected the worst in her, if you didn't trust her, she may have simply lived up to your expectation.

> Forgiveness is a gift you give yourself.
> - Suzanne Somers

Most of us need to heal our Inner Self by apologizing and forgiving him or her. Apologizing, because he/she may have tried to "warn" you, but you either ignored or denied him/her. Have you ever been in a situation that was harmful in some way and, after the fact, say to yourself, "I just knew I shouldn't have done that!" or "Why did I go out with (do business with, etc.) that person? I knew I shouldn't have trusted him or her!" Our Inner Self gives us these kinds of warnings all the time – we just sometimes don't listen. By the same token, we need to forgive our Inner Self for not giving us stronger warnings.

Fear of Evil

Evil was defined in the Basic Assumptions as: "morally bad or wrong; harmful injurious; unlucky, disastrous; wickedness and sin." Now you know that most of the so-called evil in the world can be explained by (pre-enlightened) Survival of the Fittest and the Five Reasons Why.

The good thing about evil is that it's predictable, especially when it's a function of someone fighting for survival. When people of a lower-consciousness are backed into a corner or feeling threatened, they're predictable. They will almost always act in their own self-interest, which can include greed, violence, anger, hatred and revenge.

> Knowing your own darkness is the best method for dealing with the darknesses of other people.
> – Carl Jung

This doesn't mean everyone is selfish or capable of viciousness when challenged. Thankfully, there are loving, understanding, enlightened people all over the planet, who realize generosity and fairness result in not only a loving attitude but also, ultimately, produce a much greater Reward.

In the next chapter, I'll help you become better prepared for (and even prevent) evil. In this chapter, we need to address any fear of evil you may have, as a result of your crisis. You may be worried about revenge, continued abuse, or residual violent emotions.

OTHER COMPONENTS OF FEAR

> Fear is the mind-killer. Fear is the little-death that brings total obliteration. I will face my fear. I will permit it to pass over me and through me. And when it has gone past, I will turn the inner eye to see its path. Where the fear has gone there will be nothing. Only I will remain.
> – Frank Herbert

In James Redfield's book, *The Tenth Insight*, he suggests the following solutions for moving past fear:

- Attune with the Divine by asking for guidance.
- Align with courageous and wise individuals who inspire us.
- Remember that even though we may feel insecure, we're not alone.

Fear vs. Desire

Fear and desire seem to be opposite emotions; however, sometimes they're two sides of the same valueless coin. When we want something badly, we need to look at the desire and determine if the main reason we want it's because we fear its opposite. For example, we may want love, because we fear we're unlovable, or that we'll be lonely. We may want financial success, because we're afraid we'll be left homeless or because being wealthy is the only way we feel like we're worthy of someone's love or attention.

> If you want happiness because you fear unhappiness, happiness remains unreachable. If you want happiness for its own sake and not because you fear its absence, nothing will block its attainment.

> The key is the element of fear.
> – Pathwork Lecture #130

We need to see if your crisis is masking a destructive fear as desire.

Resolving Grief and Loss

Although grief is a result of the loss of someone (or something) and not the cause of a crisis, in order to resolve the crisis, you're going through, it may be helpful to have tools to cope with your anguish.

As mentioned in My Story, I recently lost a great love (in addition to my business, my house, my dog, etc.), and I did one thing that proved to be very helpful.

I made a list of all the things I loved about him. Every time I thought of something that made me miss him, I wrote it on the list. (I used an electronic list, which I preferred for a few reasons. First, it allowed me to edit and rearrange the items on the list. Second, I could make sure I didn't repeat anything and third, I liked that it was on my hard drive on my computer, which was more permanent than a written list, yet also less "in my face" as putting it in my journal.)

The exercise was very helpful for a number of reasons. It allowed me to acknowledge and honor the things I loved about him. It gave me something to potentially share in the future. And, most importantly and most powerfully, once I typed something into the list, I could let it go. The conscious and subconscious thoughts and feelings I had were now established and preserved, allowing me to stop thinking about them.

Whether your loss was of someone, or if your loss was of a way of life (freedom, independence, mobility, etc.) or of something tangible or material (money, home, possessions, etc.), you may need to dig deeper into your feelings.

ENDING THE KARMIC CYCLE

There are four simple steps for ending the Karmic Cycle:

- Stop the harmful, destructive behavior
- Apologize and offer to make amends
- Forgive yourself
- Forgive others

DISCONTINUING SUBCONSCIOUS SABOTAGE

As you know, Subconscious Sabotage can come from your own Inner Self, the Inner Self of another person, or through group thoughts (the Collective Unconscious).

To End Self-Sabotage:

- All the exercises for releasing emotions (Face it, Feel it, Free it) and connecting with your Three Selves will help immensely.

To Halt Subconscious Sabotage from others:

- Connect with your Higher Self, to ask for signs of negative thinking and energies coming from others and how to prevent them.

To Stop Group Subconscious Sabotage:

- If you find that you're very upset at world events, follow the advice of Dr. Andrew Weil and take what he calls a "newsfast," which means not watching the news for a period of time. According to Dr. Weil, there has been research that demonstrates "the emotional content of television news can affect mood and aggravate sadness and depression. Addictive watching of news programs can also promote a negative view of life." Personally, I don't watch the news. I don't want to be exposed to events that I cannot influence.

- Consider the group consciousness of any company, club, organization, political party, or religious group you may belong to, and re-consider your participation if you recognize any of the following:

- Acting superior or Subjugating (putting down) another group as being inferior or beneath them. (Social Darwinism).
- Vicious and/or unfair competition.
- Acts or endorsement of violence.
- Condemnation or judgment toward others.
- Lack of compassion or understanding for the less fortunate or people who are different.
- Responding with anger or hatred, instead of peace and love.

LEARNING THE LESSONS

Review the Lessons again, and ask yourself the following questions:
- When you read the Lessons in that chapter, did any of them resonate with you?
- How are you doing in learning that lesson?
- Are you prepared to pass a test to ensure the learning?

Now let's address and resolve some of the key Lessons.

ACCEPTING OTHERS – EVEN ACCEPTING THAT SOME PEOPLE ARE NOT HIGHLY OR FULLY EVOLVED

Who in your life have you not accepted for being who they are? What about the groups or organizations you belong to or participate in, and the groups or individuals they may have judged or not accepted? You should have considered these people in your life review exercise. If you didn't, please make a list of these people and go back and do the exercise to resolve these judgmental feelings.

> Resolve to be tender with the young, compassionate
> with the aged, sympathetic with the striving,
> and tolerant with the weak and the wrong.
> Sometime in your life you will have been all of these.
> - Dr. Robert H. Goddard

Useful Anger

Anger can be useful, if it's a motivator for change. For instance, injustice stimulates people to work for justice. War can encourage people to rally for peace. Outrage at global warming can increase awareness and communication. Irritation with unreasonable health care practices incites people to protest traditional medicine. If no one had transformed their anger into action, we would still be facing the tyranny, social injustice and human rights violations that plagued the past.

> Nobody got anywhere in the world
> by simply being content.
> - Louis L'Amour

APPRECIATION

Debt and Paying Bills

Why do people get themselves in debt? Debt is created by not listening to – and taking care of – our Inner selves. In this way, debt is like overweight, addiction and many other problems we face – only rectified by facing, feeling and freeing our emotions and staying connected to our Inner Self.

To most of us, paying bills is an unpleasant experience. Some of us even get angry and feel "ripped off" by the company we're doing business with, whether it's a utility company, our mortgages or a credit card. It's a natural response of the "Survival of the Fittest' part of our Inner Self. We want to hold onto our possessions and money. The more unhappy our Inner Self is, the more tightly we hold.

In order to live happier lives we need to first, of course, face, feel and free the negative emotions, but then it's crucial that we compel ourselves to remember the pleasure received by the experience that generated the expense. The phone calls made. The heat or air conditioning provided. The comfort of our homes. The TV shows enjoyed.

Every time we exchange money, we receive something in return, and it's our choice to make that exchange. Capitalism usually allows us to make a choice between providers, so we're given some level of control. It isn't "us versus them." It's a mutually agreed-upon transaction.

The problem with credit cards is that there's too much detachment from the experience of receiving the item. We're usually paying for more than one item with one payment, which means that we cannot identify the source of the pleasure that initiated the bill. And it's likely too much time has passed between the interaction and the pleasure of the item. Another problem with buying on credit is the potentially endless debt generated, which can create a crisis in itself.

Here's a radical idea: give thanks when you're paying your bills. Thank every person involved in every transaction. Thank the person who did the installation. Thank the people who are there for customer service. Thank the people in accounting, HR, legal, marketing and every other department. Asking for Help

In a children's book I wrote called, "Sometimes I Wonder," I offer the following verses:

Or do we stew and we fuss
And blame someone else?
Instead of taking
A look at our self

Do we ask for help?
And give in return?
It's best when we realize
There's a Lesson to Learn
© Brownell Landrum

Just about anything you're going through has happened to someone else who can help you. You just have to find and reach out to them. There are a number of resources to meet people who can help you, including therapists, healers, books, websites, organizations, self-help groups and many others.

> Other people may be there to help us, teach us,
> guide us along our path,
> but the lesson to be learned is always ours.
> – Unknown

BOREDOM

The most difficult thing about resolving boredom is recognizing it. Because it can manifest as either laziness/apathy or by turning someone into a drama addict, it's sometimes difficult to diagnose and detect as being the reason for your crisis.

> When we are no longer able to change a situation - we
> are challenged to change ourselves.
> - Viktor Frankl

The Solution: Change!

Whichever your manifestation of boredom is, the solution is to change! Make a choice to make a positive difference in your life and that of others. Realize that you created the crisis (at least subconsciously) because you were bored and had too much time on your hands. The quote "an idle mind is the devil's workshop" is applicable here.

Find something fun and healthy you're interested in and focus on it! If you really are concerned with something "out there" then immerse yourself in trying to find a solution instead of worrying about it. The more you learn about something, the less you fear it and the more you can control it.

CONNECTING WITH INNER SELF (SUBCONSCIOUS)

Our subconscious minds will take direction from our conscious selves, but only when two factors are present:

- The direction/guidance should be clear, and

- We recognize and acknowledge the needs and emotions of our subconscious.

The first factor suggests we need to have clear, consistent alignment on what we want at all times. When we fail to make up our minds or change our minds, it confuses the subconscious mind.

The second factor is a reiteration of the point made throughout this book: to develop a relationship with our subconscious and connect with what our Inner Self needs.

In the previous chapter, and throughout this chapter I discussed several ways to connect with your Inner Self, to help you diagnose your Reason Why: Self-Questions, Dreams, Astrology, Free-Flowing Writing, Mind-Mapping, Kinesiology, and more. These same tools are also helpful tools to use on a regular basis.

> We are so captivated by and entangled in our subjective consciousness that we have forgotten the age-old fact that God speaks chiefly through dreams and visions.
> – Carl Jung

Daydreams: Daydreams are visions of our desires. When we pay attention, we can learn a lot about our subconscious (Inner Self). Keep a record of the thoughts that float through your head.

Affirmations

Affirmations are simple, positive statements that your conscious mind gives as a direction or "command" to your subconscious (Inner Self). Affirmations can be very helpful and influence positive change, but only if the following is considered.

- First, you need to Face, Feel and Free any negative emotions in your Inner Self. Otherwise, we can experience resistance to manifesting the visualizations.

- Affirmations should be done with the help and cooperation of your Inner and Higher Selves.

- Statements need to always be positive. For example, we should say, "I feel good," instead of "I don't feel bad."

Because your Inner Self sometimes abbreviates and focuses on the key words, he/she may read the second sentence as "I feel bad."

- Proclamations should always be supportive of each other. For example, saying both "I am relaxed and peaceful" and "I have a lot of excitement in my life" may be conflicting messages.
- Ideally, affirmations are statements in the present tense. For example, "I am healthy" instead of "I want to be healthy" or "I will be healthy."
- Affirmations should be in alignment with Divine Will, which means they should be loving. Always.

CONNECTION WITH YOUR HIGHER SELF AND YOUR HIGHER POWER

The Higher Self or Superconscious Our Higher Self is our connection to God, Divine Intelligence, and Unconditional Love.

As you now know, your Inner Self is the pathway to your Higher Self and Divine Guidance. If he/she isn't heard, rested, exercised or well-fed, he/she won't open up the communication. (This is actually a blessing, because our physical and emotional being is so important to our life and Lessons on Earth). Therefore, we need to connect with our Inner Self before we can have open communication with our Higher Self or Spirit.

> The wise man in the storm prays to God, not for safety from danger, but deliverance from fear.
> - Ralph Waldo Emerson

> Never pray for an untroubled life; Ask the gods to give you an enduring heart.
> - Menander of Athens

Simple Prayer to Align with Divine Will:

"Let Divine Will Fill My Heart
And Guide My Actions"

As you say these words, notice how naturally you'll be able to breathe in the first line, and breathe out the second line – so that you breathe in when you let Divine Will fill your heart, and that you breathe out when you say "guide my actions." The more you practice it, the more it will fall in rhythm with your breathing.

> Look at every path closely and deliberately, then ask ourselves this crucial question: Does this path have a heart? If it does, then the path is good.
> If it doesn't, it is of no use.
> - Carlos Castaneda

Meditation Techniques

Several meditation techniques can help you resolve problems, most of which we discussed in the previous chapter on diagnosing the Reasons Why.

Creative Visualization

Creative Visualization is a form of self-directed meditation in which you close your eyes and create mental images. Visualization uses the integration of your conscious (Outer Self) and subconscious (Inner Self), because you're directing the meditation, but you allow your creative self to imagine the five senses (sight, smell, taste, sound and feel) of the scene. It can be used to relax, to solve problems in the present or to "program" your future. It can be beneficial in many ways, including healing, success, Higher Self communication, sports performance and eliminating destructive emotions and habits.

Done consistently and repetitively, creative visualization works with your Inner Self to re-set your self-image and/or "encode" the direction for your future.

Deep Breathing Exercises:

Deep breathing exercises are easy to do. Just relax and breathe deeply in through your nose, hold gently for a few seconds, and release slowly through your mouth. You can imagine that the breaths in are healing or bringing in light or love, and you can imagine the breaths out are releasing toxins, cleansing, or letting out negative energy.

> The process of breathing is one of the great miracles of existence. It not only unleashes the energy of life, but it also provides a healing pathway into the deepest recesses of our being.
> - Dennis Lewis

Yoga Exercises:

There are many kinds of yoga exercises, some focusing on breathing, some on stretching, and others on strengthening or healing. Some variations can work on every muscle, ligament and internal system in your body, while others are gentle. Look into yoga as a way to find physical as well as inner, healing.

DESPAIR

> Action is the antidote to despair.
> - Joan Baez

If you don't know where to turn or what to do, if you're afraid you can't get through what's ahead of you, I know how you feel. My advice is to learn to ask for help.

> There's no place like hope.
> – Kobi Yamada

FORGIVENESS

When we're reluctant to forgive, our Inner Self is holding onto emotions we need to face, feel and free, whether they're resentment, guilt, blame, anger or fear.

One of Dr. Phil McGraw's common sayings is, 'If you do what you've always done, you'll get what you've always gotten." And, "The past is a great predictor of the future." He's clearly right. If someone has been abusive in the past, he'll probably continue his behavior (unless he has extensive psychotherapy).

The message: don't fear him – get away! Pray for their recovery and peace – *from afar*!

GIVING UP AND LETTING GO

To learn to give up is to release your fears and worries to a Higher Power. In a later chapter I'll discuss prayer. When we can't "give up" it means one of two things. We either haven't resolved the emotions or fears using one of the Face it, Feel it, Free it exercises, or we don't fully trust God.

> Giving Up is Releasing to a Higher Power.
> - Brownell

> And the reason it was life changing for me is because in that moment of surrender, I realized that when you've done everything that you can do, when you've given it the best that you know how, you surrender it to that which is greater than yourself. You survive everything. And when you make peace with that, that is when you open up the space for what is to come to you, to come. And that lesson has changed me forever.
> - Oprah Winfrey

HOPE

> When the human is exhausted by grief or remorse, covered with shame and abandoned by the world, hope glimmers and brightens into a ray of light. The human, in his darkest hours, looks for hope. While he looks for hope he cannot fail altogether. Hope shows the way by which one can save himself and earn his conscious immortality.
> – Harold Percival

Like Divine love, hope is avaliable to all of us, all the time. All we have to do is close our eyes and ask, and open our eyes and remember.

IMMORTALITY

One of the reasons we fear death is because we feel like we haven't finished what we came here to do. In some small way, we want to become immortal by leaving a legacy. The Life Review exercise can help you discover a list of people you helped make a difference in their lives, which is the first step. What are other ways to leave a legacy?

LIFE GOES ON

If you've lost someone to death and have been wondering how they're doing, I would suggest reading some books and other material from George Anderson, Michael Newton, and the website Afterlife101.com. The consistent answers from these sources are:

- They are happy; they have a new "life" on the other side.
- Whether they passed away quickly or after an illness, they want you to know that there's no pain where they are.
- You will see them again. (As a verse in my book, Sometimes I Wonder suggests, "We have friends who'll meet us, with warm open hands, and music to greet us, like grand marching bands!")
- It helps to send them good thoughts and prayers.
- It doesn't help (and in fact can hinder them), if you hold onto your grief and don't get on with your life.
- They can communicate with you, if you're listening (but they're busy, so it isn't all the time).
- They want you to be happy and joyful. They want to see you laugh and get pleasure from life. They don't adhere to the concept that it's disrespectful of the dead to release them and move on. In fact, it's a great tribute if you can move toward happy memories.

LOVE

If there is only one Lesson, it is Love.

If there is only one Solution, it is Love.

Unconditional Love

We're often told to love others unconditionally, but this is often misunderstood. Isn't all love conditional on how someone treats us? How can we love someone unconditionally, when she does something harmful to us?

Unconditional love comes from our Higher Self and the Divine. Another way to think of unconditional love is UC love – or "You See" love, a feeling that comes from opening yourself to the "sight" of higher love. From this part of ourselves we know only love and acceptance.

> Sending unconditional love to someone is like sending a signal to a satellite that then transmits the signal down to the one you love. It is detached and enhanced with much more power with the energy of Spirit.
> - Brownell

For many years, I was a volunteer counselor for a bereavement camp for children. A few years ago, we had a very troubled – and troubling girl in our cabin. She'd been abusive and violent to the other girls in camp, forcing the administration to call her father to take her home. Afterward, we got all our girls together in the cabin and instructed them to send good thoughts to this girl. They resisted at first because they were still upset and angry. But I suggested we should all send her wishes for her health and recovery – from afar. They learned that unconditional love means we can release someone to their highest level of healing and growth, without having to spend time with them.

> Anger management, health, empathy, compassion, patience and understanding, nonviolence, relationships, security, destiny and free will, contemplation and mediation, spirituality; all these are steps to immortality. All these are facets of the greatest virtue, which is love.
> Love is the ultimate lesson.
> How can you retain anger if you love?
> How can you not be compassionate or empathetic?

> How can you not choose the right relationships?
> How can you strike another? Foul the environment?
> War with a neighbor?
> Not have room in your heart for other viewpoints,
> different methods, divergent lifestyles? You can't.
> – Brian L. Weiss

MAKE AMENDS

Making Amends relates to both giving and receiving forgiveness, and is a wonderful way to alleviate anger, resolve Karma, and end Subconscious Sabotage from others.

Making Amends

Who can you think of right now who is angry or annoyed with you, or is hurt or resentful of something you've done? Have you apologized and asked for their forgiveness? Have you offered to make amends? Even if you have already apologized, it's not too late to offer to make amends. Think of what you could do to make it up to them. Make a list, if possible. This will help in your discussion with them, because it will demonstrate your true sincerity, and it will also serve to provide ideas for your talk. Accept and understand that the other person may not want you in their life anymore, but it still may help to make amends. You could do something for their charity or cause, for example.

Asking Others to Make Amends

If you're still hanging onto animosity or bitterness toward someone in your life, but you feel like he might like to make it up to you, all you have to do is think of the things that he or she could do to make it up to you, and then ask him/her to do it. I remember the first time I tried this. I had gone over 3000 miles on a business trip, to meet a work colleague, and he completely stood me up. I was furious. That is, until I thought of what he could do to make it up to me. I strongly suggested he buy me a mini refrigerator for my office, which he did. It felt so good! I could no longer be angry or try to get him in trouble and I got something in return!

If your matter is more serious – perhaps you're the victim of a crime or your mate cheated on you – your approach will be different, but the effect can be the same. If you're victimized, you need to release the emotional baggage and forgive, before you face your attacker. But once you do, if you're prepared to offer suggestions to make amends, it could be a very healing experience.

For more on Making Amends, see the chapter on Forgiveness.

RESPONSIBILITY

Now that you know there is a Reason Why everything happens, it means no one is a truly a victim. If the Reason Why is Karma or Subconscious Sabotage, then we have direct responsibility for the cause – and cure – for what is bothering us. If the Reason Why is a Lesson, Test or Reward, we have responsibility to resolve the purpose of what has plagued us.

Accepting Responsibility

Look at all the things in your life that you've blamed on someone else. Now, identify the Reason Why these things happened. Can you now see the purpose of the situation, and see where your taking responsibility for the resolution can help?

SELF-ACCEPTANCE AND SELF-LOVE

Accepting and Loving Yourself

It can be difficult for some of us to love ourselves. But we're all able to love our Selves, and we are all able to receive Divine Love at any and all times.

> Human potential is the same for all.
> Your feeling, "I am of no value", is wrong.
> Absolutely wrong. You are deceiving yourself. We all have the power of thought – so what are you lacking? If you have willpower, then you can change anything.
> It is usually said that you are your own master.
> - Dalai Lama

WILL TO LIVE/SURVIVAL

It's impossible to heal, if you have no will to live. What's the point? Sometimes people hold on for the people around them, which is at least one reason. But in order not to just survive, but thrive, it's critical to have good reasons for living.

> Keep a notebook or journal of lessons learned.
> - Rick Warren

PASSING THE TESTS

The key to passing any Tests is to know you're handling your situation with love, peace, respect and kindness.

REWARD

Have you found the Reward in your situation yet? Even if all you can see now is the potential for increased compassion for others, going through what you've been through, it's a gift. But hopefully by now you've seen ways to dig deeper and find even more Blessings in Disguise.

OTHER SUGGESTIONS

Advice From 12-Step Programs

The following "steps" from the Alcoholics Anonymous Twelve-Step Program coincide with many of the suggestions provided in this book. Whether your crisis involves an addiction or not, these are good suggestions for resolution and healing, because we:

- #4: Make a searching and fearless moral inventory of yourself.
- Be entirely ready to have God remove all defects of character.
- Make a list of all persons you had harmed and become willing to make amends to them all.
- Make direct amends to such people wherever possible, except when to do so would injure them or others.

- Seek though prayer and meditation to improve your conscious contact with God, as you understand Him, praying only for knowledge of His/Her will for us and the power to carry that out.

Attention Whiners

Sometimes it feels good to vent your problems to a trusted friend – even if all you want for her to do is listen. But whining isn't only unproductive, it can also be destructive, if continued for too long. A good friend will listen – up to a point. Eventually, she'll get tired of the tapes you keep playing over and over again. Even a paid therapist will get weary of unproductive complaining.

Be careful who you whine to and about what. It's insensitive and destructive to whine to people less fortunate than you are. Also, be careful not to talk in absolutes. "My whole life is going to hell" is rarely, if ever, accurate. Eventually, if it goes on long enough, you'll have to make one of three choices:

- Keep finding new audiences for your whining
- Make the necessary changes in your life
- Accept your life as it is (and hopefully make the best of it).

Several of the exercises in the Reasons Why Workbook will help you process the things you have to complain about, so you can make the necessary changes. Remember – it's all about change.

The Remedy: Resolving the Reasons Why

CHAPTER 15: THE BIG REASON WHY: WHAT DO YOU NEED TO CHANGE?

The objective of this brief chapter is to give you the tools for change. Has it started yet? What else do you need to change?

> I have learned over the years that when one's mind is made up, this diminishes fear; knowing what must be done does away with fear.
> - Rosa Parks

Your plans for the future may have changed, perhaps even dramatically, because of what you've been through. Therefore, it will be helpful to you to re-plan your future.

Of course, the first clue is the Reason Why your "bad thing" happened in the first place. Hopefully, you've gotten an idea about that by now. (If not, the Reasons Why Workbook has several activities to help you plan your future. And there are multitudes of other goal-setting guides and sources to help.)

CIRCLES OF CONTROL

Next, let's look at Control. What you can control and what you can't. The following diagram is from a business I started called DrawSuccess. It's called the Circles of Control.

Basically, what this concentric circle diagram is showing is that the inside circle are the things you can control, which includes where you put your effort, what your goals are, the things you focus your attention toward, your behavior, your actions and reactions, your emotions, desires and motivations.

The middle circle are the things you might not be able to fully control, but you can Influence. These include your opportunities, your health, how you spend your time, personal crises, outcomes and people you know.

© DrawSuccess

And then there are the things out of your control, like the economy, your competition, natural disasters, widespread crises, technological change, people you don't know, the weather, etc.

For the things Outside of Your Control: Prepare.

How can this help you going forward?

For the things inside your control you Act. Look at where you put your effort and attention. Define your goals. Monitor your behavior. Understand and evaluate your desires. And watch your actions.

For the things inside your Influence – you need to Understand. Before you can influence someone, understand him or her first. Get a handle on the outcomes you can influence. Identify how you spend your time, and how other people might control your schedule instead of you. And do whatever you can to take care of your health.

And for the things Out of your Control? Prepare! You might not have any control over the economy, but you can prepare for the fluctuations! And while natural disasters might be difficult to predict, many are "predictable surprises" – things that will happen someday.

The Remedy: Resolving the Reasons Why

CHAPTER 16: SPIRITUAL DARWINISM: PREVENTING FUTURE BAD THINGS

Anthony de Mello offered the following insight on suffering: "Some of us get woken up by the harsh realities of life. We suffer so much that we wake up. But people keep bumping again and again into life. They still go on sleepwalking. They never wake up. Tragically, it never occurs to them that there may be another way. It never occurs to them that there may be a better way. Still, if *you* haven't been bumped sufficiently by life, and you haven't suffered enough, then there is another way: to *listen*."

What are you listening to? Hopefully this chapter will help!

> That's the difference between me and the rest of the world! Happiness isn't good enough for me! I demand euphoria!
> - Calvin & Hobbes (Bill Watterson)

Spiritual Darwinism is a proposed new approach to "Survival of the Fittest" which reveals that the strongest and most powerful strength one can have is a close spiritual connection. With this awesome ability, each of us can't only survive and thrive as individuals, but we can also ensure endurance of the human race. Spiritual Darwinism is the key to preventing Bad Things from happening to us, our fellow human beings and the planet.

> Extraordinary claims require extraordinary proof.
> – Carl Sagan

I realize I'm making a pretty huge claim: that we can prevent future Bad Things from happening to us, and that Carl Sagan's above quote is certainly an appropriate expectation for you to have. By the end of this chapter, I plan to clearly demonstrate how you can avoid being negatively affected by problems, crises and tragedies – which is what Spiritual Darwinism.[63] is all about.

You have learned a lot up until this point. You now know the Five Reasons Why: Karma, Subconscious Sabotage, Lessons, Tests, and Reward, plus the Big Reason Why: Change. You also know how to diagnose each and have found out which of the Reasons Why are behind your recent problems. And in the Reasons Why Workbook you've been given the information and exercises to take you through the remedy to resolving the underlying cause of your crisis. You're clear and in the process of healing and moving on with your life – or at least well on your way.

Now you want to learn how to prevent future Bad Things from happening. And, while we're at it, we'll talk about how you can create more joy in your life. After all:

> Enlightenment is a waste of time unless it can help you get a better parking space.
> - Alan Marsh

---

[63] Spiritual Darwinism was first introduced in the Commitment and Basic Assumptions chapters as this author's proposed antidote to Social Darwinism.

You may be a little skeptical, but hopefully your experience has shown what a difference it can make to connect with your three Selves, release negative emotions, eliminate fears, and stop negative Karma and Subconscious Sabotage. You can now realize how empowering it is to identify and learn many of life's Lessons, just as you can feel better that you know what you can do to pass Earth School Tests. Your optimism has increased, because you've recognized the potential for Reward in even the most tragic of circumstances.

This chapter, along with the Reasons Why Workbook, will expand on what you learned in the chapter on Resolving your Reason Why and take you through additional insight, experiences, and information, to help you live a happier, healthier, more meaningful life. We'll look at the Five Reasons Why again, but instead of as a cause for Bad Things, as a source of greater joy and fulfillment. We'll also review the general categories of crises, including death, disease, crime, problems faced by people near you, and various kinds of loss (freedom, material, job, relationship, etc.) and show you how to avoid being influenced or hurt by them. And, finally, we'll have FUN STUFF to learn and practice to make life more enjoyable. Are you and your Inner Self ready?

> Behold, I show you a mystery; we shall not all sleep, but
> we shall all be changed, in a moment,
> in the twinkling of an eye...
> - Corinthians

KARMA

Resolve All Past Karma

Balance any and all Karma you've possibly created in the past using exercises provided in the workbook and preceding chapter on resolving your Reason Why, including Life Review, Forgiveness and Make Amends.

Prevent Creating New Negative Karma

To prevent creating negative Karma, always ask yourself these questions:

- Are you doing your very best?
- Are you asking for Divine Guidance?
- Are you staying connected to your three Selves? (See Integrated Alignment, below).
- Are you considering the alternatives and select the most loving, fair and respectful option for all concerned?
- When faced with conflict, are you asking what you might have done to contribute to the situation – and forgive yourself, as well as ask for forgiveness?
- Are you offering to make amends right away?
- Are you forgiving your transgressors – even if they don't ask for it? (See the chapter on Forgiveness).
- Are you having mental conversations between your 3 selves and their 3 selves, understanding their motivations?
- Are you aware of your hurtful thoughts, so you either prevent them or reverse them immediately?
- When you pray, are you following the Prayer Guidelines.[64]?

Avoid Involvement in Other People's Karma

When you become involved in other people's Karma, you take on the responsibility and influence of their Karma as well. This can happen, even if your intent is pure. An obvious example is if a friend is involved in a fight and you join in to "defend" them, harming their transgressor in the process. A gentler example is if a nation goes in to an underprivileged country and "fights" for their freedom. As soon as you take on anger or violence, you take on negative Karma, no matter what your intention is.

---

[64] Discussed in the chapter on Prayer.

This doesn't mean you can't help other people – you absolutely can, and we'll discuss it in the next chapter. But you need to act in love and peace. I know some would argue that the only way to abolish evil is to fight it. I disagree. There is always a loving solution to every conflict. Always.

> When I despair, I remember that all through history the ways of truth and love have always won. There have been tyrants, and murderers, and for a time they can seem invincible, but in the end they always fall.
> Think of it - always.
> - Mahatma Gandhi

Praying for Others

I was discussing prayer with someone recently and he said he follows a Native American belief that the only time you should pray is for someone else. Although I understand the influence and benefit in praying for others, I disagreed with him, at least in the way most people pray.

Praying for others can be a tricky – if not dangerous – situation. For example, what if someone prayed for you and you didn't agree with their religious beliefs? Or what if you prayed for someone to avoid a crisis, and it meant that he'd miss out on the Reward that would follow? I'll discuss praying for others in a later chapter, but the point here is that even praying for someone else can involve you in their Karma. And don't forget: all thoughts are prayers of some kind.

Clear Negative Karma Every Day

Even when we're integrated with our Inner Self, we'll still experience the negative emotions of anger, guilt, resentment and jealousy. The problem isn't experiencing these feelings – the problem is with allowing them to influence our behavior. Sometimes we aren't able to resist reacting strongly to situations, creating negative Karma. It may be because we're threatened and feel insecure or because we witness injustice that disturbs or infuriates us.

Eventually, we may all be able to live in peace with each other all the time. Until then, we need to clear out any Karma we create as soon as possible. Ideally, as soon as we recognize our behavior but, failing this, at least once a day.

> Man should forget his anger
> before he lies down to sleep.
> - Mahatma Gandhi

The steps are simple:

1. Review the emotions and actions of the day.
2. Face, feel, and free your negative feelings.
3. Recognize and forgive your Inner Self.
4. Apologize and ask for forgiveness from the person or people you harmed.
5. Think of ways to make amends and make a plan to follow through.
6. Send love to everyone involved.
7. Ask for Divine Guidance, to help you act in love, peace and understanding.

Instant Karma

The more enlightened and aware you become, the more instant your Karma becomes – both bad and good. You'll see an almost instant reaction to your thoughts and actions. This is helpful for your further development, because it will allow you to clear negative Karma immediately – sometimes soon enough to prevent it entirely.

Positive Karma

By the same token, instant Karma means you will reap rewards from virtuous actions. Barbara-Ann Kipfer has produced a cute book, *Instant Karma – 8879 Ways to Give Yourself and Others Good Fortune Right Now,* which lists thousands of ways to create positive Karma, from "dance whenever the spirit moves you" to "reduce clutter – it detracts from the flow of energy" to "try to experience everything as though it were brand new." The advice emphasizes the importance of physical health, spiritual growth, harmony and peace.

With positive Karma, the more love you send out, the more love returns to you. The more you act in peace, the more peaceful you become. The more you take care of yourself, the more your Self will take care of you. And even the more thoughtful and appreciative you are, the more you're rewarded with great parking places.

The way I enhance my parking space Karma is to make sure I never choose an up-front space, unless I really need one, with the result being I almost always get a close space when I *do* need one. (For which I give thanks right away!)

~~Subconscious Sabotage~~
Integrated Alignment

I'm no longer talking about Subconscious Sabotage – our new, life-affirming, resolution and prevention phrase is Integrated Alignment (IA), when your three selves – mind, body and spirit – are integrated and aligned with the Divine.

> When we align our thoughts, emotions, and actions with the highest part of ourselves, we are filled with enthusiasm, purpose and meaning. Life is rich and full. We are joyously and intimately engaged with our world. This is the experience of authentic power.
> - Gary Zukav

In the bestseller, *Blink*, author Malcolm Gladwell said, "the adaptive unconscious does an excellent job of sizing up the world, warning people of danger, setting goals, and initiating action in a sophisticated and efficient manner." With Integrated Alignment, we bring this power of the subconscious into our conscious awareness and merge it with an even more powerful force, the Divine.

Benefits of Integrated Alignment

Amazing awareness, knowledge and gifts are yours when you become integrated and aligned. With Integrated Alignment you'll feel such incredible joy, peace and love it will feel as if you're opening your eyes for the first time.

> *The great teachings unanimously emphasize that all the peace, wisdom, and joy in the universe are already within us; we don't have to gain, develop, or attain them.* We're like a child standing in a beautiful park with his eyes shut tight. We don't need to imagine trees, flowers, deer, birds, and sky; we merely need to open our eyes and realize what is already here, who we really are – as soon as we quit pretending we're small or unholy.
> - Unknown

Love

When you're aligned, your ability to love yourself (your Selves) is significantly approved. The more you love yourself, the greater your capacity to give and receive love from others. Anyone, no matter what their awareness, enlightenment or ability, can feel the shower of love when they do the exercise "Giving and Receiving an Endless Supply of Love" from the Reasons Why Workbook on resolving your Reason Why. Those who have Integrated Alignment will not only be able to access this love more efficiently, they'll also have a much greater appreciation for this divine gift and will never be without an endless supply of higher love.

> Love is the only way to grasp another human being in the innermost core of his personality.
> - Viktor Frankl

Improved Relationships

Certainly, the more loving you are, the better your relationships are. But Integrated Alignment provides even more benefits in our interactions with others. First of all, by having a close relationship with our Inner Self, we can respond, not react to situations. This is because we immediately know our own emotional responses and can therefore prevent reacting in a destructive emotional way. Instead, we'll be calmer and more rational, even when faced with emotional behavior from others.

Second, it helps us understand other people much better. Research has shown that up to 90% of our one-to-one communication is non-verbal (telepathic and body language) – the "language" between Inner Selves. So, having the close connection with our Inner Self allows us to now translate this complex and previously hidden interaction.

Because we're free from our own hidden signals, we're more open and honest with others, creating a closer bond. And since we're now better able to measure the other person's intent and motives, we can distinguish people who have our mutual interests at heart from those who don't, allowing us to avoid unhealthy, hurtful or dangerous people.

Finally, relationships with IA are infused with Eros. Remember when we talked about Eros in the chapter on the Big Reason Why? Eros, or continuous discovery, is created when we're learning, evolving and changing, and is what sparks relationships with interest and excitement.

Preventing Accidents and "Being in the Wrong Place at the Wrong Time"

Integrated Alignment provides us with innate awareness and Divine protection that helps us avoid accidents of all kinds, from stubbing our toes to auto collisions and airplane crashes. When we're integrated and aligned, all of our Selves are focused on a unified goal, preventing the confusing communication that leads to all kinds of accidents.

For example, have you ever noticed how you stub your toe or run into something when you're going one direction and then suddenly change your mind and go another way? This happens because you (your Outer Self) have "programmed" your Inner Self to a certain path and then haven't re-aligned them to a new "goal."

In a similar way, this is how auto accidents occur. When we "zone out" while driving, we're allowing our Inner Self to take over. This isn't bad, in fact it's actually critical: we can't consciously put our mind on every task we have to do. It would drive us crazy to have to remember to breathe and blink and so on. But we need to make sure to give clear direction to our Inner Self at all times to:

- Follow our instructions
- Let us know when something is bothering him/her
- Alert us to potential dangers

Because our Inner Self is aware of the Inner Self of others and of the Collective Unconscious, it is able to perceive possible threats and help us avoid them. This happens when your Inner Self is working in alignment with your Higher Self to look after your well-being. (See also Divine Intervention, below).

This phenomenon explains why two-thirds of the passengers of a doomed airplane routinely "miss" a flight. Or why some of the World Trade Center worker were late for work that tragic day in September 2001.

We "fight" Integrated Alignment when we don't listen to our Inner Self and try to "force" our conscious will.

> Are you aware of your body's wisdom?
> Our bodies usually know us better than our minds do.
> If you have a decision to make, consult your body
> before making a final choice.
> - Osho

Eliminating Destructive and Addictive Behavior

Destructive and addictive behavior occurs when we do something "without thinking about it." It can be when we eat a second donut without realizing what we've done, when we have "one too many" drinks or when we "deserve" that sweater we can't afford. It happens as a result of a wounded Inner Self's feelings have been ignored.

Once we face, feel and free our emotions and take good care of our Inner Self, we no longer need harmful habits. With the functional (inner) happiness that comes from Integrated Alignment, we're more fulfilled in each moment, and if we eat a donut we relish every bite and don't need a second one.

> As you become more clear about who you really are,
> you'll be better able to decide what is best for you –
> the first time around.
> – Oprah Winfrey

Preventing Life's Little Annoyances

When our Inner Self is ignored and trying to get our attention, it can play all kinds of annoying games with us, like losing our keys, forgetting an appointment, or turning off an alarm. Sometimes their actions come from mischief and are a way to mess with us a little, so we become aware of them. The solution is to recognize your need for Integrated Alignment.

Sometimes these things happen to help us achieve another goal we've set. For example, have you ever been found yourself so late that you miss a trip or a meeting that you really didn't want to go to in the first place? With IA, we can recognize these subconscious influences, and either prevent or appreciate them.

Instant Manifesting

One of the fun benefits of Integrated Alignment is being able to instantly manifest wishes. You'll be amazed at how you can say to yourself, "I wish I could find" an object and it instantly appears. Or, "I hope so-and-so calls" and the phone rings.[65] Because of its connection with the Inner Self of other people and the collective unconscious as a whole, our channels of communication are vastly opened.

---

[65] Please remember, however, we should never interfere with someone else's energy or destiny. And *they* have to be open, too, for the communication to be complete.

Additional Brain Power

Our Inner Self can open us up to the extra 3.997,999 bits of information per second we process but don't remember with our conscious minds. This explains why law enforcement will use hypnosis to help a witness remember events more clearly. Their conscious minds may not have any idea they even saw a car, but the subconscious can remember the license plate number!

Add to that the extrasensory awareness from our subconscious. Then add the potential information from the Collective Unconscious. Finally, supplement that information with Infinite Intelligence and we have unlimited knowledge and awareness within us at all times. This explains the 90-95% of our brain that we currently don't "use."

When our Selves are aligned and integrated, we're also better able to focus without distraction. For example, let's say you're very hungry in the midst of taking an exam. If you have IA, you'll be able to develop an inner agreement with your Inner Self to "hold off" the hunger pangs, until you complete the exam.

Creativity and Inspiration

Research has shown that your creativity can increase up to ten times, when you achieve IA, for several reasons. First, you can remember more ideas and apply them to a current situation or problem. Second, creativity comes out when your Inner Self is happy and having fun. Third, you're better able to "listen" to ideas and messages inside and around you. And, finally, creativity happens when you can see beyond the obvious and find a unique idea or solution.

Inspiration means "in spirit" or the breathing in of Spirit. Webster's defines inspiration as "a Divine influence or action on a person believed to qualify him or her to receive and communicate sacred revelation". It happens when our Outer Self releases control and our Inner Self is content, allowing an opening for messages from Spirit.

I get most of my inspirational communication when I am either just waking up or doing repetitive cardio exercise. (When my Inner Self is happy). The ideas just "pop" into my head. To help me recall the thoughts later, I keep a pad beside the bed and use the voice memo on my cell phone.

> The song was there before me, before I came along. I just sorta came down and just sorta took it down with a pencil, but it was there before I came around.
> - Bob Dylan

Enthusiasm

> Every memorable act in the history of the world is a triumph of enthusiasm. Nothing great was ever achieved without it because it gives any challenge or any occupation no matter how frightening or difficult, a new meaning. Without enthusiasm you are doomed to a life of mediocrity but with it you can accomplish miracles.
> - Og Mandino

The word enthusiasm means "to be filled with (or inspired by) God." But we also know of enthusiasm as "intense enjoyment or interest." Enthusiasm happens when our inspiration is propelled forward, with a focus toward the enjoyment of the future, with a vision of hope, faith and optimism, which is only possible with IA.

Intuition

Intuition gives us information beyond our five senses, defined as "understanding without apparent effort, quick and ready insight seemingly independent of previous experiences or empirical knowledge. "It helps us filter information that comes to us, so we can find meaning and direction. Intuition helps us recognize synchronicity in what we might otherwise call "coincidences" and makes us aware of serendipity, both of which are evidence of the Divine in our lives.

> Intuition is a spiritual faculty and does not explain, but simply points the way.
> - Florence Scovel Shinn

Intuition can also help us gain insight into other people's motivations, which not only protects us, but also connects us to each other.

Success

> To laugh often and much; to win the respect of intelligent people and the affection of children.
> To earn the appreciation of honest critics and endure the betrayal of friends. To appreciate beauty, to find the best in others. To leave the world a little better place than we found it, whether by a healthy child, a garden patch, or a redeemed social condition. To know even one life breathed easier because you lived.
> This is to have succeeded.
> - Bessie Anderson Stanley

Enthusiasm, Intuition, Additional Brain Power, and Creativity and Inspiration all contribute significantly to success in life. In addition, Integrated Alignment also means your Selves are now in partnership with Divine Will, which helps you reach more fulfilling goals. The prayer "Let Divine Will Fill My Heart and Guide My Actions" becomes as natural as breathing in and out. Because anything connected with the Divine is a reflection of love, the result will be receiving more love with everything you do. IA also means you're able to release attachment to the outcome, allowing your Higher Power to bring the highest good to come to you.

Wellness and Health

> In Tibet we say that many illnesses can be cured by the one medicine of love and compassion. These qualities are the ultimate source of human happiness, and our need for them lies at the very core of our being.
> - Dalai Lama

Cures and Prevention

A cure for the common cold? When you're able to have an ongoing dialogue with your physical Inner Self, you can't only heal diseases but also prevent them, even something so common as a cold or flu virus.

There appears to be a conflict between the scientists and "moms" on this subject. Scientists say that the only way to prevent a virus is to prevent contact with someone with the virus or at least do preventative measures, like washing hands after possible contact. "Moms," however, tell children to "bundle up or you'll catch a cold." Scientists say this is bunk. Who is right?

Let me make things clear. Both are right. Scientists are right when they say you cannot prevent a cold by keeping warm and dry. But, moms are right in that you can prevent yourself from getting sick from a virus by taking better care of yourself. If you abuse yourself, either with disregard to extreme temperatures or through other physical or emotional stressors, you're more likely to feel sick from the virus. It's scientific fact that depressed people have more vulnerable immune systems. Why? Your Inner Self is rebelling against your abuse! It figures, if you won't take care if him/her, then you'll suffer the consequences. (Remember: they just want to get your attention and love)..[66]

---

[66] By the way, while we're on the subject of colds and viruses, I have another trick that I use when I don't want to get sick. Most people I tell don't take the advice (probably because they actually wanted the excuse to stay home and be sick), but here it is: when I feel my body being worn down and achy at the onset of a cold, I drink about ¼ cup of apple cider vinegar blended with about 1 cup of water. I don't like the taste – some people do – but it absolutely works. What it does is changes your body's "system" from an acidic system (created usually, by eating highly processed, sugary or acidic foods including, believe it or not, orange juice) and turns it into an alkaline system. And a cold virus cannot live in an alkaline system. I'm not professing to be a scientist and prove any of this, but try it yourself. It WORKS!

Conversely, if you're in touch with the needs and desires of the Inner Self on a daily basis, you can prevent a whole host of physical problems. I was visiting a friend the other day who, had a serious stomach flu. She'd caught it from someone she worked with and several others were very sick. After I left her room, I could actually feel the physical effect of the virus in my energy field. So, I had a talk with my Inner Self. "I'd appreciate it if you could fight this off for me. Let me know when you need a rest, and I'll take care of you. But we have too much to do – including having fun! – to get sick right now."

> Serious illness doesn't bother me for long
> because I am too inhospitable a host.
> - Albert Schweitzer

When healing yourself of something more serious, cancer, for example, the processing is more involved. This isn't to say that all healing can be accomplished with IA, but the efforts of the best doctors, healers and medicine in the world are enhanced, when we have integrated and aligned our selves. We're able to participate more effectively in our diagnosis and healing. Now that we understand there's a Reason Why, we're open to full and complete – holistic - healing.

Happy People Are Healthier

Louise Hay's books, including *You Can Heal Your Life,* explain the emotional causes of disease. By the same token, positive emotions create positive physical experiences and sensations. In fact, research has proven a direct link between a positive attitude and the body's immune response. Neurologists at the University of Wisconsin-Madison found that the happier subjects (those with more activity in the left prefrontal lobe) had more antibodies in their system, while less positive subjects had a weaker immune response. This is because Integrated Alignment motivates us to exercise and eat healthier food, because when our Inner Self is happy, they take care of "us."

Better Sleep

We sleep more soundly when we've been able to "face, feel and free" our emotions. If we do have difficulty sleeping, it's for one of two reasons. The first, and most probable, reason is we have emotions that need to be resolved. The second reason is that we're being alerted for an important message. Once our Inner Self is relaxed, we're more open to Higher Self communication. Either way, these times are meaningful and should be recognized.

Meditation helps us release the daily electrical impulses (otherwise known as extraneous thoughts) from the day to help us attain peaceful rest and also achieve more meaningful dreaming.

Physical Pleasure

Did you skip ahead to this heading? It's interesting how quickly our Inner Self directs us to topics of sex and physical pleasure. Of course, physical pleasure includes more than human contact or sex. It also includes all enjoyable activities that involve the senses. The smell of cookies baking, the sound of a child laughing, the sight of an ocean sunset, the texture of a crisp apple, the taste of a ripe strawberry. And the "sixth" sense provides joy as well: the elation of discovering the solution to a problem, the excitement of Divine Inspiration, the peace of agreement, the directed energy of commitment.

But your Inner Self wants to hear more about physical pleasure – especially sexual union. Tantra is considered to be the unification of two souls to connect to each other in a profoundly pleasurable way, both physically and spiritually (which inherently means "with love").

Integrated Alignment allows us to connect in this way with another person. Because we've been able to recognize and release any fears or destructive emotions, only our highest intentions are expressed. And because we're connected with our Selves on all three levels, we're able to connect with our partner on all three levels. We're fully open to experiencing the highest levels of physical pleasure – and love.

And If You Do Get Sick...

Yes, you may still get sick from time to time. You may be experiencing IA most of the time, but still have bouts of fleeting disconnection. Perhaps, illness is the way to help you remember your Integrated Alignment. The following quote is a remarkable example of this:

> Strangely, perhaps, I now regard my tumor as my very young and very good friend...one who harbors no ill intent towards me...one, in fact, who has provided me with what I now regard as the greatest of all gifts...Transformation... yes... hyperbole... no...my cancer changed me for so much the better... where I myself was completely unable to help myself.
> - Man recently diagnosed with Cancer

Perhaps you're still "paying" for previous destructive behavior (to yourself or to others), and the illness is a result of Subconscious Sabotage or Karma. Illness can also contain a Lesson, Test or reveal a Reward. Being integrated and aligned with our three selves can not only help us recognize the underlying meaning of an ailment, it can always help us know the best way to proceed with our own treatment, whether it is in the correct medication to take, or procedure to have performed.

As you become more integrated and aligned, you'll be able to stop most of the problems that create disease:

- Instead of ignoring your body, you'll pay attention to it.
- Instead of hurting your body, you'll nurture it.
- Instead of abusing your body, you'll take care of it.
- Instead of hating your body, you will love it.

Inner Peace

> Of one thing I am certain, the body
> is not the measure of healing – peace is the measure.
> - George Melton

© 2006, 2016 Brownell Landrum

David R. Hawkins, M.D., Ph.D. identifies 17 levels of human consciousness in his book, *Power vs. Force*, beginning with Shame as the lowest, and up through the levels of guilt, apathy, grief, fear, desire, anger, pride, courage, neutrality, willingness, acceptance, reason, love, and joy, and then up to the highest levels of peace followed by enlightenment. According to Dr. Hawkins, peace is "extremely rare, attained by only 1 in 10 million people."

However, although there are few people who attain and remain at the level of inner peace, we all have the capacity to experience this overwhelming ecstasy. Even a tiny glimpse of inner peace can change our lives profoundly.

Heightened Ability to Help Others

I'll talk more about helping others in a later chapter. It's important to know that we often heal ourselves when we help others. We're more able to make a difference in the lives of others and in the planet when we, ourselves, are integrated and aligned. Then our gifts are pure, boundless, life-changing.

Increased Attractiveness

There's nothing more attractive than the peace, love and happiness generated by Integrated Alignment. A smile that comes from functional happiness and inner contentment makes you look years younger. Increased vitality improves your complexion and your optimism will be contagious.

You'll find people drawn to you just to share in the energy you radiate. Because you're feeling and conveying only positive, loving emotions, others will be transformed in your presence. With IA, you can channel this energy in awesome ways. The exercise in the Reasons Why Workbook on resolving your Reason Why: Feel and Send Love is a magnificent way to make a difference in yourself and the planet as well – make sure to integrate it into your daily life.

The following quote exemplifies the feeling an individual has when he/she interacts with someone with IA:

> When we talked, I felt brilliant, fascinating; she brought out the version of myself I liked most, a person self-consciousness normally held down.
> - Nuar Alsadir

Sending Positive Messages and Creating Positive Energy

In a lecture, Deepak Chopra described an experiment on meditation, where serotonin levels were measured before and after the session. After the mediation, the participants were more peaceful, as indicated in their levels of serotonin. However, the interesting part of this study is that the meditation of this group affected others nearby who were not meditating. Their serotonin levels were also significantly increased! This experiment is similar to studies done about Transcendental Meditation to demonstrate the 1% Solution we discussed in the chapter on Karma.

> Live your beliefs and you can turn the world around.
> - Henry David Thoreau

Other Benefits: Parking Places, Taxi Cabs, Etc.

Once you're connected to your Inner Self and the Divine, numerous additional conveniences come your way. You'll find convenient parking spaces when you need them most, recover lost items, and receive extra help from others.

More to Be Thankful For

With heightened awareness comes elevated joy and appreciation for even the smallest things in life, from the green of leaves to the miracle of the human body to the vastness of the universal mind. Integration with your body (Inner Self) brings a new perspective of the body you took for granted before. Every breath is magic. You're fascinated with the instinctive blinking of your eyes. The processing of food and nutrition through digestion is incredible. A sneeze is suddenly really cool. You're now blown away by the astounding power of the body to heal from even the smallest splinter. Things you may not have noticed before are now amazing and spectacular.

Even when challenges come your way, you recognize the gift within them. They could be an invitation to change something or an adventure to learn or try something new. Gratitude and appreciation become a new way of living every day.

Good Things Created by a Positive Collective Unconscious

The Collective Unconscious or Spiritus Mundi (The Spirit of the World) is the combined energy of human thought. As each person elevates his or her consciousness and reaches IA, the rest of the planet is influenced and uplifted. The results include:

- Natural beauty
    - Healing of the planet
    - Progress and learning
    - Peace between nations and individuals

LESSONS

The great thing about Lessons is that all you have to do is learn them – and remember the Lesson – in order to prevent Bad Things. Remember, the purpose of Lessons is to help us become more evolved, loving and enlightened beings. There would be no need to go through a tragedy to learn a Lesson if you've already mastered the Lessons identified in that chapter.

Remembering Past Lessons

First, we need to keep reminding ourselves of what we have already learned. It doesn't matter if you took Spanish in high school, if you no longer remember how to speak the language today. The same is true of Lessons. The following passage exemplifies this message:

> "I've gotten cancer; it's shown me things – the important things that people don't realize until they're 65. I'm going through so much, the pain of it but I'm

also getting good things, all these important lessons. I don't want to forget them quickly because the way I think life works, it keeps giving you lessons over and over until you learn them, until you remember them...I don't want to lose sight a year or two years from now of what I've learnt. Then, it might sound silly, but I think the cancer will come back to show me again, to put things back in perspective. I've got to keep in mind what I've learned and take that along...if I go back to the way I used to think, putting value on the wrong kind of things...I wouldn't be surprised if I relapsed again."
- Woman in her 20's undergoing treatment for leukemia

Learning Lessons In Advance

I was in a work situation where one of my colleagues lied to me about why I had been excluded from a particular meeting, one where a significant and unethical decision was made. When I found out about the meeting, it was clear to me why I wasn't wanted: I would have identified the mistake with conviction, and management wanted to proceed anyway. I confronted the colleague, and he falsely told me something else. This happened on a Friday.

However, on Monday he came to me and confessed what had actually happened. He'd been feeling bad about it all weekend, not just how he'd treated me, but that he had violated his personal ethics. By confessing so quickly and earnestly, it was clear to me he was preventing any potential negative Karma from coming back to him – from me or anyone else. He reinforced that he learned his lesson about year a later, by avoiding another business situation that could've put him in a position of responsibility, but also potentially compromised him ethically.

This is a good example of how we can learn our Lessons and prevent negative repercussions from our actions. We're not perfect – we wouldn't be here if we were. We all make mistakes. We have years of patterns, addictions and hard-wired brain synapses to learn from. But we can - and I certainly hope we will – learn from them, and I sincerely want each of us to learn in advance, *before* Bad Things occur.

The Lessons

The best way to measure your attainment of a Lesson is to go through each of the Lessons and ask yourself the following questions:

- Have I learned this Lesson?
- Do I model the attributes of the Lesson?
- Would others say that I exhibit this behavior?
- If tested on this Lesson, would I pass?
- Do I know enough to be able to teach it to others?

While all of the Lessons need to be mastered in order to prevent a crisis in the future, the following Lessons are the most involved in Spiritual Darwinism:[67]

ACTION AND ADVENTURE

Action takes on an entirely different meaning, when we're living with Spiritual Darwinism. When we're integrated and aligned, the path is clear. We know what direction to take and we look forward with a sense of excitement and adventure.

APPRECIATION

> Dear Lord: The gods have been good to me. For the first time in my life, everything is absolutely perfect just the way it is. So here's the deal: You freeze everything the way it is, and I won't ask for anything more. If that is OK, please give me absolutely no sign. ... OK, deal. In gratitude, I present you this offering of cookies and milk. If you want me to eat them for you, give me no sign. ... Thy will be done.
> – Homer Simpson, The Simpsons

---

[67] Note: Enthusiasm, Intuition, Peace, Pleasures and Relationships are discussed earlier in the chapter.

Being appreciative allows us to focus on the things that are going right in our life. The more you show your gratitude for the blessings in your life, the more gifts you will receive. Integrated Alignment allows us to keep our focus on the light in our life.

Asking for Guidance/to see the Signs and Awareness

Awareness is constantly unfolding, when we're connected with our three Selves and the Divine. Our eyes are always open, and signs are everywhere.

Balance

To prevent Bad Things from happening, we should keep our lives in balance. Even if our work is our true passion, it isn't healthy to work more than a certain number of hours a week. We still need time to relax, spend with friends and family, explore, learn, play, walk in nature, teach, exercise, laugh, regroup, organize, plan and breathe!

BOREDOM

> Are you bored with life? Then throw yourself into some work you believe in with all your heart, live for it, die for it, and you will find happiness that you had thought could never be yours.
> - Dale Carnegie

If you feel like you're either bored or too stressed-out, you need to look at your lifestyle. Either way, you're setting yourself up for drama and crisis. Once you learn how to love and listen to your Inner Self, and face, feel and free your destructive emotions, you'll seek out new ways to live a healthy, balanced, fun and enjoyable life.

COMPASSION AND ETHICAL BEHAVIOR

While Social Darwinism, or Survival of the Fittest, doesn't provide room for compassion (because humans in that state are too competitive), it's the natural state of enlightened beings living in a world of Spiritual Darwinism. Spiritual people know that the health, safety and survival of the less fortunate is important to the health, safety and survival of the planet.

In addition to compassion, we exhibit other forms of ethical behavior: understanding, harmony, patience, respect, tolerance, caring, acceptance, cooperation, dependability, forgiveness, courtesy, responsibility and other values that come from the highest value of all: love. By demonstrating high ethics ourselves, we're able to prevent much of the conflict and disharmony in our previous lives.

CONSCIOUSNESS

Conscious thought and action, the key to prevention, is only consistently possible with Integrated Alignment. Mistakes and errors in judgment are eliminated when we're fully awake and any disruptions are recognized as opportunities, not as a nuisance.

EVIL – ITS SOURCE, ITS WAYS, AND HOW TO AVOID IT

> You can block out or protect yourself from negative vibrations from other people by believing and connecting with God in whatever environment you are in, asking for the love of God and the protection of God to completely surround you and to be with you at all times.
> - Afterlife 101

Evil is a cancerous outgrowth of Social Darwinism and it can be both prevented and avoided. The first step is to recognize that most humans will act and react in ways to ensure their survival. When threatened, they can become evil. But when they encounter someone who is exhibiting the ways of Spiritual Darwinism, they'll be much less likely to be threatened. After all, why would they feel challenged by someone who's loving and accepting them?

343

This is not to say we can always transform evil with love. Sadly, this isn't always possible. But we can avoid evil when we're spiritually aware and aligned. Not only will we be able to distinguish who we can trust and who to steer clear of, we'll have more alignment with the Divine, to help us in dangerous situations. Stories abound of people who, when presented with a potentially perilous situation, were protected by a Divine influence. Some became invisible to criminals and others projected the illusion of being protected by large guards, thereby frightening off attackers.

FAITH, SECURITY, TRUST AND EASE

When you become integrated and aligned, Faith comes easily and naturally, because you know that you are protected and can handle anything that comes your way. When you have nothing to fear, you reach the ultimate state of ease, which is the essence of Spiritual Darwinism.

> Security comes from Trust. Trust comes from Faith.
> Faith comes when you eliminate all fear.
> Ease comes when you are fearless.
> - Brownell

The following quote comes from the Very Special Epilogue to DUET stories Volume III:

> Fear doesn't come from lack of love;
> It comes from lack of trust.
> The solution is to trust yourself, to trust each other, and
> to trust your connection with the
> Source of all Love and Light.
> To trust God.

FRIENDSHIP

Friends are like sails – they help shield us against storms and provide the force that helps direct us on course. Friends enhance our lives in many ways: they listen to us when we need someone to talk to; they support us when we feel vulnerable; and they empower us when we're facing challenges.

By helping us shine the light on the true nature of our souls, friends facilitate our becoming integrated and aligned.

> True friendship multiplies the good in life and divides its evils. Strive to have friends, for life without friends is like life on a desert island...to find one real friend in a lifetime is good fortune; to keep him is a blessing.
> - Baltasar Gracian

As you evolve, your friendships will evolve as well. You may go through a period of what I call the "Eliza Doolittle Syndrome" – where you may find that while you're changing, your "previous" life doesn't fit like it used to. But when you live the Lessons – especially acceptance and non-judgment – you're able to continue to love your old friends, as you meet new ones.

FUN

Hey, it's FUN to be enlightened! It's fun to see the meaning in the simplest things. It's enjoyable to appreciate life. When you are without fear, your laughter is ready and pure. What is more fun than a life of discovery and adventure? Later in this chapter I'll explore even more fun ways to live a meaningful life.

HAPPINESS

Happiness is inherent in IA, because we're able to connect – and appreciate – everything life offers.

> Find something to be happy about every day,
> and every hour, even if only for a few minutes,
> and if possible moment-to-moment.
> This is the easiest and best protection you can have.
> - Gregg Braden

HONESTY

Honesty is both inherent and irrelevant in the communication with someone who is integrated and aligned. This is because, when you're connected to your three selves, you can communicate telepathically with the Inner Self and Higher Self of other individuals. Hidden agendas and motivations are routed out and identified, so they can be addressed and resolved and Truth becomes the only language.

IMPERMANENCE

Knowing that all of life is transitory and impermanent provides you with two things. First, you have more appreciation for the gifts that are in your life today. Second, because you know change is constant, you have an enhanced sense of adventure.

LEARNING AND TEACHING

Most people would say that teaching is one of the most admirable professions one can pursue. Even if we don't choose education as our career, however, we all have opportunities to teach others. One of the things you learn as a teacher is that there are always things you know that someone doesn't and vice versa. There are always things to learn from others as well.

If we look at teaching from a purely selfish point of view, it can be one of the most meaningful learning experiences. The old joke, "Those who can't do, teach" is amusing, but has a hidden message: we can learn a lot by teaching others. Have you ever been asked to make a presentation and realized that you learned a lot through the preparation? Therefore, teaching is both a gift to others and ourselves.

LOVE AND VIRTUES

Love is the shared message within all of life's Lessons and virtues, because love is what unifies us with the Divine and with each other. When spiritual teachings talk about separation from God or human's fall from grace, the Lesson is that when we don't act with love, we separate ourselves from God. But when we think and feel and express love to all, we become one with Spirit. Since Divine Love is available to all of us all the time – all we have to do is ask for it – we can all experience the ecstasy of alignment with the Divine. Spiritual Darwinism tells us that the more we love, the more we will thrive, both individually and collectively.

It Pays to Be Nice - Literally

I read a fascinating article several years ago about New York City taxi drivers who were paying to take a course on how to be nicer to their customers, and I was captivated by its simplicity and effectiveness.

What they found was that it paid to be nice. Literally. Their tips increased significantly, if they followed the suggestions of courtesy and pleasantness. While the findings are not really that surprising, the repercussions are fascinating. First, it shows us all that it pays to be nice. What an interesting way to create Karma for yourself: become friendlier and you make more money.

If you take this example and apply a common economic theory, called the multiplier effect or the ripple effect, you can see the potential of this class affecting the people of New York and possibly beyond. The cab drivers are more pleasant and friendly. The customers arrive at their destinations, likely feeling more positive toward whomever they're meeting. If the passenger is from out of town, he or she may carry those good feelings across the country. Friendliness is contagious.

The "Pay it Forward" movement uses a similar approach of creating a better world (and positive personal Karma), by helping others with no desire for anything in return – except for the recipient to "pay it forward" and do something nice for someone else.

MAKE A DIFFERENCE AND MOTIVATION FOR POSITIVE CHANGE

There's nothing like making a difference, to both enhance and extend someone's life. This is clearly evident in spending time with patients given a terminal diagnosis. Those who have accepted the potential for death and eliminated fear of it, then found a way to make a difference in the time they have left on Earth, are the ones who beyond any medical reason.

Since every one of us has a terminal diagnosis – we will all die – we'll all get more life out of life when we're motivated for positive change.

> I truly believe that individuals can make a difference in society. Since periods of change such as the present one come so rarely in human history, it is up to each of us to make the best use of our time to help create a happier world.
> - Dalai Lama

PURPOSE FOR EVERYTHING

The more you become conscious of the messages from your three Selves and Spirit, the more you realize there are no coincidences and there is meaning and purpose in everything. This recognition provides more energy and excitement in life and it also helps us become aware of the things and people in our lives that don't provide health, joy and love.

PURPOSE – YOUR LIFE'S PURPOSE, SELF-FULFILLMENT, TALENT AND UNIQUENESS

From a macro level, we all share the same life purpose: Love. We express love through our uniqueness and talents. Self-fulfillment is only possible when we can express our talents through our connection with the Divine.

> Each person is given something to do
> that shows who God is.
> – Corinthians

There are many great books to help you find your soul's goal for this lifetime. But for all of us, the overarching goal is the same: Love. Expressing love, feeling love, living love. How we do this comes from our unique talents and interests.

> Work is love made visible.
> - Kahil Gibran

> Everyone has his own specific vocation or mission in life; everyone must carry out a concrete assignment that demands fulfillment. Therein he cannot be replaced, nor can his life be repeated, thus, everyone's task is unique as his specific opportunity.
> - Viktor Frankl

RECOGNIZING BEHAVIOR PATTERNS

With awareness comes the ability to recognize behavior patterns, both in ourselves and in others. As you know, recognition is the first step toward change. Even though we can't change others, when *we* change ourselves change occurs in our relationships. By displaying acceptance and sending love, miracles happen.

SHARING

Sharing, when both giver and receiver are connected with a higher source and open to giving the best of themselves, is both an indication and a result of Spiritual Darwinism. When sharing through Integrated Alignment happens, one plus one equals infinity.

> In Sharing, $1+1 = \infty$
> - Brownell

349

TESTS

Have you ever studied and studied for a test, only to go to class and find the exam had been cancelled? In a similar way, preparing for life's tests helps us prevent them. Or, if not prevent them, we can be so prepared for tests they are a "piece of cake" and we breeze right through them.

Most of us know firsthand that Tests are either easy or difficult, depending on whether you've studied. We've gone into exams unprepared and felt the trepidation and nervousness. We also know what it's like to be so prepared that we eagerly anticipate the Test, ready to demonstrate what we know. The difference is in how prepared we are.

Many years ago, I went to a lecture entitled, *Looking Forward to Being Attacked*,[68]" delivered by the Memphis police department. Not only was it a clever title, it was accurate. When I finished the course I was left feeling armed and ready to say, "Bring it on!"

Remember Lieutenant Dan's response to the hurricane, in the movie *Forrest Gump*? He said, "Come on! You call this a storm? Blow, you son-of-a-bitch! Blow! It's time for a showdown! You and me. I'm right here. Come and get me! You'll never sink this boat!"

Lisa Aspinwall, Ph.D., of the University of Maryland, suggests that "proactive coping" (anticipating crises) any crises can reduce their impact and even prevent them altogether.

The basic question behind every test is, "How will you handle it?" The best way to handle a test is to be prepared. So, let's get you prepared for any tests that could come your way.

Preparation

> It is better to look ahead and prepare
> than to look back and regret.
> - Jackie Joyner-Kersee

---

[68] The book provided by the course had the same title and was written by Lt. Jim Bullard.

Preparation is the key. Not only does it alleviate fear, it gets us ready to take on whatever challenges life can throw at us.

Looking Back

Look back at your crisis and ask yourself this question: How would it have been different, if I had prepared for this?

For many of us (me included), not being better prepared is one of my biggest regrets. I got caught up in the "think only of the positive" mentality. I thought that if I entertained the possibility of failure, I would draw failure to me. Hogwash, I say now. Yes, we need to focus on the positive – but our subconscious Inner Self can't help but look at all the possible outcomes, including failure. Unless we face it, we fear it.

> Unless we face the potential for failure, we fear it.
> Only when we know we can handle any outcome,
> can we be truly open for success.
> - Brownell

Preparation relieves the fear. First, I'll talk about preparing for Predictable Events.

Predictable Events

Now that you know how past behavior – Karma and Subconscious Sabotage – brings about events, and how to use the tools for resolving negative Karma and Subconscious Sabotage, you're now equipped to prevent self-created crises. When we add the ability to learn Lessons in advance, the only crises you'll face will be either Tests or predictable events: the inevitable experiences of human life.

Ask yourself the following questions:
- Do you live in an area that has a risk of a natural disaster?
- Are you unhappy in your job?
- Do you have any unhealthy habits, like smoking or drinking too much?
- Are you a risk-taker, either with risky activities or business ventures?

351

- Are you faced with a lot of stress in your life, either with daily stressors like traffic driving back and forth to work, or with larger-scale stressors such as a sick relative?
- Do you have children? Pets?
- Are your parents still alive?
- Do you have other significant relationships?
- Have you been in more than one accident?
- Do you ever have trouble sleeping?
- Are you bored, lethargic or unmotivated?
- Do you have high blood pressure, digestive problems and/or headaches?
- Do you own your home?
- Do you have a car?
- Do you have anyone in your life who is disrespectful, abusive, dishonest or in any other way destructive to you?
- What are you most attached to?
- *Who* are you most attached to?

If you answered yes to any of these questions, it's a sign pointing toward something you may have to face in the future. It doesn't mean you shouldn't have relationships or children, it just means that the more people and responsibilities you have in your life, the more risk you have and the more you'll have to face in your life. If you take a risk, that's okay – it's part of life! - but it's important to face the potential outcome and be prepared.

> Once you know what to expect
> it's hard not to see what's going on.
> - Cate Montana

Our Own Death

Every one of us will die, but we can have some control over how we die. In the Reasons Why Workbook, you went through several exercises to help you prepare for your own death. You decided how you want to (and don't want to) die. You wrote your own obituary, and looked at ways to become immortal. And you were given ways to resolve any fear of death you may have had, including a life review and suggestions for learning more about the afterlife.

Death of a Loved One

Just as every one of us will die, if you're old enough to read this, there's nearly a 100% chance that you'll experience the death of a loved one, whether it's a grandparent, parent, other relative, friend or colleague. If you work or volunteer in the healthcare field, you're probably exposed to death on a regular basis.

While we shouldn't become numb to the death of others, we all need to prepare for the inevitable experience of having someone close to us leave us to go on to the afterlife. To do this, we need to do two things: open up our communication with our loved ones on their deaths, and become prepared to cope ourselves when it happens.

The Alternative: Aging

The alternative to death is, of course, to live as long a life as we can. But, if that happens, it's a good idea to be prepared for what that will bring, including the need for money, options for housing and care, and the potential for disease.

Calculate Your Life Expectancy

To calculate your life expectancy, based on factors ranging from family history, education, and personal lifestyle, you can use a tool on the internet.[69] This information can be helpful in many ways. First, it identifies many of the habits and factors that cause death, which can point you toward creating a longer, healthier life. Plus, it can help you prepare better for your financial needs throughout your remaining lifetime.

---

[69] One life expectancy calculator is on the following website: http://gosset.wharton.upenn.edu/mortality/perl/CalcForm.html

Illnesses

Yes, many illnesses are completely – or at least largely – preventable, and it's possible to live a long life with full vitality and health and just peacefully "blink out" like a light bulb at the end. But, illness is still a probability, whether it's the result of something we have created or for a Lesson, or even to potentially be a gift, and we need to prepare for it.

To help you prepare, here were the leading causes of death in the United States in 2003:

Number of Deaths for Leading Causes of Death.[70]

- Heart Disease: 685,089
- Cancer: 556,902
- Stroke: 157,689
- Chronic lower respiratory diseases: 126,382
- Accidents (unintentional injuries): 109,277
- Diabetes: 74,219
- Influenza/Pneumonia: 65,163
- Alzheimer's disease: 63,457
- Nephritis, nephrotic syndrome, and nephrosis: 42,453
- Septicemia: 34,069
- AIDS/HIV: Number of deaths: 14,095
- Unintentional injury deaths: 109,277
- Homicides: 17,732
- Suicides: 31,484
- Motor vehicle traffic deaths: 43,340
- Firearm deaths: 30,136
- Poisoning deaths: 28,700

---

[70] National Center for Health Statistics. For Additional information, visit http://www.cdc.gov/nchs/fastats/

Relationship Changes

Relationships change and evolve throughout our lifetime. Marianne Williamson, in her beautiful book, *A Return to Love,* based on the teachings of *A Course in Miracles*, identifies three levels of teaching in relationships, from casual encounters to those that last all our lives.

> "When physical proximity no longer supports the highest level of teaching and learning between them, the assignment will call for physical separation," she explains. "If both people learned what they were meant to learn, then that relationship was a success."

The key questions to ask ourselves in relationships are: Did we do our best? Have we resolved any subconscious (Inner Self) emotions? Have we forgiven? Asked for forgiveness? Can we still love this person, even if we're separated from him or her? (See chapter on Forgiveness!)

Business Failures

Starting a business of any kind requires taking a risk. But to mitigate risk we should prepare for the possibility of failure. While we shouldn't let naysayers get us down, we should look at the possible stumbling blocks and prepare contingency plans.

Denial is dangerous. - Brownell

Crime

Integrated Alignment will help you avoid being a victim of most crimes, but you can gain additional strength when you're prepared for it. Self–defense courses, CPR, and knowledge about what areas of town to avoid will help significantly. The advice given in the book, *Looking Forward to Being Attacked*, by Lt. Jim Bullard tells us that we should "Look forward to being attacked, not with fear, but with a properly controlled, well-channeled response of outrage and anger."

Police Lieutenant Bullard said, "More than anything else, your attitude will determine whether or not you'll be a victim of an attack. Fear is crippling but anger will give strength of courage to do what you have to do." However, for both men and women, anger will need to be controlled – which is easier when you're prepared.

> Physical strength can never permanently
> withstand the impact of spiritual force.
> -- Franklin D. Roosevelt

Look Forward to Being Attacked

Whether you're a man or a woman, you should take a self-defense course. We need to all be prepared. If you can't find one, try to organize one for your office, club or organization. Ask your local police to help you. Know the points of weakness in a potential attacker. Understand their motivations.

Try to incorporate a directed meditation or visualization into your class. "See" yourself warding off attackers in a variety of situations. Be ready.

I learned an interesting trick: get a bottle with a long-distance spray nozzle and fill it with ammonia and food coloring. The ammonia will supposedly knock out your opponent, and the food coloring will help you identify them in a lineup!

The point isn't to develop a violent personality. The point is to be prepared, so that you can react with strength as efficiently and peacefully as possible.

Financial Problems

Many of us are one disaster away from a financial crisis. According to a nationwide Bankrate.com poll, fewer than four of 10 American adults have an emergency fund to fall back on in the event of some financial disaster.

Debt happens when we have a wounded, ignored, bored and/or unhappy Inner Self. I like something Buddha said. To paraphrase, he said there's nothing wrong with wanting the best for ourselves. But when we want it at the expense of someone else, it's greed. I'll add to that my philosophy: there is abundance in the universe – there is no limit to riches, just as there is no limit to the capacity for love. The only problem comes when our motives for the things we buy are maligned. If we want something to enjoy, or to share, we'll not only get the "thing" we wanted, but the enjoyment as well. But, when our motives are greed or to display superiority, even if we acquire something, we won't be able to experience the positive feelings of joy associated with the acquisition.

The truth is, the more miserable we're in our jobs, the greater the potential for debt. Why is that? It's because we placate our Inner Self with expensive, unnecessary treats when they feel hurt, in order to produce pleasurable feelings.

Preventing Debt

For many of us, the word "budget" is a dirty word. This is because our Inner Self doesn't like restrictions on opportunities for pleasure. Heck, for that matter, neither does our Outer Self!

But much of life's pleasure is free, or at least inexpensive, especially when you realize that it isn't stuff we want – it's the feelings we get from stuff! If we want new clothes, it's to make us feel better about ourselves. It we want a new car, it's usually more for status or comfort, than it's for transportation or safety.

Often what you'll find is that your Inner Self will prefer a day off from work, to take a walk, relax, or meditate – all are free! But we don't do it, for reasons we should deeply explore, (usually having to do with work or other obligations that are not that important in the big picture). If we ignore the simple requests from our Inner Self, we won't be integrated and aligned!

Work/Career

When we're discontented or unfulfilled in any area of our life, it's an indication that something needs to change. Our career is the most obvious example of this. Very few people who get fired (or laid off) are truly happy in their jobs. What would you do if you lost your job? What would you do that day, the next day, the next week, etc.? Are you prepared? Do you have financial backup? Would you feel any extra pressure from family? These and more questions are pursued in the Reasons Why Workbook.

Loss of Home and/or Possessions

The more we're attached to our "stuff," the greater the chance we could lose it all. Losing our homes and/or possessions can be a shock, but it isn't all that rare. Whether it's because of a natural disaster (fire, flood, hurricane or tornado) or an accident or from financial reverses, there are many things that can cause us to lose our home or possessions.

Ready for some irony? The day I was writing this a giant tree fell on my house. (Yes, the one facing impending foreclosure). I think I surprised the tree removal expert with my demeanor. Even though the problem brings a lot of serious issues to deal with, I'm not concerned. I'll deal with it. (I'm thankful, however, that it wasn't a fire – I would not have wanted to lose the months of writing I've put into this book!) But I have learned something valuable about prevention. To back up my data!

Even if you fear losing your home, it helps to realize you weren't likely to be living there the rest of your life anyway. You might envision living somewhere else. This can help you release your attachment to your home, and help you see "the bright side," if you were to lose it.

Accidents

We often fear the things we cannot control more than the ones we can, but the sad truth is, the things we can control are often the more dangerous things. For example, more people worry about being in a plane crash, but your odds of being in a fatal plane crash are one in 1.25 million. However, the odds of being in a deadly car crash (something we have more ability to control) are one in 237.

Awareness and Integrated Alignment are what we need, to prevent accidents of all kinds. But, in case an accident happens, we need to be prepared.

Problems Faced by People We Care About

As discussed in the chapter on Karma, we need to be careful, when interfering with other people's Karma. However, as you know, when someone we care about is facing a crisis, it can have a significant effect on our own lives. We may be affected financially and/or emotionally. We may even become responsible for many activities that we inherit from the situation the loved one is going through.

Legal Disputes

The most important Lessons in any legal dispute are Anger, Forgiveness and Make Amends. Controlling anger can help you resolve (and prevent) many legal problems. Forgiveness – offering forgiveness as well as seeking it – is also critical. The entire purpose of any legal dispute, whether it's a criminal or civil case, is restitution - to Make Amends.

Family History

The past is the best way to predict the future. Knowing your family history is a good way to help you see the red flags that could pop up along your future path. looking at all the members of your family – parents, siblings, grandparents, etc., as far back as you can go...Has anyone had cancer? Is there any heart disease or stroke? Has anyone committed suicide? Have there been any legal difficulties? Has anyone had a particularly short life? Has anyone had genetic difficulties? Has anyone been the victim of a crime? Has anyone been guilty of a crime? Have there been any cases of mental disease, dementia, etc.? What bad habits would describe your family members? What other problems has your family experienced?

Other:

Smoking: if you smoke, not only will you probably die from smoking, it also produces many miserable diseases. For example, in 2003, there were 3.6 million adults with emphysema.[71] You know you need to stop – and your Inner Self knows it, too. Once you connect with and start loving him or her, you'll *both* be able to quit. (Bribery with other pleasant, healthy alternatives also helps a lot!).

Skin Cancer: is can be preventable with sunscreen. Many other problems we face are preventable. We just need to stay informed, and stay connected to our Inner Self. He/She knows what's best for us.

Preventing Large Scale Events

Hopefully, you now feel much more empowered and prepared for any Tests you may encounter in life. But what about the big stuff, environmental changes and war? Certainly I can't expect you to prevent being affected by them, can I?

The answer is *absolutely…*

Preventing Natural Disasters

Gregg Braden, in his book, *The Isaiah Effect*, explains our individual impact on global events:

> We are offered two precepts to guide us through the greater challenges of our modern time:
>
> First, we are reminded that imbalances imposed upon the Earth are mirrored as conditions within our bodies. Such traditions view the breakdown of our immune systems and cancerous growths in our bodies, for example, as the inner expression of a collective breakdown that prevents our outer world from giving life.
>
> Second, this line of thinking invites us to consider earthquakes, volcanic eruptions and weather

---

[71] Lung cancer kills 166,440 a year, and other effects of smoking include cancer of the bladder, esophagus, pancreas and cervix among other cancers, emphysema, heart disease and stroke.

patterns as mirrors of great change occurring within human consciousness. Clearly, from such a worldview, life becomes much more than a group of daily experiences occurring on a random basis. The events of our world are living barometers showing us our progress on a journey that began long ago. As we look to our relationships within the pattern of societies and nature, we are actually witnessing changes within ourselves.

If our outer world does in fact mirror our beliefs and values, is it possible to end the pain and suffering of Earth through our choices of compassion and peace made in our lives?...The key to addressing such events is the timing: the sooner we recognize our relationship with the world around us, the sooner we'll recognize our inner choices of peace mirrored as gentle weather patterns, the healing of our societies, and peace between nations.

We can make the changes – each of us – to save our planet.

> The environment is very important in the aspects of peace because when we destroy our resources, they become scarce and we fight over that.
> - Wangari Maathai

In the meantime, we need to prepare for the probability of some kind of natural disaster. Depending on where you live, it could be an earthquake, thunderstorm, hurricane, extreme heat, tornado, mudslide, fire, flood, tsunamis, droughts, or other problem.

What is Your Plan?

Some questions to consider: Do you have smoke detectors and/or other methods of alarm? If any of the above disasters happened, do you have an escape plan? How would you protect your family? Do you have an efficient way to communicate your plan? Have you practiced your plan? What financial resources do you have to help? What other resources are available to you? Do you know how to contact them? Are you prepared for the potential emotional responses of anger, frustration, depression, blame, guilt, despair, etc.? Have you considered moving to a place that is safer?

Advice from the Red Cross

The American Red Cross website provides the following advice to victims of disasters (natural and terrorist):

- Avoid media coverage of the event.
- Talk it out!
- Ask for help when you need it
- Listen to other people.
- Be especially kind to others.
- Spend time with your family.
- Return to your usual routine.
- Sit under a tree, look at a brook, lake, river or ocean.
- Remind yourself of other times when you were afraid and how you coped.
- Do something that could help others.

Preventing Terrorism and War

Remember the exercise on Karma, where you were asked to consider your response to your neighbor's "rutting" your yard? The message was that responding in anger and aggression is going to generate cyclic negative Karma. The alternative is to get a closer understanding of the motivations of your potential attacker. As discussed in the chapter on Tests, the pre-emptive approach to terrorism is to ask, "Why?" "Why would someone want to attack us?" And, "What can we do to prevent it?"

Communication is the key to understanding and we need to select leaders who are expert in negotiation and open communication. I don't know about you, but I would rather have a president who can look an "enemy" in the eye and say, "If you have a problem with me, punch me. Don't attack my people" than one who sends someone else out to settle his or her arguments. But even better is one who displays consideration and cooperation and not respond in anger or violence.

In his book, *Power vs. Force,* Dr. David R. Hawkins describes the difference between the two energies. Force, he said, is when "society has tried to 'treat' social problems by legislative action, warfare, market manipulations, laws and prohibitions," only to see the problems continue. Real power, he asserts, comes from an enlightened perspective, with "unconditional kindness to all life, including one's own…Whenever force meets power, force is eventually defeated."

Our leaders should set an example for the rest of us by demonstrating Integrated Alignment. With IA, violence is never the solution. This might be the most challenging part of this book for most people to accept: Spiritual Darwinism – acting in love and peace – can create peace and prevent war.

> Oh, *great warrior*, hmm? Wars not make one great.
> - Yoda (Frank Oz) in *Star Wars: The Empire Strikes Back*

The Test of Terrorism and War: Asking "Why?"

Answer the following questions:
- Why do you think terrorists attack any country or people?
- Why do you think wars are fought?
- Why do you think the terrorists attacked the World Trade Center and the Pentagon on September 11, 2001?
- Can you see the underlying fear that motivates any act of war?
- Do you recognize the influence of "Survival of the Fittest?"
- Can you see the similarity between the exercise about your neighbor rutting your yard and disputes between neighboring nations?

- Do you think everyone in the country is guilty of terrorism, if one person within the country is guilty?
- Do you think it's appropriate for innocent people to pay for a crime someone committed in their nation? What about families – do you think everyone in a family is responsible if one member of a family has done something wrong?

> Fear is generally the motivating factor for all negative acts that you see upon your earth. It is all based on fear of one form or another, fear of not being accepted, fear of not being good enough, fear of being eliminated. Fear is the biggest contributor to the dark side of mankind, followed by anger. Those are the two largest reasons.
> - Afterlife 101

> As individuals come together in a collective consciousness of love, of peace, of harmony and good will towards everyone, this coming together could most definitely be used to affect large worldly events.
> – Afterlife 101

Other Ways to Prevent Terrorism and War

- Vote for Peace: Select leaders who are most likely to engender a sense of love, understanding, acceptance and cooperation.
- Be Nice! Just as the taxi drivers learned that it pays to be nice, being nice yourself has a contagious effect on the world around you.
- Pay it Forward: Doing nice things for others without expectation or attachment is a gift you can give yourself because it feels so good!

> Visualize Whirled Peas
> - Bumper Sticker

Preparing for Traumatic Events

In the chapter on Tests, I discussed two phases of trauma – the Impact phase and the Recoil phase. Just knowing that these phases exist can help us prepare for them.

But large disasters also provide an opportunity for the expression of great love, charity, appreciation and heroism. Not only does responding this way create positive Karma and increases your opportunity for Reward, it also helps you maintain a feeling of responsibility and control.

> To put the world in order, we must first put the nation in order; to put the nation in order, we must put the family in order; to put the family in order, we must cultivate our personal life; and to cultivate our personal life, we must first set our hearts right.
> - Confucius

Lessons in Predictable Events

There is always a Lesson in any predictable event:

- How we take care of ourselves
- How we take care of others
- How we are in relationships
- How prepared we are
- How long we mourn
- How we seek answers/solutions
- How connected to our 3 selves we are – because they can warn us.

The Secret to Passing Tests

The Secret to Passing Tests is to ask three questions with every action you take:

- Is it best for me?
- Is it best for all concerned?

- Am I doing the absolute best I can, coming from a place of love and acceptance?

Look for Tests and Have Fun "Passing" Them!

When you're prepared for a Test, it can be fun to take them. You find out how much you know and how strong you are. And you're more likely to find the synchronicities that lead to serendipity and Reward.

Experts have shown that optimistic self-appraisals of capability (self-confidence) that are in accordance with what is possible can be advantageous, as they increase motivation and persistence and reduce fear.

One big aspect of passing Tests is to always look for the Reward. It's usually there if we search hard enough.

REWARD

Divine Intervention

When we're integrated and aligned with our Higher Self and the Divine, we are more open to "Divine Intervention" – when the highest level good seems to "swoop" into our lives, bringing us awesome gifts.

Expecting Miracles

Cambridge University Professor J. E. Littlewood has published research findings in mathematics dubbed "Littlewood's Law" that states that individuals can expect a miracle to happen to them at the rate of about one per month.

The key ingredient missing in Littlewood's Law is the awareness and perspective of the individual. The more we expect a miracle and are looking for one, the more we will find them. Have you ever noticed that when you meet someone significant in your life and find out what kind of car he drives, you see that kind of car everywhere you look – and may never have noticed it? The more we look for miracles, the more we'll see them.

> In addition to praying for miracles to happen,
> ask to see the miracles that are already there.
> - Brownell

Inattentional Blindness and Preparation

In the movie, *What the Bleep Do We Know?*, the writers present an interesting message about awareness. When Columbus arrived in the Caribbean, the natives were unable to see his ship in the water. All they could see was the movement in the water. This was because they had no ability to "see" something they couldn't conceive of. The village shaman, however, had the openness of vision to be able to actually see the ship, and were therefore able to explain it to the natives, in order for them to "see."

This phenomenon is called "Inattentional Blindness," which is defined as "the failure to notice unusual and salient events in their visual world when attention is otherwise engaged and the events are unexpected."[72]Researchers Mack and Rock conclude that "without attention, nothing is consciously perceived."[73]

Similar research by Simons and Chabris establishes what is called "change blindness," which proves that people rarely notice changes in their environment. Certainly, we all acknowledge that when we're focusing on something, we often "tune out" – visually and auditorily – things that are happening and changing around us, but change blindness also occurs when we miss changes in the things we concentrate on as well.

> Will you believe it when you see it?
> – Or will you see it when you believe it?

Chabris' experiments showed that "people often *do* have a representation of some aspects of the pre-change scene, even

---

[72] Research conducted by Daniel J. Simons, Ph.D., University of Illinois, and Christopher F. Chabris, Harvard University
[73] Mack & Rock (1998) explored the nature of perception, when attention is directed away from a target object.

when they fail to report the change. And, in fact, they appear to 'discover' this memory and can explicitly report details of a changed object in response to probing questions."[74]

What this means is that we do possess the ability to remember the things we "miss" through unintentional blindness and change blindness. As discussed in the chapter on Subconscious Sabotage, our conscious minds process a tiny fraction of the information we receive, the rest being retained in our subconscious minds – our Inner Selves. The solution? Getting in touch with our Inner Selves and asking them to recognize – and report – miracles every day!!!

How to Be Rich

One of my favorite books is a children's book called, *How to Be Rich* by Michael Twinn. Like the Dr. Seuss book, *Oh, The Places You'll Go!* this book is as relevant to adults as it is to children. In a simple and endearing way, the author demonstrates the riches we all have (at least to some degree), as well as the gifts we're able to give, no matter what our station in life.

Another way to feel rich is to measure your quality of life versus the rest of the world. Enter your annual income in the website: www.globalrichlist.com and you'll find how rich you are compared to the rest of the world. For example, if you enter $50,000 as your household income, you're the 59,029,289th richest person in the world, or in the top ninety-eight percent. Not bad, huh?

Look for Reward

If we don't get angry when something happens, but instead try to uncover the benefits, we can usually find them.
- If someone slows down in front of you in traffic, it might be for the best. It might prevent you from an accident.
- If you miss a plane, you might avoid a disaster.

---

[74] Simons, D.J., Chabris, C.F., Schnur, T., & Levin, D.T. (2002). Evidence for preserved representations in change blindness. Consciousness & Cognition, 11(1), 78-97.

- If you don't get a promotion, it might be for the best. You could find out that you'd have hated the job or it would have been eliminated in the next "cut."

- If someone leaves you, it might be for the best. You could either find someone better for you, or discover that you prefer being alone.

- If you get caught doing something wrong, it might be for the best. It could've prevented you from a more serious and dangerous outcome.

- If someone passes away, it might be for the best. This may be a difficult one – but it is often true. It could be their relief from pain, the moving on to a better place, or the end of great turmoil. For survivors, it can mean liberation from burden and stress, and helps you move on.

- If your home is destroyed, it might be for the best. You may move somewhere you like more, or you could've the chance to rebuild it the way you want.

- If your business fails, it might be for the best: You might either find that you learned enough to ensure success the next time, or you find another career/business you enjoy more – and which is more profitable!

> The province of philosophy is not so much to prevent calamities befalling as to demonstrate that they are blessings when they have taken place.
> - Ernest Bramah

Reward Your Self

Don't forget to Reward your Inner Self. Thank him or her when you:

- Handle situations with ease
- Respond with understanding and compassion
- Feel good – healthy and happy
- Accomplish a challenging task
- Forgive someone or ask for forgiveness
- Complete an exercise, meditation or other worthwhile activity

- Experience the feeling of love: from above, from others and toward others. You'll both enjoy it, and any behavior becomes easier and more fun to do when it comes with a Reward at the end.

CHANGE

> Enjoying success requires the ability to adapt.
> Only by being open to change will you have a true
> opportunity to get the most from your talent.
> **- Nolan Ryan**

Love Change!

 This symbol offers a great philosophy of life: Love Change. Look forward to new opportunities. Embrace challenges.

Changing Your Destiny

> Nothing is absolutely fixed and everything depends on
> how we choose to use our own free will.
> Even those events that are already predestined
> can be changed or modified by a change
> in our own way of relating to them.
> - Afterlife 101

Becoming Fearless

Just imagine what you could do if you were fearless! What would you do or try if you had absolutely no fear? Would you travel more? Try a sport or activity? Express yourself better? Take a risk? Start a new career or business?

FUN STUFF

The best way to prevent Bad Things is to remember to enjoy life. Recognizing what makes you and your Inner Self happy is crucial in preventing crises of all kinds. As you become integrated and aligned you will find a new level of fun that is healthy and life-affirming, while also achieving a Divine purpose.

> Fun is fundamental. There is no way around it. You absolutely must have fun. Without fun, there is no enthusiasm. Without enthusiasm, there is no energy. Without energy, there are only shades of gray.
> - Doug Hall

What Kind of Life Do You Want?

Now that we have addressed the things you don't want, what *do* you want in your life?

> Follow your bliss and the universe will open doors for you where there were only walls.
> - Joseph Campbell

The movie, *The Secret,* discusses the "Law of Attraction" or the power of deciding what you want. Although the film misses the points made previously in this book – that there are Reasons Why Bad Things Happen and that we cannot just wave a magic wand and make them disappear – it's a powerful film to see, once you have a full understanding of Karma, Subconscious Sabotage, Lessons, Tests and Rewards, and are now ready, with the assistance of Integrated Alignment, to manifest the positive, loving things you want in life.

The Perfect Day

In as much detail as possible, construct your idea of the perfect day. When will you wake up? Where will you be? Who will be with you? What will you have for breakfast? What will the weather be like? And so on. You may want to create more than one day. For example, you could have the perfect weekday, the perfect weekend, or the perfect vacation day.

> "I would rather have thirty minutes of wonderful than a lifetime of nothing special."
> - Shelby Eatenton Latcherie (Julia Roberts), in the movie Steel Magnolias

Learning Through Joy

Yes, we do learn through our crises, but we can also learn through happy experiences such as love, joy, and success.

Old Crisis Mantra: "Lord, please prevent _____ from happening" or "Lord, please bring me _____".

Evolved Crisis Mantra: "Lord, help me find love, peace and compassion in times of need."

New Prevention Mantra: "Lord, please help me learn through Joy"

Make a Wish!

Twice a day the clock strikes 11:11 – the time many people recognize as an opportunity to make a wish.

Love Yourself

Now that you're integrated and aligned, your three selves will work in harmony to such a degree that you no longer distinguish the motivations from your Inner Self, Outer Self and Higher Self – they're all one. Now you're able to love all of your selves as a unified being.

Feng Shui, Colors, and Other Reminders

Anything you can do to help remind you of the wonders of life, the strengths you have, and the opportunities ahead of you can help you stay aligned. Feng Shui is the Asian art of environmental design. A good book on the subject is *The Western Guide to Feng Shui* by Terah Kathryn Collins. The principles of Feng Shui are to draw your home into a nine-square (tic-tac-toe) grid pattern, with each square representing a part of your life: knowledge and self-cultivation; health; wealth; fame and recognition; travel, etc. Even if you don't "believe" in it, it's still a good idea to remember the important things in life.

Colors have energy to them and can affect your mood. Do some research on the effects of different colors, but basically, black is depressing; white is uplifting; red is passion (both bad and good); orange is physical; yellow is will and determination; green is love, earth and healing; blue is communication; indigo is foresight and purple or violet is connection to Spirit. Surround yourself with colors that bring out the best in your energy.

> We have to keep dancing
> in the face of insurmountable odds.
> We must refuse to succumb to the world of death and
> despondence and negativity. All we need is energy,
> idealism, and the capacity to dream.
> - Archbishop Desmond Tutu

Predicting the Future

The problem with predicting the future is that it can allow us to live in the future, which creates either hope or fear, depending on our level of strength and resolve.

> 'Always in motion is the future."
> - Yoda (Frank Oz), in *The Empire Strikes Back*

However, I've discussed many ways to prepare for the future, so you may have the inner power to be able to handle any crisis that can come your way.

CONCLUSION: YOU *CAN* PREVENT BAD THINGS!

> Power is having control over your own life.
> - Brownell

Remember in the chapter *Bad Things Defined* when we went through your definition of Bad Things? You were asked to check a list of physical pain and/or emotional pain that characterize your general definition of Bad Things. Now, let's look at the list again:

- Physical pain

- Emotional pain – Something that makes you feel: depressed, frustrated, discouraged, angry, guilty, ashamed or embarrassed, alone, neglected, deserted/abandoned, unworthy/worthless, lost, vulnerable, helpless, defenseless, unhappy, weak, blocked/ obstructed, hopeless, useless, desperate, ignored, inconsolable, betrayed or deceived, unloved / unlovable, sad, miserable, gloomy, lonely or isolated, unsatisfied, pessimistic, bitter, abused or mistreated, or afraid.

By our definition, Bad Things are not events they're defined by either physical or emotional pain. In fact, we realized that "Bad Things are difficult to define because it depends on the emotions involved and perspective (how you look at it)."

First, you know the "Big Reason Why," that anything you'd define as "bad" or a crisis is a sign that something needs to change.

Second, let's review physical pain. If your physical pain is strong enough and you need relief and time to resolve the Reasons Why for the pain, the medical and pharmaceutical community can certainly accommodate.

But you now know that even physical pain can be a gift and is a strong signal that something needs to change in a person's life. It's counter-productive to cover pain, so that someone can return to a self-destructive life.

For emotional pain, the following list outlines each problem and provides the resolution to each:

PROBLEM		SOLUTION
Feeling abused or mistreated		Feeling protected, helped, assisted
Feeling afraid		Feeling brave, valiant
Feeling alone		Feeling accompanied, helped
Feeling angry		Feeling calm, peaceful
Feeling ashamed or embarrassed		Feeling proud, happy
Feeling betrayed or deceived		Feeling protected, informed

Feeling bitter		Feeling accepting, understanding
Feeling blocked / obstructed		Feeling open, successful
Feeling defenseless		Feeling armed, secure, safe
Feeling depressed		Feeling happy, optimistic
Feeling deserted /abandoned		Feeling connected, self-sufficient
Feeling desperate		Feeling calm, hopeful
Feeling discouraged		Feeling positive, encouraged
Feeling frustrated		Feeling calm, successful
Feeling gloomy		Feeling bright, light
Feeling guilty		Feeling innocent, guilt-free
Feeling helpless		Feeling self-reliant, helped
Feeling hopeless		Feeling hopeful, optimistic
Feeling ignored		Feeling heard, understood
Feeling inconsolable		Feeling consolable, relieved
Feeling lonely or isolated		Feeling connected, accepted
Feeling lost		Feeling found, directed
Feeling miserable		Feeling happy, bright
Feeling neglected		Feeling cared for, attended to
Feeling pessimistic		Feeling optimistic, confident
Feeling sad		Feeling cheerful, positive
Feeling unhappy		Feeling happy, joyful
Feeling unloved / unlovable		Feeling loved, lovable
Feeling unsatisfied		Feeling satisfied, fulfilled
Feeling unworthy / worthless		Feeling deserving, valuable
Feeling useless		Feeling useful, helpful
Feeling vulnerable		Feeling impervious, invincible
Feeling weak		Feeling strong, invulnerable, powerful

You have been given tools, exercises, suggestions and insight. You're now equipped to resolve the emotions and have a new, healthier perspective!

SPIRITUAL DARWINISM

> "I desire for the whole life process to be an experience
> of constant joy, continuous creation, never ending
> expansion, and total fulfillment
> in each moment of now."
> - "God" (Neale Donald Walsh)

> Instead of falling prey to your subconscious, which is
> constantly compelling you to embrace a future that is
> predictable, you can seize control of your talent for
> projection. Live the highest ideal now. See a future
> based on the belief that you are cared for in the universe,
> that you are growing toward higher consciousness, that
> love, truth, and self-acceptance are already yours. You
> do not have to achieve these states in order to live them
> now. Living them now is how you will achieve them.
> – Deepak Chopra

Imagine...

- Imagine having an invisible shield around you that could protect you no matter what occurs…

- Imagine knowing with absolute certainly you'd be able to handle anything that happens to you…

- Imagine knowing that if someone came at you, to attack you, you'd be able to quickly, peacefully and effectively get him to surrender his weapon and reconsider their way of life...

- Imagine you're in the middle of a war zone, with bombs flying and gunfire sounding around you, and you remained calm and unaffected…

- Imagine hearing that you're dying of a terminal disease and having no fear of what will happen…

- Imagine never feeling guilty again, because you know you always did your best…

- Imagine your home being ripped away by a natural disaster and you're able to react with both action and compassion…

- Imagine someone being very angry with you, screaming and yelling, and your immediate response is to calmly ask what you did to make her angry, sincerely apologize and lovingly offer to make it up to her...

- Imagine all your friends abandoning you and having nothing but love for them...

- Imagine your child is attacked and being able to freely forgive their attacker...

- Imagine finding out that you have two months to live and being grateful for every minute you can spend between sharing your love for your friends and family and figuring out how you can leave a lasting impact on the world...

- Imagine your country is being attacked and your reaction is to pray for guidance and how to respond in the most peaceful way possible...

- Imagine being stranded on a deserted island and looking forward to having the time alone to connect with your Higher Power...

- Imagine your child being abducted and your response is to send loving, peaceful thoughts to the kidnapper...

- Imagine being financially wiped out, losing everything you own, and you couldn't care less...

- Imagine your worst fears being realized and having an immediate plan to confidently address the situation...

- Imagine no longer having these fears...

- Imagine nothing ever bothering you again...

Preventing Bad Things

CHAPTER 17: PRAYER

As established earlier, prayer is talking to the Divine (or your Higher Power) and meditation is listening to God. Both are critical in our communication with the Divine and we have previously discussed ways to meditate or listen. But what about the prayer side of the discussion?

WHAT IS PRAYER?

The following quote from Betty J. Eadie's book, *Embraced by the Light,* is a beautiful description of what she learned about prayer during a Near Death Experience,:

> "I saw the sphere of Earth rotating in space. I saw many lights shooting up from the Earth like beacons. Some were very broad and charged into heaven like broad laser beams. Others resembled the illumination of small pen lights, and some were mere sparks. I was surprised, as I was told that these beacons of power were the prayers of people on earth.
>
> "I saw angels rushing to answer the prayers. They were organized to give as much help as possible...I was distinctly told that all prayers of desire are heard and answered. When we have great need, or when we're praying for other people, the beams project straight from us and are

immediately visible…. Our prayers for others have great strength, but can only be answered as far as they don't infringe on the others' free will…"

Prayer is Infinitely More Powerful Through Integrated Alignment

As discussed in the chapter on Subconscious Sabotage, human thought has awesome power, and conscious, directed, loving thought (prayer), through Integrated Alignment, has even more power. Larry Dossey, M.D. in his book, *Healing Words – The Power of Prayer and the Practice of Medicine*, said, "We will never be able to take full advantage of the power of the mind to shape our health – including the mind's use of prayer – until we broaden our concept of "consciousness." This means including the unconscious."

> The unconscious mind can initiate or cooperate with prayer and even mediate the effects.
> - Larry Dossey

Directed Prayer vs. Non-Directed Prayer

Directed Prayer is used to request and manifest something we want in our lives – health, money and material objects, success, acceptance, etc.

> "Bart, with $10,000, we'd be millionaires!
> We could buy all kinds of useful things like... love!"
> – Homer Simpson, *The Simpsons*

Non-Directed Prayer is more open-ended, asking more for guidance and positive feelings than for specific items or outcomes. Research has shown that, although both types are effective, non-directed prayer is twice as effective as directed prayer.[75] This isn't surprising when you consider two things. First, Non-Directed Prayer is a request for feelings, which all

---

[75] Research from Spendthrift, cited by Dossey in his book *Healing Words*..

stem from love – which is in infinite supply from the Divine. Second, Non-Directed Prayer is detached and surrenders the specific outcome – a key to successful prayer.

Are All Prayers Answered?

What is the answer to the quintessential question: Are all prayers answered? I remember going to a spiritual talk as a high-schooler where the priest said that all prayers are answered in one of three ways: "Yes" (and you get what you ask for), "Wait" or "I'll give you something better." I've thought about that talk ever since, and would like to amend it with my own viewpoint.

Not to sound trite, but it depends on the request – not only whether it's a directed prayer vs. a non-directed prayer, but it also depends on the requestor as well as who is being prayed "to." Assuming that all prayers are to a benevolent, loving, Divine Higher Power, some prayers are always answered "Yes", some are answered "No," some are "Wait" and some are "I'll give you something better."

- If we ask for love, the answer is always "Yes." But we need to remember to keep asking!

- If we ask to experience inside of us, or express to others, any of the following feelings that are expressions of love, the answer is always "Yes":

  Awe, Acceptance, Admiration, Allegiance, Appreciation, Assertiveness, Beauty, Bliss, Brilliance, Caring, Cleanliness, Commitment, Compassion, Confidence, Consideration, Contentment, Cooperation, Courage, Courtesy, Creativity, Delight, Dependability, Detachment, Determination, Devotion, Diligence, Discernment, Ease, Enjoyment, Enthusiasm, Esteem, Excellence, Faith, Faithfulness, Flexibility, Forgiveness, Friendliness, Generosity, Gentleness, Grace, Gratitude, Happiness, Harmony, Heaven, Helpfulness, Honesty, Honor, Humility, Idealism, Integrity, Joy, Joyfulness, Justice, Kindness, Love, Loyalty, Magnificence, Marvel, Mercy,

Moderation, Modesty, Obedience, Order, Orderliness, Patience, Peace, Peacefulness, Perseverance, Pleasure, Prayerfulness, Purity, Purposefulness, Quality, Reliability, Respect, Responsibility, Reverence, Righteousness, Sacrifice, Satisfaction, Self-Discipline, Serenity, Service, Steadfastness, Tact, Thankfulness, Tolerance, Tranquility, Trust, Trustworthiness, Truthfulness, Understanding, Unity, Value, Wisdom, Wonder, Zeal

- If we ask for peace within, the answer is always "Yes." But, as with love and other loving feelings, we can get distracted and need to keep asking.
- If we ask for learning, the teaching is provided, but the learning is up to us.
- If we ask for guidance, the direction is provided, but it's up to us to follow the path.
- If we ask for alignment with Divine will, it will be provided, but we need to trust that what we receive *is* in accordance with Divine will.
- If we ask to exhibit selflessness, it's up to us to fulfill that prayer (and we'll be shown how to do it).
- If we ask for material things, the answer can vary, depending on what we're asking for, whether we're too attached to the outcome, and whether providing it's for the best and highest good of all concerned. To ensure success, we need to dig deeper to the "why" of the thing we want – what internal feelings we want to generate instead of the external "stuff." If the feelings are genuine and come from love, and generate a true expression of appreciation, we're more likely to get what we pray for.
- If we ask for help with relationships, it depends on what we are asking for. If we ask for more love and acceptance, then we're guaranteed to get it. If we pray for someone to do something, we're infringing on the other person's free will. Not only is this outside of the domain of the Divine, getting it

may actually cause harm in the situation (to ourselves or the other person). If we ask to be released from attachment and to allow the relationship to unfold according to Divine Will, our wish will be granted.

Are You Listening?

As discussed earlier, prayer is talking to God, but we need to meditate in order to listen. Simply put, it means we need to get centered, be quiet, and pay attention. We can do this through the types of meditation discussed earlier (Sitting, Guided, Mind-Clearing), or through other avenues, like when exercising, dreaming, mowing the lawn, etc.

Even if we're listening, sometimes we have a problem recognizing the answer to our prayers. This could be for several reasons. It could be that we're too attached to the outcome and we can't recognize the open window because we're pounding too hard on a door to open. It could be because we're limited in our view and have blinders on. The solution to both of these problems is to keep an open mind and be open to solutions that give you the feelings you asked for, not the "stuff."

Another reason we could have a problem recognizing the answer may be that we really don't trust our Higher Power to bring what is best for us. This could be a challenge of faith, which is an opportunity to dig deeper to connect your three Selves and the Divine.

Suggestions from Philosophers and Theologians

- "The function of prayer is not to influence God, but rather to change the nature of the one who prays." - Soren Kierkegaard
- "The wise man in the storm prays to God, not for safety from danger, but deliverance from fear." - Ralph Waldo Emerson
- "Being mortal, never pray for an untroubled life; But ask the gods to give you an enduring heart" - Menander of Athens
- "Love your enemies, bless them that curse you, do good to them that hate you, and pray for them which despitefully use you, and persecute you." - Matthew 5:44

- "Pray as though everything depended on God. Work as though everything depended on you." - Saint Augustine
- "Rejoice always; pray without ceasing; in everything give thanks; for this is God's will for you." - I Thessalonians 5: 16-18
- "Humanity is never so beautiful as when praying for forgiveness, or else forgiving another" - Jean Paul Richter

Detachment and Surrender

In an interview with NBC's Ann Curry, Oprah Winfrey described the power of detachment and surrender to a Higher Power when she had auditioned for a role in "The Color Purple." She desperately wanted and prayed for the role because, she said, "I remember sitting home and I think it took my breath away literally. I remember closing the book and weeping, because my God, this is my story."

Although she had heard they were looking for an experienced actress to play the part, she was crushed, even hating herself, blaming herself for not getting the part because she was overweight. She entered a fat farm, trying to "lose 50 pounds in 2 weeks."

She "realized at that time that my obsession had gotten the best of me. I'd never wanted anything more than I wanted to be in "The Color Purple." Never. And it was life changing for me, because I decided I had to let it go. So I go out on the track by myself. It's cold. It's raining. I'm alone, running around the track. And I start asking 'God, dear God, just like Celie. Please help me to let it go so that I can move on with my life.' And I start singing, 'I surrender all. I surrender all.'"

Miraculously, just at that moment she received a call from the movie's director, Steven Spielberg, offering her the part, with one condition, "If you lose a pound, you will possibly lose this part."

This story shows how important it is for prayer to include surrender and detachment to Divine will for the outcome. It also demonstrates a great example of how we need to love and accept ourselves the way we are – because we may already be perfect for our destiny!

Wouldn't It Be Nice?

Two key factors of asking for Divine assistance are no attachment to the outcome, and that you'd be appreciative if you received your request.

"Wouldn't it be nice?" is the perfect way to ask Spirit for what you'd like to see in your life. First, it demonstrates that you're making a simple request, not a demand, with no expectation or attachment to the outcome. And second, it shows your Higher Power that you think "it would be nice" if the request came through, indicating that you'd appreciate it!

> When we pray for a specific outcome in a particular
> situation, we are presuming to know
> how the world should proceed.
> – Larry Dossey

PRAYER GUIDELINES

The following are some guidelines for prayer to connect with your Higher Power:

Integration

Before beginning any prayer, engage all three of your Selves in the process. Make sure your Inner Self is cleared of all negative emotions and fears, and is aligned with the intent of the prayer.

Gratitude

Be sure to give thanks to your Higher Power.[76] for:

- The gifts you have in your life
- Infinite Divine Love

---

[76] Note: if you pray to the Universe, remember that The Universe" is a big place and not necessarily Divine. Instead of a deity, please be sure that you ask for the highest level guidance available.

If the purpose of your prayer is to manifest something in your life, it's helpful to indicate your appreciation of the gift – as though you already have it.

Praise

Show reverence and love for your Higher Power. This means that you recognize that you're calling upon an energy greater than yourself.

Love and/or Peace

Ask for love: To feel love, to find love, to express love, to act in love. Love is the most powerful energy in the universe, and it's available to all of us, at all times. Peace is also a very powerful expression of love.

> Experiments in prayer suggest that love is one of the most important factors influencing its effectiveness.
> - Larry Dossey

Alignment

Ask for Alignment with Divine Will. A few famous prayers requesting alignment include, "Let thy will and mine be one" and "Let me delight in thy will and walk in thy ways." And, of course, the simple alignment prayer provided in the chapter on resolving your Reason Why: "Let Divine Will Fill My Heart and Guide My Actions."

Guidance

Ask for Divine Guidance. How you can:
- Do the best you can with in every situation you encounter.
- Help others, either directly or indirectly by serving as a model of love.

Awareness

Ask for help to see the signs from Spirit, including asking:
- To see the potential silver lining or Blessing in Disguise.

Selflessness

When asking for something, ask "if it's for the highest good of all concerned." It is important to never infringe on the rights of others, especially through prayer.

Commitment/Loyalty

Demonstrate that you're committed to following through and are loyal to the Divine by doing so.

Release

Release the message from yourself up to your Higher Power, to bring you what is best for you. This also includes detachment from the results, if you're using the prayer to ask for something.

What Prayer Should *Not* Do:

- Infringe on another's rights or free will.
- Restrict or limit the Divine from providing what's best.
- Nag. Don't nag when you pray! Your Higher Power knows what you want; you don't have to nag Him. The more you pester and nag for what you want, the more you'll find it to be elusive, because you're showing that you're too attached to the outcome (an important Lesson!)

Be Careful What You Pray For

In addition to the Lessons discussed earlier from Larry Dossey's book, *Be Careful What You Pray For*, about the potentially harmful effects of prayer, we should also pay close attention to the things we think we want in our lives, including success, health, abundance, etc. If we're not integrated and aligned, we may receive exactly what we ask for – but find that we're either not satisfied with the result, or perhaps are even deeply troubled by it.

Affluenza is a term that describes the stress associated with money and financial success. Many of us know that financial adversity can cause anxiety, but having a lot of money can create problems as well. Research has shown that the larger the square footage in a home, the greater the likelihood for divorce. And the more possessions you have, the more problems you can have. We may dream of having a vacation home, for example, but not realize it would mean twice the bills and upkeep.

This doesn't mean that it's wrong to ask for external possessions – as long as we realize that not only doesn't it produce functional (internal) happiness, but there can also be a downside to every request.

Having Someone Pray for You

If someone asked if she could pray for you, what would you say? Would it matter if you knew her or not? What if you were facing surgery and your physician asked if he/she could pray? What if you found out that someone prayed for you without your permission? Would it bother you, or would you be grateful? Would it matter what their belief system is? Would it matter how they prayed – what they said – and to whom?

As we know, there's amazing power in thought. Having others pray for us can be extremely helpful. But it can also be uncomfortable – or perhaps even counter-productive – if it isn't delivered and received with the highest energy and intent.

There can be problems with having other people pray for you:

- They could be trying to influence your belief system. For example, they could pray that you go to a particular church, a place that isn't comfortable to you.

- They could have a hidden wish or agenda in the outcome of your experience. For example, they could hope that you keep your job so that you can help them find a position with the same company – while the best thing for you could be to move onto another career.

- They could misunderstand what you'd like, yet want something different for you. For example, you could say you want a particular relationship to work out, and you pray that you stay married. However, the outcome of their prayer could be that you do, indeed stay married, but are still unhappy.

- Even if their wishes are aligned with yours, they could be troublesome. For example, say you want to be healed from a serious illness. They could pray for your healing as well, and it works – your illness is gone. But if you didn't figure out the Reason Why, you may have to face a bigger problem in the future.

These interferences could come from the best intentions, or they could include Subconscious Sabotage from the other person. It can be very complicated! However, the guidelines provided below offer the best advice for praying for others and having others pray for you.

Praying for Others and Why the Prayer Study Didn't Work

Praying for others is just as complicated. In 2005 a study was done to measure the effect of prayer. As reported by Rob Stein of the Washington Post, "Praying for sick strangers does not improve their prospects of recovering, according to a large, carefully designed study that casts doubt on the widely held belief that being prayed for can help a person heal. The study of more than 700 heart patients, one of the most ambitious attempts to test the medicinal power of prayer, showed that those who had people praying for them from a distance, and without their knowledge, were no less likely to suffer a major complication, end up back in the hospital or die."

Although this study was widely debated by scientists and theologians, the "Reason Why" the study didn't work was crystal clear to me: *Because no one should interfere with the rights of others.* Each of these patients had their own Reason Why they got cancer.

For some, Subconscious Sabotage was the cause. Their own negative thinking produced the disease. For these people, praying for the removal of the disease would only have been a temporary "cure."

For others, developing cancer might have been a Karmic payback to something they had done. Unless the Karmic debt was paid, the disease would continue. Conversely, perhaps the disease offered a chance to earn some positive Karma by helping others.

Some of the patients may have been learning a valuable lesson through their disease, which could've been thwarted if the outsider's prayers for their healing had worked.

The cancer could've also been a test, to see if the patient would react to the disease with anger or with faith.

And, finally, perhaps the cancer held a Reward for the patient. If the study was effective, the people praying could've robbed the patients of the blessings often found through disease.

However, if the study had followed the guidelines listed below, I believe it would have been significantly more effective.

Guidelines for Praying for Others and Having Others Pray for Us

Both praying for others and having others pray for us are safest and most effective when the following suggestions are applied.

Ask for:
- Divine love, guidance and support
- Help to learn any Lessons involved
- Strength to handle anything that comes with grace and dignity
- Faith to keep believing and find meaning
- Compassion to and from others
- Awareness to look for signs and find guidance
- Connection to their 3 selves and the Divine
- Alignment with Divine Will
- Help to face, feel and free any fears or harmful emotions.
- Forgiveness toward a perpetrator

And the simplest thing is also the most influential:
- Send love and ask for love.

Great Times to Pray

When you:

- Wake up
- Go to sleep
- Eat
- Pay bills
- Are trying something new or embarking on an adventure
- Are in a potentially risky situation
- Are trying to connect with people (especially challenging people)
- Are grateful
- Are happy!

> Old Man: "It goes like this. Let's see now: 'Protect me from knowing what I don't need to know. Protect me from even knowing that there are things to know that I don't know. Protect me from knowing that I decided not to know about the things that I decided not to know about. Amen.' That's it. It's what you pray silently inside yourself anyway, so you may as well have it out in the open."
> Arthur: "Hmmm, Well, thank you - "
> Old Man: "There's another prayer that goes with it that's very important, so you'd better jot this down, too."
> Arthur: "OK."
> Old Man: "It goes, 'Lord, lord, lord...' It's best to put that bit in, just in case. You can never be too sure. 'Lord, lord, lord. Protect me from the consequences of the above prayer. Amen...' And that's it. Most of the trouble people get into in life comes from missing out that last part.'"
> - Old Man Oracle's prayer given to Arthur Dent in The Hitchhiker's Guide to the Galaxy

Prayer

<u>Chapter 18: Forgiveness</u>

As I looked for quotes on forgiveness, it was interesting how many I disagreed with. Things like, "Forgive many things in others; nothing in yourself," and "It's far easier to forgive an enemy after you've got even with him," or even "Forgive your enemies, but never forget their names." Ugh!

I realized it's because forgiveness is a concept that can create a lot of confusion and misconception. Which is a travesty, because not being able to forgive – or to be forgiven – can not only lead to more "bad things," it can prevent healing or change!

Therefore, as it's such a crucial – and complicated – lesson, I decided to create an entirely separate chapter on the subject. And since forgiveness is something you can either give or receive, we'll look at it from both perspectives, starting with the Four Steps to Forgiveness, the things you need to do if you want to regain another person's trust.

Is there someone you've hurt? A relationship that needs healing? While you can never control how someone will react, and you can't force someone to forgive you, the following Four Steps will help immensely.

As you read, you may find yourself being challenged, even possibly wanting to argue about some of the points being made. Sorry to say, but any resistance you're showing indicates that you may not be ready – to give or receive – forgiveness. At least not yet. Pay attention to your reaction: there's a(nother) lesson in there! Another opportunity to "heal the hurt" so you can have the triumphant life you want.

STEP 1: ADMIT WRONGDOING

> The three most difficult things for a human being are not physical feats or intellectual achievements. They are, first, returning love for hate; second, including the excluded; third, admitting that you are wrong.
> Anthony de Mello

Forgiveness is not just about saying "I'm sorry." Getting someone to forgive you requires that *they* know *you* know what you did was wrong. You shouldn't have done it.

All too often, when people say they're sorry, it's more that they're sorry you're upset – and less an indication that they really regret what they did, or even understand how their actions impacted you.

What this means, is that it's likely they'll do it again! So, the first step – admitting wrongdoing – is the key to opening the dialogue that leads to healing. And the clearer and more sincere you are, the greater the chance the relationship will be able to move forward.

By admitting you were wrong, and being specific, you're not trivializing the infraction. For example, you can say, "I'm sorry I didn't take out the trash when I promised I would." Okay, that's good. You said what you did wrong. But how about instead you say, "I'm sorry I broke my promise to you. I shouldn't have made a commitment I wasn't able to keep." Or even better, "I sorry I didn't take out the trash when I said I would. I should've kept my word to you, even when it was difficult. I know you count on me, and by not doing the things I say I will, it makes it harder for you to trust me."

See how even something "trivial" isn't, really, in the other person's eyes?

If you're seeking forgiveness, and not exactly sure of how "wrong" your actions were – ask! Find out! Sometimes we might not know the whole story, so dig deep! As with the above example, it's usually not about the trash, is it? And be prepared to listen – really listen – if you want to heal the relationship.

Since we're talking about commitment and trust, I'll divert here a little and share a little test I use when trying to discover whether someone's values are in alignment with mine. I pose a hypothetical situation: Suppose you and I were single and best friends 20 years ago, and we made a pact: if one of us was arrested, the other would bail him or her out of jail. Now, fast-forward 20 years. You're married; I'm not. We're not really in touch that much anymore. Yet one day, you get the call from me: I've been arrested and need your help. Now, let's say your spouse says there's "no way" he/she will allow you to go to the jail to bail me out. (For whatever reason). What do you do?

For me (and this is just for me, okay?), if that person says he won't keep their commitment to me, it's a deal-breaker. To me, to the relationships I want to cultivate, I need people who value their commitments – over everything else. (And, honestly, if I had a friend whose spouse didn't understand this, I'm not sure I could relate to him very well anyway!)

Some people might argue that their commitment is more to their spouse than to you. I hear this argument, but don't buy it. It's not (at least to me) really about their prioritization of the people in their life. It's about the value they place on keeping their commitments. (It's not like I wouldn't be understanding if, when I call them from jail, I find out their child is in the hospital, and they say they can't come. But I'd still hope my friend would find a way to get me out of the slammer! I know I'd do the same!)

STEP 2: APOLOGIZE

The second step, those three magic words, "I'm really sorry," are both crucial and cathartic, especially when combined with the other steps. For most people "I apologize" just doesn't carry the same kind of punch. And please have the courage to do it in person, looking him or her in the eye when you speak those words. Flowers and gifts can be nice, but they still can't make up for the impact of saying you're really sorry.

Here's an "inspirational" quote about forgiveness that bothered me immensely: "Apologizing does not always mean that you're wrong and the other person is right. It just means that you value your relationship more than your ego." Why does this statement bug me so much? Because it IS your ego that's choosing to placate the other person instead of getting to the real issue! He or she isn't angry with you for no reason! He or she feels hurt! For the apology to be sincere it has to mean you start listening to the other person to find out what they think you did was wrong.

How NOT to Apologize...

If you are really serious about fixing the relationship, the last thing you want to do is say the wrong thing, right? Hopefully! Otherwise, what's the point? (If that is a rhetorical question for you, and you think the answer is "To prove my point," or "to defend myself," or something even more heinous, then you might as well stop reading this book, because you'll have missed the point entirely!)

If you're still with me, and really want to know the things *not* to say...here they are:

First, never say, "I'm sorry you're upset." What that's really saying is that you're not sorry for what you've done; you're just sorry you got caught! Or at least you're regretting the reaction, not the action. To be really sorry, you need to admit wrongdoing – step #1.

Second, don't try to defend yourself. You're still looking at it from your point of view and not theirs. If (you think) your action is defensible, then it's something you're probably going to do again without the slightest restriction or remorse. You'll always have an excuse. "I'm sorry I didn't meet you for our date. I got really busy" is really saying "I'm not that into you to even call to cancel" and probably "I was flirting with another girl." Is that "forgivable?" Didn't think so...

Third, please don't say "I didn't mean to hurt you." Again, you're still focused on yourself. For most offenses, the other person probably didn't intentionally go out of her way to hurt you. But still, when she delivers this message, what she's really saying is she wasn't thinking, which ultimately means they didn't care if they hurt you or not. How can you forgive someone so immune to how her actions affect others?

Remember when we talked about Karma, that there are two factors related to karma: intent and effect? "I didn't mean to hurt you," might mitigate some forms of transgressions, but it doesn't eliminate the effect. If he cut you off in traffic because he wasn't thinking (or on the phone or…), but his action caused you to spin off the road and crash your car and break your back, do you really think he's innocent because he "didn't mean to?" No. Didn't think so. (The law calls this "recklessness" or "reckless disregard" and is defined (by Wikipedia as "a person pursuing a course of action while consciously disregarding the fact that the action gives rise to a substantial and unjustifiable risk." And, yes, it's a crime; both legally and morally.)

If the other person is really so unconscious to have no idea what he said or did but really does want to make things work, see "safe word" below. If he agrees to this tactic, and really appreciates it when you call him out, then you can start to get through to his subconscious (Inner Self) and make him conscious of his actions.

You might be asking, "What if the other person is just too sensitive?" Good question! How you treat the situation will depend on three things: (1) your history with that person; (2) how much you care about him or her, and (3) if this has happened to you before with other people. If there's a history, then the reaction is likely a build-up of past offenses and the latest "minor" infraction is the proverbial straw. If not, then you might want to decide if there's a future. If other people being "too sensitive" happens a lot to you, then you're missing an important opportunity for learning and personal growth!

Fourth, never, never, never say "I was just being honest" or "I was just being myself" if you want to have any possible hope of healing the relationship. You might as well be saying, "You mean so little to me that I have no interest in trying to control my words or actions around you." (You might be asking: what if someone asks my opinion and then don't like what I have to say? Don't I have the right to be honest then? My answer, if you want it, is "No." Not really. Any human being who wants to get along with another needs to be able to filter what he or she says to save the other person's feelings. (Yes, sometimes "tough love" might be required. Sometimes. But, again, if you want to know what I think, "tough love" is all-too-often a euphemism for "verbally abusive.") Don't you deserve better? Don't they? If you can't say "yes" and be willing to move on (away), then you're probably setting yourself up for future "bad things."

Finally, don't use deception or lies. This should be blatantly obvious. No further explanation needed. This includes not making commitments you are unlikely to keep. (See below).

When apologizing, can you add, "Please forgive me."? Yes – but only if you're willing to go the next step and make amends...

STEP 3: MAKE AMENDS

Do you really want the relationship to move forward in a positive direction? Offer to make amends. Do something to show you're serious about earning their forgiveness. You can come up with something on your own, but it's even better when you ask him what he'd like you to do. Some people might say, "nothing," but don't let her get away with it! Make her give you some task, large or small, to demonstrate your appreciation for her forgiveness. You'll both feel much better!

Have some amusing ideas? In one of my DUET stories novels, I tell the story about a vanity license plate that said, "ASN9." It was seen on a man's treasured, expensive vehicle. The license plate was the wife's way of getting even for the husband's infidelity. It was fictional and intended for humor, but it also conveyed an important message. The fact that his wife selected this form of "revenge," and the fact that the man agreed to it suggests he wouldn't have agreed to the plate if he hadn't admitted he was wrong and wanted to make amends. Did the punishment fit the crime? You'll have to decide. But you can't deny she had to have had some form of satisfaction! (Not to mention significantly reducing his chances of repeating the offense!)

Again, it's a fictional story. Can you think of some solutions for making amends that aren't vindictive, but can help balance the scales? Share your thoughts in our Reasons Why online discussion group!

STEP 4: NOT DO IT AGAIN

You've admitted what you did was wrong. You've apologized sincerely. You've even paid your price by making amends. You wouldn't want to lose all that work, would you? Hopefully not! But just to be clear: DON'T DO IT AGAIN! Whatever you did before, if you repeat the offense, you're not only stupid (sorry, but I have to call it as I see it), you probably don't deserve another chance. That old adage, "Fool me once, shame on you; Fool me twice, shame on me," comes into play here. Do you really think the other person would - or should - keep letting it happen to him or her? Really? If so, you need to consider...perhaps you weren't looking for forgiveness in the first place. Perhaps your motives were, let's say, less enlightened?

A Safe Word?

Also in my DUET stories novels, one of my characters does something that really ticks off the other. She's angry, but doesn't know how to express herself. The relationship is in the early stages, so there's no history for her anger, the issue is isolated. But, if she "drops it," it can fester in the subconscious and come out later. (By now, you know the Inner Self can be quite devious when being ignored!)

So – what does she do? Does she utter those four treacherous words, "We need to talk? No, thankfully, she's too smart for that. But she is annoyed. So, she starts by sending a text, "I've got some explaining to do." This was good; it allowed her to start out by taking responsibility for her reaction!

Then, when she meets with him, he's ready, but open to listening. They finally decide on an approach I think real-life people can learn from. They come up with a "safe word" when one has done something to upset the other. The safe word they come up with (I won't tell you here – no spoilers! You'll have to read the book to find out), but I will say it is one that is quite clever and humorous, and it bonds them tighter as a couple.

So...how can having a safe word help in forgiveness? I'm sure you've figured it out by now, but for the sake of clarity...

Sometimes we do things unconsciously. (Especially before we get to know our Inner Self!). By using a safe word, we can re-program ourselves (and, potentially, even others), by building awareness of our activities.

Now, what if you're on the other end, the one who needs to do the forgiving? And what if the other person doesn't follow through on the four steps? Here's some advice on forgiving someone else:

ACKNOWLEDGING YOUR ROLE IN WHAT HAPPENED

There are usually two (or more) sides to a story. And it's pretty rare when one person is 100% guilty and the other pure as the driven snow. When one partner cheats, for example, there's usually some problem at home he or she is avoiding. Maybe not always, but usually. When someone steals from another, he may be taking something he thinks he "deserves." Again, he's probably still over 50% wrong - maybe even 98% wrong, but as you learned in the Reasons Why, it happened to *you* for a reason. What was it?

Anthony de Mello suggests, "Every time you find yourself irritated or angry with someone, the one to look at is not that person but yourself. The question to ask is not, 'What's wrong with this person?' but 'What does this irritation tell me about myself?'" Pretty good advice! (He had a lot of that!)

Acknowledging your role in what happened is, in a word: Accountability. Taking (at least) some responsibility for what happened. As discussed under Lessons, it's one of the most important lessons of all! Without it, you'll likely never get to the Reasons Why – or forgiveness!

LETTING GO OF THE ANGER AND RESENTMENT

At some point, you've got to just let it go. In fact, some philosophers have said the definition of forgiveness is "to drop it." Others suggest forgiveness is "giving up the hope of a more enlightened past." (Think about that one a while!). But in the end, if you hang on to the resentment you're only hurting yourself. You know that, don't you? How many ailments arise from the stress of anger, hatred and resentment? If not, do the research. And keep reading.

SEEING SOME GOOD IN THE OTHER PERSON THOUGH IT MAY BE DIFFICULT!)

Everyone has good points and bad. No one is 100% dark. As Goo the Guru, from DUET Stories Volume III: *A Chorus of Voices*, might say, "There are infinite shades of gray between pure light and lure darkness." So... what are some good things about the other person? Make a list. Write it down. If your anger has been raging, perhaps this can stifle it a bit. Just one caution: just because someone isn't all bad, it doesn't mean that he or she is good for you. Often, you need to distance yourself and just send them away with good thoughts...

SENDING GOOD THOUGHTS

Yes. It might be difficult, but it really helps to send someone who's wronged you good thoughts. When I first heard the following story, it blew me away...

Forgiveness Can Save Your Life

Forgiveness can save your life. Exemplifying this truth is the powerful story of Marietta and Bill Jaeger. In 1973, Bill and Marietta took their children camping in Montana. In the early hours of June 27th, their seven-year old daughter, Susie, was kidnapped from her tent. As the horror turned into days, then into weeks, the Jaegers felt their hatred for the kidnapper grow.

One night, however, Marietta heard a voice inside her say, "I don't want you to feel this way." She decided the best thing she could do for herself – and for her daughter – was to forgive. While it didn't mean she had to pretend to like him or ignore what he had done, she would pray for him, sending him good thoughts.

Some days, she would wish for him to experience good weather. Other days that he would find something he had lost, and so on. "I felt that I would better honor Susie's life and Susie's spirit by having an attitude of concern and compassion towards the man who took Susie away from me, than by wanting to have him killed in her name. That would be a violation of all the beauty and goodness and sweetness that was in her."

Conversely, her husband, Bill, let his anger and hatred destroy his health, and ultimately his life, dying of a heart attack at 56. "If you remain vindictive, you give the offender another victim. Anger, hatred and resentment would have taken my life as surely as Susie's life was taken," reflects Marietta.

> Forgive others as quickly as
> you expect God to forgive you.
> Unknown

ASKING FOR "AMENDS"

As discussed above, offering to make amends when you've done something wrong is a key step in earning that person's forgiveness. But what about the other way around, when you're the one who wants to forgive? Can you ask for amends?

Yes! Sometimes people don't realize they can fix the problem! For example, I used to travel a lot, and one time something happened with the airline that was 100% their fault (not the weather or something out of their control, but something egregious they should've *never* done), which caused serious problems for me and my schedule. I was furious!

I could've gone online and ranted, but this was (thankfully) before the internet. And how healthy would that be? Would I be able to change anything? Probably not!

So, what did I do? I wrote the airline a "strongly worded letter" (not too angry or it would've backfired!) and suggested they should give me 10,000 frequent flyer miles for my trouble. You know what? They did! You know what else? I not only forgave them, they earned my loyalty from that day forward!

Can this work with personal relationships? Maybe, maybe not. It takes two, as they say. But you won't know if you don't ask! You can say, "I'm really angry, but I've figured out a way for you to make it up to me. If you (fill in the blank), I'll let it go. And then, if they do it, keep your word! Have some ideas for amends that fit the "crime?" Let us know on our Reasons Why website! (Something really good the internet is for!)

GETTING HIM/HER TO SEE YOUR POV

If someone comes to you and he is angry/upset/hurt, defending yourself is usually ineffective (and potentially destructive).

But if someone hurt you and you want to (gently) get her to see what she did through your eyes, here's a suggestion:

I had a relationship that was decidedly one-sided, where I gave and gave and gave and the friend not only didn't reciprocate, it was often rudely dismissive of my needs and wants. (Note: (this happened to be a friendship, but could apply as equally to a work or romantic relationship) I finally confessed, but started with a "what-if" question. "If you told me you (did something wonderful, needed help, etc.), how do you think I would've responded?" She answered as I suspected: she knew I'd do whatever I could to help and be supportive.

Then...I set the stage so I could shift the discussion to find out: why isn't she doing the same for me? I give her immense credit for trying to heal the relationship, but she started by defending herself. "You didn't ask," and "I have my own issues." I finally said to her, "I'm reaching out to you and telling you because I care. And want to talk about it. But before we do, I want you to think carefully on the question, How do you think your (doing whatever it was) made me feel? When you come back, the closer you get to understanding how I felt, the more likely we'll be able to heal our relationship."

So, if you can, see if you can get the other person to see things from your point of view. It's worth a try!

LEARN TO DETACH

One of my favorite teachers/philosophers/spiritual leaders is Anthony de Mello. (As you'll notice, I'm referring to him several times in this chapter). Reading his books (several times!) provided a profound breakthrough in my life, and the recurring theme throughout all his teachings related to attachment.

I agree with de Mello that it's our attachments that produce unhappiness. It can be attachment to a person, concept or belief. And, yes, we can have an "attachment" to our own anger. Yet, as de Mello asserts, "An attachment destroys your capacity to love."

Reflecting on the story above about Marietta Jaeger, then, what if we give up our attachment to our anger and, instead, seek out a more loving solution?

Anthony de Mello offered the following advice:

> The happier the other person is, the more you can detach from him, the happier you can be. The key is that the other person has to be really happy, sincerely happy, happy that comes from learning and growth, deeply changed happy – then you can detach.

The truth is, the happier and more enlightened the other person becomes, the more it will improve their chances of realizing what she did was wrong. And, of course, it reduces the chance she'll ever do it again!

> Life becomes easier when you learn to accept an
> apology you never got.
> Robert Brault

AND, IF APPLICABLE, ACCEPT HIS/HER APOLOGY

When an apology is given, when you're lucky enough to hear those words, accept them graciously. Hopefully, the other person will want to follow the Four Steps. But even if not, be the better person - STAY the better person and say, "Thank you."

SHOULD YOU TAKE ACTION?

> I think the first step is to understand that forgiveness
> does not exonerate the perpetrator. Forgiveness liberates
> the victim. It's a gift you give yourself.
> T. D. Jakes

As the above quote implies, just because you forgive, it does NOT mean that you have to continue the relationship. Nor does it mean you should "exonerate the perpetrator," sit back and do nothing, not have a role in the "punishment," or become passive in what happens next. Remember the quote by Edmund Burke: "All that is necessary for the triumph of evil is that good men do nothing." Besides, it's possible you have an unwritten "spiritual" contract with that person to be the one who helps him or her learn! If you do nothing, then you: (a) cannot claim any honor that this kind of assistance brings, and (b) might not be able to truly – and lastingly – forgive. Especially when you sense that you could've prevented someone else from the same kind of pain you went through. Just make sure your energy is coming from as high a level as possible (your Higher Self), and not out of anger and the need to "get even," or you'll just bring on more of your own karma!

OTHER VARIABLES TO CONSIDER

Finally, it might help to consider the following variables:

Forgiveness

- Most issues have two sides. Do you understand both?
- There can be a range of responsibility. As suggested above, it's rare for someone to be 100% wrong. Usually, both parties have some level of responsibility in what happened.
- The angrier you get, and the less forgiving you are, the more "in the wrong" you appear. Have you ever seen this happen? I remember seeing this on a reality TV show. (I don't watch them much, but sometimes there is wisdom, as Edie Brickell would say, "on a cereal box.) Anyway, the man was rude and insensitive (and, frankly, a few fries short of a happy meal, if you get my drift). The woman was angry about it, and wanted to stand up for herself and express her displeasure. Nothing wrong with that. But at one point, she got so angry it ended up making *her* look bad!
- Find out: what's going on in that person's life? Does he or she have problems or issues outside of the one at hand? This can be really helpful in being able to forgive someone, when you find out her daughter's got a serious illness or he just lost his job!
- Could you remind him of someone else, and his actions against you were just reflections that had nothing to do with you at all? It's easier to forgive someone for ignoring your calls when you find out her parent is dying.
- Is the problem ongoing? The answer to this question can have a significant impact on forgiveness. If it's the first offense, forgiveness is usually easier. Maybe the person didn't know you'd take offense. But if it's ongoing, it can build up over time, making the anger accumulate. However, consider this: if you let the offense go the first or second time, weren't you, in some way, condoning (or at least tolerating) the behavior? Was this fair? (Note: in my second DUET stories novel, my characters discuss the "Predictable Surprises" that can occur in relationships. This includes the way that people are more "forgiving" (translation: more likely to ignore) problems in the beginning of a relationship. But over time, they build up and suddenly leaving a towel on the floor becomes a major offense!

- Is the problem a result of something that might've happened before? Could your anger or resentment be about something else entirely? For example, a wife may get angry with a husband for leaving dishes in the sink, but the thing she's really upset about is how he doesn't listen.

- Is it not really about you at all? The person may be lashing out to you because they remind you of someone. Or because you're the safer (or closer) target.

- Going forward, consider your commitments carefully. This can be easier said than done. I have a staunch policy not to ever make a commitment unless I know I can keep it. I'm not saying that I'm perfect (far from it!), and I sometimes forget/make mistakes, etc. But I do make sure I never tell someone I'm committed when I'm not. It's not so easy! A lot of people will do whatever they can to force you to behave in a certain way, and it can be very tempting to appease them. Very tempting! But the truth is, to placate someone with a half-hearted vow or guarantee is (sorry to be so blunt) not that far from a lie. Talk about bad karma! And practically guaranteeing another "bad thing" in the future! (By the way, this goes both ways. Don't try to coerce someone to promise you something!)

- And try to make sure you manage the other person's expectations! By saying, "I'll take out the trash this week," instead of "right now," you're giving yourself - and the other person – a very precious gift! Sure, it might stink up the house for an extra day, but at least it gives you something to negotiate.

- On that note, please be patient with me in getting out the Reasons Why workbook! I'm going to do my best to get it out as soon as I can, I promise! (I just have a long, long to-do list these days!)

Forgiveness

CHAPTER 19: HELPING OTHERS

> If there's any kind of magic in this world, it must be in the attempt of understanding someone, sharing something. I know, it's almost impossible to succeed, but... The answer must be in the attempt.
> – Celine (Julie Delpy) in the film *Before Sunrise*

First: Process Your Own Feelings

When Bad Things happen to people we care about, it can be almost as bad as their happening to us. For example, let's say you have a loved one with a serious illness. Even if you don't physically feel their pain, you're affected. You could need to face the potential for losing him or her, your schedule may be taken up with caring for him, or it could make you realize that "it could have been me."

Because you don't want to subconsciously sabotage someone else, you need to process your own feelings about the situation. At first this may seem selfish. After all, it's their problem, not yours. But it's actually completely self-less and considerate, to both your Selves and your loved ones.

You may have already recognized the effect of their tragedy and gone through your own emotions and Lessons from the other person's crisis throughout this book. (Remember, in the chapter

Bad Things Defined, when you identified your role in the crisis?) However, if you haven't done so, the exercises in the Reasons Why Workbook should help you process your emotions.

How is His/Her Crisis Affecting You?

How is the other person's crisis affecting you? Is it affecting your Schedule? Finances? Emotions? Lifestyle? Health? Job or Career? Change in Future Direction?

What fears and emotions do you have regarding your loved one's crisis? Are you afraid that you'll hurt him/her? Are you angry – at them, yourself or someone else? Are you afraid you will lose them – or their love? Do you have any guilt? Resentment? Do you feel helpless? Do you have any judgment of him or her, either because of what happened or how he/she's dealing with it? What fears and emotions have been projected to you, either from the other person or someone else?

> The best way to find yourself
> is to lose yourself in the service of others.
> - Mahatma Gandhi

HOW YOU CAN HELP

Be a Good Listener

Sometimes all they want to do is talk with someone who cares and who won't judge or condemn. Many of the problems we face are the result of our actions, but we don't need someone reminding us of that. We need someone to listen, someone we trust.

> The friend who can be silent with us in a moment of
> despair or confusion, who can stay with us in an hour of
> grief and bereavement, who can tolerate not
> knowing…not healing, not curing...
> that is a friend who cares.
> - Henri Nouwen

Ask How You Can Help

Sometimes people in a crisis just want to be left alone. And sometimes they need help in the most unusual or insignificant ways.

A friend of mine was telling me about an acquaintance of hers who was ill. Her mother was strongly suggesting that she visit this person in the hospital. But my friend didn't feel comfortable, and I understood completely. When I've been hospitalized, I'm very particular about who I want to see me in such a vulnerable state. However, I would have really appreciated someone visiting my dog or feeding my fish.

Show Compassion (Not Pity)

Compassion comes from love and the Higher Self – pity comes from a wounded Inner Self. There's a great difference between the two energies. Can you feel it? Compassion lifts both people, pity lowers both.

Sometimes just asking is a big help. It shows you care and are willing to be a support. But it wouldn't hurt to think of some things you could do to help out. Bringing food, checking mail, feeding or walking pets can all be a way to help out. A simple reaching out makes a huge difference.

Give Your Opinion ONLY If They Ask For It

Hopefully you've been able to face, feel and free any judgment you may have toward the other person. If not, I would advise not providing your opinion until you've removed all judgment you could have of them. Even then, wait to be asked for your opinion, before giving it.

> "Why does God allow any suffering at any time? There is perfection in the process – and all life arises out of choice. It is not appropriate to interfere with choice, nor to question it. What is appropriate is to observe it, and to do whatever might be done to assist the soul in seeking and making a higher choice. Be watchful,

> therefore, of the choices of others, but not judgmental. Know that their choice is perfect for them in this moment now – yet stand ready to assist them should the moment come when they seek a newer choice, a different choice, a higher choice."
> - "God" (Neale Donald Walsh)

Send and Show Love

Even if your loved one (or your "enemy," as the case may be) isn't receptive to help and would rather be alone, you can always send and show love. Love is the highest, most inspiring and healing energy there is and you can send it from any location to any location, including the "other side."

> Finding love within oneself is the love that turns around and goes out to others as God's love.
> – Afterlife101

Ask Them: Why Do You Think This Happened to You?

If you feel comfortable, and are sure you won't be judgmental, you may casually ask them, "Why do you think this happened to you?" The answer may be very interesting. I have asked several people this question and their answers are fascinating and enlightening for both of us. One time I asked man, who was a friend of a friend, this question and he provided a fluid and inspiring explanation. But then, a moment later, he nearly forgot what he had said! What seemed clear to me was that the reply came from Higher Self, while his conscious Outer Self was completely aware. Your friend's answers may also be revealing.

> Don't urge your friend to move on—instead, help her tolerate her emotions. Distress can be a catalyst for change, and processing pain may be essential to deriving meaning from a life-shattering experience.
> Don't shut it down. Help them manage it so they can think straight without going numb,
> - Rich Tedeschi, *Psychology Today*

Praying for Others

The chapter on Prayer gave guidelines for praying for others. The important thing to remember is to ask the Divine to help them through their crisis with love, guidance and support, and to try to avoid asking for a particular outcome. Remember that Integrated Alignment means we can find the silver linings and blessings in disguise through any tragedy, so the best thing to desire is to achieve IA.

> It is not for me to change you.
> The question is, how can I be of service to you without diminishing your degrees of freedom?
> - Buckminster Fuller

An Answer to the Question: How Can a Human "Heal" Another Human by Spiritual Means?

The following is an answer to the above question from the souls speaking from "the other side" as reported on the website, www.afterlife101.com.

"One human can never heal another human. It is the choice and responsibility of the individual who perhaps is not even seeking to be healed. We can never assume that a person is choosing to be healed. We can never put ourselves into their situation. But as we view an individual who we view needs to be healed, whether it be physically, emotionally, spiritually, mentally, whatever that healing is, however we view it, we can call forth and ask for the highest good of that individual and pray that that individual receives its highest good. The highest good for that individual might not be what we see. We might selfishly wish for that person to be physically healed and to continue life with us but for the person who we view that needs to be healed, maybe it is not what is right for them. Maybe it is a time for their crossing, so we can never take the responsibility of knowing what is the highest good for each individual. We can only pray for their highest good and pray that we as their loved ones are doing what is best for them in praying for their highest good.

"There are many, many healers upon your Earth and the person who is seeking a healing may go to someone who has the ability to heal, whether it be a doctor, a mechanic to heal their car--whatever the healer is--they may choose to see a financial healer, a mental healer, it does not matter what the healer is. If the individual goes to the healer and is seeking healing, it is then their choice to be healed and they along with the healer have the responsibility of working together. And in the healing, again, you ask for the highest good at that time. Please know it is not the healer that is doing the healing. It is the person's responsibility who has come to the healer to be healed."

> Jesus did not heal those he healed because he saw their condition as imperfect. He healed those he healed because he saw those souls asking for healing as part of their process. He saw the perfection of the process. He recognized and understood the soul's intention.
> - "God" (Neale Donald Walsh)

Teach a Man to Fish...

Helping others help themselves is the most powerful way to offer aid, because it's least likely to interfere with their Karma or Lessons. The beneficiary would need to join in the ownership of the problem and be actively involved in the solution. The following advice, from Chinese Philosopher Lao Tzu, is perhaps the best there is:

> Give a man a fish and you feed him for a day.
> Teach a man to fish and you feed him for a lifetime.
> - Lao Tzu

Or, perhaps comedian George Carlin's...?

> Give a man a fish and he will eat for a day.
> Teach him how to fish, and he will sit in a boat
> and drink beer all day.
> – George Carlin

Seriously, though, we need to remember that, even if we could wave a magic wand and eliminate all of the problems our loved one's face, it isn't in the best interest for them. Even if their problem is eliminated, they won't have the tools to cope with another problem down the road, unless they have been able to face what they're going through now.

Remember what Harold Percival said about reaching the ultimate goal, which is ease.

> "Ease is a further development of trust. Only a developed person can feel at ease in riches or in poverty, in sickness or in health. Ease comes to a person only after he/she has been the victor in many battles and difficulties and has learned their ways and how to live with them. Ease does not depend on easy circumstances, but the person maintains their ease notwithstanding any outward conditions, favorable or adverse. Ease is a feeling of confidence that the person will find its way through life."

We shouldn't want our loved one to miss out on the confidence that comes with ease. But what we *do* want is to help them get there. (Just as we want to get there ourselves.) To do this, we can first teach ourselves "to fish", and then be available to share what we've learned.

> To ease another's heartache is to forget one's own.
> - Abraham Lincoln

Pray for Those Who Have Passed On

In all the books I've read about the Other Side, all of them have said that our prayers for loved ones who have passed on helps them immensely, especially in times of severely stressful transitions like murder and suicide. It isn't that they're being punished or sent to hell, but our offering love, forgiveness and appreciation can help them and us at the same time.

If you went through the life review exercise and imagined everyone you've ever harmed, through thought, word or deed, you can appreciate how those who have passed on might feel – except they don't' have the chance to apologize! So, offering forgiveness and acceptance, even to those who have hurt you, is very influential. We can also send thoughts of appreciation – although hopefully we'll remember to do it while they're alive!

> Strange is our situation here upon earth. Each of us comes for a short visit, not knowing why, yet sometimes seeming to a Divine purpose.
> From the standpoint of daily life, however, there is one thing we do know: That we are here for the sake of others...for the countless unknown souls with whose fate we are connected by a bond of sympathy.
> Many times a day, I realize how much my outer and inner life is built upon the labors of people, both living and dead, and how earnestly I must exert myself in order to give in return as much as I have received.
> - Albert Einstein

Should You Give Them a Copy of This Book?

If you have gotten this far, you know that this book can be very enlightening and helpful. But it does take a commitment to get through it, doesn't it? My suggestion would be to first demonstrate what you've learned by reading it. If your loved ones can see that you've become more peaceful, trusting and connected, it will go a long way toward your being able to help them, and set an example they could want to follow. If they ask, certainly feel free to tell them what you've learned. And you could tell them that you've read an interesting book which you found helpful, but please don't "force" it on them. There are other books on the website that can help others through difficult times as well.

SHARE YOUR STORY

> Let us not be satisfied with just giving money. Money is not enough, money can be got, but they need your hearts to love them. So, spread your love everywhere you go.
> Mother Teresa

If you want to help others, one way you can do this is by sharing your story.

> A great book should leave you slightly exhausted at the end. You live several lives while reading it.
> - William Styron

Helping Others

<u>Appendix</u>

- Extensive List of Bad Things
- Prayer Examples

EXTENSIVE LIST OF BAD THINGS

- You're diagnosed with a chronic, painful illness.
- Your business fails and you lose everything.
- Your home is destroyed by fire.
- Your mother is diagnosed with terminal cancer.
- Your best friend gets divorced and has to move in with you.
- Your infant is diagnosed with an incurable disease and will need a transplant or he will die.
- Your wife leaves you for another man.
- Your husband loses his job and stays home every day drinking.
- Your spouse leaves and takes everything and you're forced to file bankruptcy.
- You get into a car accident and kill someone.
- You're sent to prison for a crime you did not commit.
- Your car is stolen.
- Your home is broken into and you're raped.
- You are exiled from your country
- You're exposed as a fraud on national TV
- Your child is abducted
- Your sister is injured in a car accident and is paralyzed on one side of her body.
- Your son goes to war and is a prisoner of war.
- Your wife gets breast cancer.
- You lose all confidence in yourself and become a hermit.
- You're fired from your job.
- Your boyfriend sexually abused your children.
- You're in the witness protection program and are forced to leave everyone and everything you know.
- Your boyfriend leaves you after 10 years together.
- You have to have a hysterectomy and won't be able to have children.

- You have an illness that puts you on long-term disability.
- You have prostate cancer and will no longer be able to perform sexually.
- Your husband leaves you alone when you're 8 ½ months pregnant.
- Your home and neighborhood is destroyed in a hurricane.
- You flunk out of college.
- You get arrested and are sentenced to 10-20 years in prison.
- You have to pay child support for a child you didn't want.
- You're 15 and pregnant.
- You lost all your money and savings.
- Your child runs away from home and lives on the street doing drugs and working as a prostitute.
- You think of suicide all the time.
- You know other people's problems may be worse than yours, but you're still devastated.
- You're forced to live on the street.
- Your son is arrested for rape.
- You were born without the ability to see.
- Your daughter is convicted of murdering her children.
- You're paralyzed from an accident.
- You lose your entire family in a tornado.
- You have a different, serious crisis every year.
- You have to have your arms amputated.
- You witness a gruesome murder.
- You're drafted to fight in a war you don't support.
- Someone is trying to kill you.
- You hate the way you look.
- You fail at everything you do.
- Your family thinks your beliefs are crazy.
- Your boat capsizes and you're lost at sea.
- All your friends abandon you.
- Your mother won't talk with you.

Appendix

- You lose everything and have to move in with someone who is abusive.
- Your father beat you as a child.
- Your dog is killed.
- Your country is the victim of a terrorist attack.
- You're stranded on a deserted island.
- You were falsely accused of abuse and lost custody of your children.
- Your business manager steals all your money.
- Your spouse/partner cheats on you.
- You're diagnosed with an illness that makes you lose your ability to think clearly.
- You have a lifelong struggle with your weight/body image.
- Your daughter is murdered by her husband, but he's free and has custody of their children.
- You contract an incurable sexually transmitted disease.
- Someone close to you is dying.
- You are at death's door.
- Other _____.

PRAYER EXAMPLES

Christian

The Lord's Prayer

Looking at the Lord's Prayer as an example, it includes the following elements:

Praise:
- "Hallowed be Thy Name"

Alignment:
- "Thy Will be done"

Guidance:
- Asking for forgiveness from others:
- "Forgive us our trespasses"
- Forgiving others:
- "As we forgive those who trespass against us"
- Asking to be guided away from the things that may be bad for us:
- "And lead us not into temptation"
- Asking us not to be a victim of – or a perpetrator of – harm, disaster, etc.
- "But deliver us from evil."
- Release and praise
- "For Thine is the kingdom, the power, and the glory."

Commitment/Loyalty:
- "For ever and ever."

Release:
- "Amen".[77]

St. Francis

---

[77] Although "Amen" may be used as an expression of release, it does not send a strong message, and may just convey an ending.

The following prayer, attributed to St. Francis, clearly demonstrates Love/Peace, Alignment, Guidance, Awareness and Selflessness:

> Lord, make me an instrument of your peace:
> Where there is hatred, let me sow love,
> Where there is injury, pardon;
> Where there is doubt, faith;
> Where there is despair, hope;
> Where there is darkness, light;
> Where there is sadness, joy.
> O, Divine Master, Grant that I may not so much seek:
> To be consoled as to console,
> To be understood as to understand,
> To be loved, as to love,
> For it is in giving that we receive;
> It is in pardoning that we are pardoned;
> It is in dying that we are born to eternal life.

A Course in Miracles/Marianne Williamson

A Course in Miracles offers prayers for many specific instances, including anxiety, happy marriage, cancer, loneliness, care giving, fear and more. The following example is from Marianne Williamson's book, *A Return to Love*, and is a demonstration of Love and Peace, Alignment, Guidance, Awareness, Selflessness and Release.

> Dear God, my desire, my priority is inner peace. I want the experience of love. I don't know what would bring that to me. I leave the results of this situation in your hands. I trust your will. May your will be done. Amen.

Here is another prayer from Williamson's book.

> "Dear God, please give my life some sense of purpose. Use me as an instrument of your peace.

Use my talents and abilities to spread love. I surrender my job to you. Help me to remember that my real job is to love the world. Thank you very much. Amen."

The next prayer, is the "Daily Prayer for Our Nation" from *A Course in Miracles,* and it shows Gratitude, Praise, Love, Alignment and Release.

O blessed Father,
One of the greatest blessings in our lives is the family that You have placed us in. Even in the midst of occasional headaches that our loved ones may cause, these families give us the stability that we long for, the love that we need, and the strength that we could not obtain on our own. Lord, help us to appreciate all of the ways that You are able to care for us through our families. Give us the energy we need so that in everything we do, we are caring for our spouses, children, parents, siblings, and all the other relatives, as they have cared for us. We offer this prayer in Your Name. Amen.

Buddhist

The following Buddhist prayer, Universal Love Aspiration, exhibits Praise, Love, Alignment, Guidance, Awareness, Selflessness and Release.

Through the working of Great Compassion
in their hearts,
May all beings have happiness
and the causes of happiness,
May all be free from sorrow
and the causes of sorrow;
May all never be separated from the
sacred happiness, which is sorrowless;
And may all live in equanimity,

Without too much attachment
and too much aversion;
and live believing in the equality of
all that lives.

Judaism

The following is a short Jewish prayer, called *Modeh Ani* or "I Give Thanks," which should be recited immediately upon waking in the morning, which shows Gratitude, Praise, and Love (compassion):

I give thanks to You, living and everlasting King, for you have returned my soul to me with compassion. Great is your faithfulness.

Another Jewish prayer, *Asher Yatzar*, demonstrates Praise and Gratitude for the workings of the physical body:

Blessed are You, HaShem, our God, King of the Universe, Who formed man with intelligence, and created within him many openings and many hollow spaces; it is revealed and known before the Seat of Your Honor, that if one of these would be opened or if one of these would be sealed it would be impossible to survive and to stand before You (even for one hour). Blessed are You, HaShem, Who heals all flesh and does wonders.

Kabbalah

The Kabbalah offers "Five Tools Of Being Sincere With God."

1. Expect The Good
2. Be Shocked If You Don't Get It
3. Listen To God's Lessons
4. Focus On What You Want
5. Make An Effort

Qur'an

The following prayer from the Qur'an includes Praise, Alignment and Guidance.

> In the Name of God, the Merciful, the Compassionate
> Praise belongs to God, Lord of all Being
> the All-merciful, the All-compassionate
> the Master of the Day of Doom
> Thee only we serve; to Thee alone we pray for succor
> Guide us in the straight path
> the path of those whom Thou hast blessed,
> not of those against whom Thou art wrathful
> nor of those who are astray.

Hindu

The following Hindu Prayer demonstrates a request for Peace, Guidance, Awareness, Selflessness and Commitment.

> O Lord, Lead Us From Untruth To Truth,
> Lead Us From Darkness To Light,
> Lead Us From Death To Immortality,
> Aum (the universal sound of God)
> Let There Be Peace Peace Peace.

Bahá'í

The Bahá'í faith requires obligatory prayer daily, as in the following, which exhibits Praise, Commitment and Selflessness.

> I bear witness, O my God, that Thou hast created me to know Thee and to worship Thee. I testify, at this moment, to my powerlessness and to Thy might, to my poverty and to Thy wealth. There is none other God but Thee, the Help in Peril, the Self-Subsisting.

427

Druid

The following Druid's prayer shows Praise, Love and Guidance.

> Grant, God, thy refuge;
> and in refuge, strength;
> and in strength, understanding;
> and in understanding, knowledge;
> and from knowledge, knowledge of what is right;
> and from knowledge of what is right, the love of it;
> and from loving, the love of God.
> God and all goodness.

James Redfield

This prayer, from James Redfield in his book, *The Tenth Insight, Holding the Vision*, is an example of several of the guidelines: Gratitude, Praise, Alignment, Guidance, Awareness, Selflessness, and Commitment/Loyalty.

> Holy Spirit, who solves all problems, who lights all roads so that I can attain my goal. You who give me the Divine gift to forgive and forget all evil against me and that in all instances of my life you are with me.
> I want in this short prayer to thank you for all things and to confirm once again that I never want to be separated from you, even and in spite of all material illusion.
> I want to be with you in eternal glory.
> Thank you for your mercy toward me and mine.

Pathwork

The following prayer is an excerpt from Pathwork lecture #138, and includes several of the key elements: Integration, Alignment, Guidance, Awareness, Selflessness, Commitment/Loyalty and Release:

Whatever I already am, I want to devote to life. I desperately want life to make use of the best of what I have and who I am. I may not be sure at this moment in what way this could happen, and even if I have ideas, I will allow for the greater intelligence and wisdom deep within me to guide me. I will let life itself decide how a fruitful interchange can take place between it and me. For whatever I give to life, I have received from it, and I wish to return it to the great cosmic pool, to bring more benefit to others. This, in turn, must inevitably enrich my own life to the exact measure that I willingly give to life, for truly life and I are one. When I withhold from life, I withhold from myself...When I withhold from others, I withhold from myself. Whatever I already am, I want to let flow into life. And whatever more in me can be utilized, still waiting to be brought to fruition, I request, I decide, and I desire that it be put to constructive use, so as to enrich the atmosphere around me.

Here is another Pathwork prayer, from Lecture #181:

I want to expand my life. I want to experience total love and pleasure supreme, without negativities or blocks. I want to give myself completely in love. I want to have health, fulfillment, abundance in every area of life. It is possible to have such a rich, good life. I am willing to give to life as much as I wish to obtain. I do not want to cheat life by secretly wanting more than I am willing to give. I want to shed all falseness, all selfishness, self-centeredness, negativity and destructiveness, no matter how hard this at may at first seem. I want to shed all illusions I have about myself, for this is the price for leading such a rich life, and I am willing to pay for it…My own happiness will contribute to the well-being of others. I am willing to shed my ego defenses and all negativity, to give and receive the best. I am willing to accept difficulties along the way, for I know that in overcoming them I will become receptive to all the goodness of life. I am willing to grow from my difficulties rather than childishly complain about them, as if someone else had given them to me. I will overcome all self-pity and exaggerated fear because I know that they are only manipulative tricks of the childish mind to avoid accepting life as it is.

Prayer of the Unknown Confederate Soldier

I asked for strength that I might achieve;
I was made weak that I might learn humbly to obey.
I asked for health that I might do greater things;
I was given infirmity that I might do better things.
I asked for riches that I might be happy;
I was given poverty that I might be wise.
I asked for power that I might have the praise of men;
I was given weakness that I might feel the need of God.
I asked for all things that I might enjoy life;
I was given life that I might enjoy all things.
I got nothing that I had asked for, but everything that I had hoped for.
Almost despite myself my unspoken prayers were answered;
I am, among all men, most richly blessed.

The author of the above prayer is unknown, but the message is powerful and lasting, and helps us understand the meaning of life.

MORE BOOKS BY BROWNELL

DUET stories Volume I: The Song Begins

Available on Amazon!

And please review and rate on both Amazon and Goodreads!

DUET stories Volume II: The Tempo Builds

Available on Amazon!

And please review and rate on both Amazon and Goodreads!

DUET stories Volume III: A Chorus of Voices

Available on Amazon!

And please review and rate on both Amazon and Goodreads!

431

by Brownell

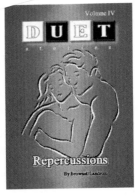

DUET stories Volume IV: Repercussions

Available on Amazon!

And please review and rate on both Amazon and Goodreads!

Wonderactive Books!
Children's books inspired by Goo!

Wonderactive Books: Sometimes I Wonder

Available on Amazon!

And please review and rate on both Amazon and Goodreads!

Wonderactive Books: This Isn't My First Time

Available on Amazon!

And please review and rate on both Amazon and Goodreads!

Fifty Shades Deeper

Fifty Shades Deeper: Sometimes the most powerful messages come wrapped in surprising packages.

Co-authored with:
Kaydee Fergus
Jewell Hennessey and
150 Author Contributors
Around the World!

And more more more coming soon! For bonus content, additional stories, articles, songs and a whole lot more, go to:

www.DuetStories.com.

Follow Brownell:
Twitter: @BrownellLandrum
Facebook:
https://www.facebook.com/brownell.landrum.author/

Made in the USA
San Bernardino, CA
06 June 2017